ISSUES IN IRISH PUBLIC POLICY

Issues in Irish Public Policy

Editor

GEORGE TAYLOR

IRISH ACADEMIC PRESS
DUBLIN • PORTLAND, OR

First published in 2002 by
IRISH ACADEMIC PRESS
44, Northumberland Road, Dublin 4, Ireland

and in the United States of America by
IRISH ACADEMIC PRESS
c/o ISBS, 5824 NE Hassalo Street,
Portland, OR 97213-3644

Website: www.iap.ie

British Library Cataloguing in Publication Data

Issues in Irish public policy
1. Political planning – Ireland 2. Ireland – Economic policy
3. Ireland – Social policy 4. Ireland – Politics and
government – 1949–
I. Taylor, George
320.9'415'09049

ISBN 0-7165-2668-9 (cloth)

Library of Congress Cataloging-in-Publication Data

A catalog record of this book is available from the Library of Congress.

Typeset by Regent Typesetting, London
Printed in Great Britain by
MPG Books Ltd, Bodmin, Cornwall

Contents

Notes on Contributors		vi
Editor's introduction	Public Policy and the Changing Architecture of Irish Politics	1
1. T. A. Boylan	From Stabilisation to Economic Growth – The Contribution of Macroeconomic Policy	9
2. G. Taylor	Negotiated Governance and the Irish Polity	28
3. E. O'Shea and B. Kennelly	The Welfare State in Ireland – Challenges and Opportunities	52
4. G. Taylor and Cathi Murphy	Environmental Policy in Ireland	80
5. R. Edmondson	Silence and the Golden Years: Older People and Public Policy in Ireland	99
6. T. Varley and C. Curtin	Community Empowerment *via* Partnership? The 'Local Community' in Rural Ireland's Area Based Development Regime	127
Notes		151
Bibliography		181
Index		199

Notes on Contributors

Dr T. A. Boylan is Professor of Economics and Dean of Research at the National University of Ireland, Galway. He has published extensively on economic theory and regional and rural economics.

Dr Christopher Curtin is Professor of Political Science and Sociology at the National University of Ireland, Galway. He has recently co-authored *Poverty in Rural Ireland: A Political Economy Perspective* and has published widely on agrarian politics, local government, disputes and dispute settlements.

Dr Ricca Edmondson is a lecturer in the Department of Political Science and Sociology and Chairperson of the Social Science Research Centre at the National University of Ireland, Galway. Her most recent book is *Ireland: Culture and Society*. She has also published in the areas of health, ageing, culture and rhetoric.

Dr Brendan Kennelly is a lecturer in the Department of Economics at the National University of Ireland, Galway. He has published articles on the welfare state, social choice, social policy and cultural economics.

Ms Cathi Murphy has completed a post-graduate Master of Arts thesis on 'Policy Networks and Environmental Policy in Ireland' at the National University of Ireland, Galway.

Dr Eamon O'Shea is a lecturer in the Department of Economics at the National University of Ireland, Galway. He has published extensively on health economics, the welfare state, social policy and ageing.

Dr George Taylor is a lecturer in the Department of Political Science and Sociology and Director of the Centre for Public Policy at the National University of Ireland, Galway. He has published papers on state theory, public policy and environmental politics.

Dr Tony Varley is a lecturer in the Department of Political Science and Sociology at the National University of Ireland, Galway. He is the co-editor of *Rural Crisis* and *Whose Law and Order?* He has published widely on rural social structures.

Editor's Introduction: Public Policy and the Changing Architecture of Irish Politics

As the new millennium begins to take shape, it seems ever more clear that the Irish polity has experienced profound change over the last ten years. The pessimism which had prevailed among political historians at the beginning of the 1990s[1] has been replaced by an overwhelming political ebullience encapsulated, if not altogether explained, in the concept of our times; the Celtic Tiger. The phrase remains all the more quixotic because definitions have thus far proven elusive.

There are those who may dispute individual features of this phrase but few would deny that it seems to possess that most ethereal of qualities, the ability to act as a prism through which our disparate, individual experiences of the contemporary Irish polity are refracted and made intelligible. On the one hand, it is capable of pervading the currency of the mundane aspects of everyday life. It confirms our intuitive sense of change, from the transformation of the workplace experience to conversations which express dismay at either escalating house prices or the time we have spent in Dublin's gridlock. On the other hand, it has found considerable favour in political and media circles, where it has rendered intelligible a period of unprecedented economic growth unimaginable a decade ago. The phrase also captures a level of dynamism previously not associated with the Irish polity. It reinforces the impression that the Irish state has embarked upon a venture to develop a new political architecture, one which befits its status as an emerging, confident, cosmopolitan European state. References to the Celtic Tiger abound and, more often than not, appear simply to relieve us of the more onerous task of providing a more detailed and thorough explanation of contemporary events.

Amid the enthusiasm for embracing all that is now 'particularly Irish' in this political and economic project, it is hardly surprising to find that dissenting voices should be few and far between. Where they do surface, they run the gauntlet of being charged with that most serious of Irish crimes, begrudgery. And yet, almost perversely, it is precisely at this point that we can locate the appeal of the phrase for it lies not in what it is, but what it is not; it is not Thatcherism. The success of the project, and the subsequent strength of its appeal, rests on its promise to deliver a 'world-class economy' which retains a modicum of political commitment to avoiding excessive social dislocation.

This is an intoxicating political elixir, formulated around the state's alleged capacity to reconcile exorbitant economic growth with political consensus. This feat has been all the more incredible when we consider that it has taken place against a political backdrop of electoral defeats for a succession of coalition governments. The downside, as current assertions now demonstrate, is that as with all 'heady brews', we should prepare for the inevitable hangover. Welcome though this startling economic growth has been, rumours are now firmly afoot that the Celtic Tiger has not delivered the financial promises to all of its citizenry, and that despite all the 'give-away' budgets of the 1990s, poverty persists.

If the 1990s were a decade of tribunals, even a decade of political excess, they were also a decade in which debate in Irish public policy was conspicuous only by its absence. Criticism of individual elements of successive budgets abounded, but the 'drift', content and ideological stance of policy received only scant attention. Exceptions to this lay largely with research reports emanating from the National Economic and Social Council (NESC), the Economic and Social Research Institute (ESRI) or the Conference for the Religious in Ireland (CORI). This is perhaps partially due to the fact that academics, politicians and journalists alike appear to have been seduced by the extravagant rhetoric which has accompanied the Celtic Tiger. Certainly, where debate has taken place it has tended to concentrate upon the salacious or 'tabloid-friendly' aspects of this era: political funding, financial embezzlement or political ineptitude. Where analysis has taken place it has alluded, albeit tentatively, to a tenuous link between an emerging political sclerosis and a neo-liberal economic strategy which has encouraged greed and excess.

It is rare to identify a defining period in which such transformations take effect, but for many the embryonic development of the Celtic Tiger can be located in the shift which took place in Irish economic policy, particularly macroeconomic policy, in 1987. As Boylan argues, the developments of the 1990s were an extraordinary achievement when considered against the backdrop of economic stagnation and political disruption of the 1980s. The impact of the oil crises of the 1970s, followed by serious policy mismanagement in the early 1980s, exacerbated disproportionately the global recession underway in other EU states. By the mid-1980s it had become clear that the Irish economy was experiencing serious problems of structural maladjustments, reflected in the fiscal and national debt crisis, rising levels of unemployment, high inflation and accompanying high interest rates. With the need to stabilise the economy, imperative direct measures were pursued, particularly in the fiscal policy domain. It was to have a positive effect on the national debt crisis and, with the pursuit of a judicious exchange-rate policy which included two devaluations in 1986 and 1993, it established a format in which economic growth was secured. As Boylan observes in Chapter 1, it has recently become clear that policies pursued over a much longer period (such as the industrial policy which centred on the critical role of foreign direct investment and the expansion of the educational system which enhanced the human capital base of the economy) have contributed significantly to the substantial rates of economic growth. In turn, these policy changes have been complemented by a neo-corporatist model of wage determination which has ensured economic competitiveness.

Few analysts would doubt that one of the defining features of Irish public policy since 1990 has been a determination on the part of successive governments to persist with macro-level bargaining agreements. Indeed, for many, including those who reside in the corridors of power in Brussels, they have contributed significantly to ensuring political stability, consistency in public policy and economic growth. Yet such agreements have not always enjoyed their current favoured status among either politicians or political scientists. For those of a conservative persuasion, such political intermediation was deemed an anathema to any 'reasoned response' to the problems which had beset the Irish polity during the 1980s. It was a set of arguments which also found accord amongst those who had 'forecast' rapid change in the new global economic order. Here, as Taylor points out, it has been widely argued that capitalism has moved firmly into a new, dynamic phase in which flexibility in personnel and organisational strategy is paramount. In such circumstances it has been argued that governments can no longer entertain the idea of sustaining agreements between business, unions and key social interests. And yet, in Ireland, macro-political bargaining has formed the backbone to public policy for over a decade.

In Taylor's opinion (see Chapter 2), this injudicious inclination to jettison the idea of macro-political bargaining so easily is based upon the misapprehension that political intermediation is incapable of engineering change to the supply side of the economy. More often than not, such arguments have been accompanied by the celebration of decentralised forms of bargaining, as if they are somehow better suited to the prevailing conditions of the new global economy. Taylor's contention is that if we are to understand the role macro-political bargaining can play, and by implication its function in framing Irish public policy over the last ten years, then we need to abandon the prevailing misconception that such bargaining schemes are simply 'deals about pay'. Indeed, the appeal of these agreements, to both management *and* unions, rests on the fact that they deliberate upon issues which extend beyond pay to include the introduction of new technology and changing work practices. More recently, he suggests, the innovative nature of these agreements has extended to the restructuring of public sector service provision where it has played a pivotal role in tentative moves toward introducing flexibility. In other words, Taylor cautions against the temptation to present a simple dichotomy between neo-liberal disengagement and a 'discredited', social-democratically inspired neo-corporatism.

The tension that resides in the drive towards a flexible economy, which avoids the social dislocation associated with the Thatcherite project, has had an important bearing upon debates about the future trajectory of the welfare state. In Chapter 3 O'Shea and Kennelly argue that the debate about welfare, and the solutions proposed to address welfare-related problems, have taken place largely within a framework disposed to assign priority to economic efficiency. This is an approach which sidelines other critical values such as social cohesion, social participation and social solidarity. In their opinion, if lasting and beneficial changes are to occur in welfare provision, there will have to be a radical reassessment of the current policy paradigm and a shift towards a higher priority for the social and distributional consequences of public policy.

The first task, in their opinion, is to establish social goals, not as residual components of general economic objectives, but as priorities in their own right. This is a position which recognises the need for new forms of social production and for social organisation to deal with the social problems that face people living in this country. Here, 'participation' represents the key to the future evolution of a welfare state which maximises individual potential through active, human-capital oriented policies of support. It is one which needs to acknowledge, and then nurture, the contribution which individuals can make to the development of society at all levels, and not only at the level of acquisition. Moving people into a future where they can realise their considerable social potential, and have a stake in the communities in which they live, is the leitmotif of the welfare state of the future.

Any serious discussion of the future of the welfare state needs to consider the changing nature of Ireland's demography and the role public policy can play with respect to ageing. On this matter, Edmondson in Chapter 5 argues that a fundamental shift in the way in which we perceive the role of public policy in this domain is required. She contends that in Ireland public policy helps to create a situation in which older people are excluded from mainstream forms of social living. Despite diffuse goodwill towards older people, and despite considerable, if sometimes erratic, financial support, public policy on ageing in Ireland fails to argue in favour of a genuinely positive approach to the last decades in the lives of its citizens. More people are living to be old, and they survive as older people for longer periods than earlier this century. If we allow the final phase of living to be devalued, then by implication we are also devaluing the stages that lead up to it. Edmondson outlines the radical changes that took place in Ireland's socio-economic structure during the twentieth century, and the changing fortunes of older people within them.

At one time, older people wielded personal and economic power in a rural setting in which children depended on inheritance for their future survival. In the current world, however, there is no obvious positive social role for older people to play. This is indicated, for example, in public policy on nursing homes, where almost no concerted effort is made to ensure that older people live in settings that support their dignity and worth as citizens with a part to play in society. It is indicated also by the residualist implications of public policy on support mechanisms for older people, which tend to communicate a view in which 'oldness' is equated with being sick, poor or vulnerable. Other policies – pensions policy, policy on housing or community care policy – also argue negatively as well as positively; among other considerations, they devalue 'flexibly' constructed life-courses (often women's), even as flexibility is endorsed in broad sections of the economy.

Edmondson suggests an alternative approach, one that would identify people who experience problems, at whatever age, as eligible for support by the social services. Policy directed specifically towards older people as such would be policy aimed at enhancing the later decades of life and ensuring that older people have access to roles which are fruitful for themselves and for the wider society. We tend currently to use misleading language for describing the needs of older people; a more positive form of public policy could help to create a new language in which a more creative vision of the human lifetime could be expressed.

The tension that resides in a political project which, on the one hand, endorses social democratic concerns, such as political participation and regulation and, on the other hand, accepts neo-liberal arguments for releasing multi-national capital from political constraints, has also figured prominently in the discourse surrounding environmental policy. This tension has been accentuated by demands from environmentalists that the degradation of Ireland's ecology should be curtailed. From the eutrophication of the lakes in Killarney to litigation about Dublin's architectural heritage, environmental protest abounds. And yet, the arrival of the Environmental Protection Agency in 1992, which had received the fulsome endorsement of all political parties, was seen initially as a decisive step towards overhauling an antiquated and discredited system of environmental regulation. Independent of government, scientifically competent and sufficiently financed, the Agency was intended to put a new ecological imprint upon the Irish polity. What is more, it sustained the impression that the Celtic Tiger would live up to its 'green obligations' – that it could successfully reconcile the problem of economic growth and environmental protection.

Taylor and Murphy, however, are sceptical of the value of such claims. In Chapter 4 they suggest that the EPA is not, as some would have us believe, the outcome of an emerging ecological modernisation within the Irish polity. Rather, it represents an institutional response to a succession of environmental conflicts which had threatened to undermine the interests of the agricultural and business lobbies. Put simply, environmental policy was shaped not by a concern with political participation or environmental justice, but with the need to accommodate environmentalist objections to the regulatory regime of the 1980s without jeopardising the free market ethos of the 1990s. As such, these authors argue that the principal problem in this revamped regime has been the failure to address its 'soft' regulatory style. It should surprise few, in their opinion, that the Irish polity finds itself once again mired in environmental protest on issues as disparate as landfills, eutrophication, wind farms, interpretative centres and mobile phone masts.

There are few areas in Irish public policy where concerns about political participation, flexibility and social dislocation are more prominent than in rural and urban development. Here, as Varley and Curtin observe in Chapter 6, the readiness with which 'local communities' have been invoked in official circles as holding part of the solution to many of Ireland's economic and social problems was a striking feature of the 1990s. Nowhere was this more evident than in the official rhetoric which surrounded the participation of 'communities' in the local development partnerships which have proliferated in Ireland since 1990. In this vein, reports published by the National Economic and Social Council (1994) and by the OECD (1995) have sought to place the area-based partnership schemes at the very forefront of the Irish state's attempt to overhaul the character of both its economic development and its attendant political structures. Sabel, for example, has been moved to note that such schemes were at the 'core of the experiment' to 'address issues of social exclusion in a more flexible, decentralised and participative way'.[2] Similarly, NESC has argued that local area-based initiatives which tackle marginalisation and social exclusion should be developed as a potentially effective strategy in promoting greater integration in social and labour market policies, and that the more closely involved local communities are in the planning and delivery of area-based projects the more they will reflect local needs and priorities.

Varley and Curtin explore the manner in which the benefits of participation to community actors in local development can be understood. The most pessimistic view they consider sees the cost to community actors of participation in partnerships as very high. This reflects the ability of the state or the EU to set the crucial parameters (priorities, funding and programme length especially), thus effectively providing them with the controlling interest in partnership-based development. This line of analysis also suggests that the participation of community actors brings with it the inherent risk of co-option – the inability to exercise an advocacy role, to oppose the state or to use confrontational tactics. To the extent that this risk is realised, the state or state-like actors can be said to be successful in constituting community groups in their own image.

At the other extreme, the most optimistic possibility holds out the hope of community actors being able to use the local partnerships to their own advantage. Participation is seen as presenting community actors with the opportunity to gain access to new resources and to deploy these in a manner that can advance their own aims in significant and creative ways. It may also happen that community actors, as a result of participation in the area-based partnerships, will come to aspire to new aims and so open up new arenas of activity for themselves.

An in-between position accepts that participation in the local partnerships may bring potential advantages to community actors, but suggests that involvement may also impose heavy costs in the form of the expenditure of time and other scarce resources. These costs can be expected to weigh particularly heavily upon small-scale local groups which are wholly dependent on voluntary effort. In view of their limited duration and terms of reference, community actors cannot really look to the local partnerships for the type of life-cycle funding they require if they are ever to realise their potential. Yet they increasingly see themselves as having little choice but to become involved if they are not to be sidelined in a local development regime ever more dominated by area partnerships.

CHAPTER 1

From Stabilisation to Economic Growth – The Contribution of Macroeconomic Policy

T. A. BOYLAN

INTRODUCTION

The achievements of the Irish economy over the last ten years and particularly since 1994, have been spectacular by international standards. The reorientation of economic policy from the late 1980s has been a crucial factor in extricating the economy from the stagnation of the 1980s and contributing to the rapid growth rates of the 1990s. As measured by the conventional criteria of comparative economic performance, these growth rates have propelled Ireland to the top of the international growth league tables. The only comparable group of economies which have generated similar growth rates were those of the Asian 'tiger' economies. The use of the label 'celtic tiger', while allowing for the linguistic hyperbole involved, nevertheless conveys the attempt at finding a plausible benchmark group of countries against which the performance of the Irish economy in the 1990s could legitimately be compared. There is some irony, however, not to mention a salutary warning, in the over-worked comparisons with the Asian 'tiger' economies even as we watch the 'Asian model' falter under the weight of a bizarre mixture of financial delinquency, poor management and deep seated political corruption.

While the Asian crisis has presented a formidable problem for economic analysts to decipher, similarly the performance of the Irish economy since the late 1980s poses an intriguing interpretative challenge to economists and students of public policy. Over an extended period in this century the Irish economy resembled the proverbial tortoise rather than a tiger in the context of the Western European growth rate experience. Its growth rate lagged considerably behind the European average from the First World War until the 1980s.[1] As recently as the mid-1980s, per capita incomes limped along close to the bottom of the Western European league table, at about two-thirds those of Britain and three-quarters of Northern Ireland's. The transformation from tortoise to 'celtic tiger' has been extraordinarily rapid and has arguably dis-orientated Irish scholars, who as a collective entity were much more intellectually attuned to the analysis of economic failure. This is clearly evident in the array of books published during the late 1980s and early 1990s, all of which addressed different aspects of Irish economic and social performance in post-independence Ireland, but which were clearly influenced by the depth and severity of the stagnation of the 1980s.[2]

Irish commentators are just beginning to come to terms with the spectacular achievements of recent years, which have also generated an increasing amount of international attention.[3] The search for explanations for the recent performance of the economy will not be an easy one, and already an expanding menu of such explanations are on offer. These include, among others, the convergence or 'catching-up' hypothesis, the strategic shift from protection to free trade in the 1960s, the impact of EU structural funds, the expansion of investment in education and training since the 1960s, and the wage moderation negotiated through centralised collective bargaining from the late 1980s. A recent study of the Irish economy noted with respect to those contributing factors that 'the research into the relative importance of such factors has not yet been done', and added that 'only time can tell' if 'they marked the beginning of a new higher-growth steady state for the Southern economy'.[4] This is a timely reminder of the difficulty of the task of interpreting the intricate interactions between the complex array of contributing factors to economic growth. They also serve to illustrate that the available corpus of contemporary growth theory, notwithstanding its rigour, formalism and the extensiveness of the research effort devoted to it, remains relatively modest in its delivery of substantive insights into the growth process when contextualised in specific circumstances of time and place. One may safely surmise that even when the applied research is eventually completed into the recent Irish growth experience, the conclusions are likely to remain highly tentative with respect to the relative contributions of the many factors identified.

This chapter will concentrate on what can be considered to be the twin pillars of achievement over the last decade, namely the stabilisation of the economy in the face of internal mismanagement and a rapidly changing external environment, along with the subsequent economic growth which surpassed the expectations of both policy makers and general public alike. That there occurred a seismic shift in the mind-set of policy makers in the mid-1980s is now taken as axiomatic, and that the contribution of the policy shifts were the principal contributing factors to current economic growth is hardly controversial. However, the path to achieving the necessary reorientation of economic policy was neither easy nor costless to this society.

AN INTERPRETATIVE FRAMEWORK

The interpretation of the contributing causes to the recent performance of the Irish economy is a complex task. There is clearly no single theory available that provides a unified account of the process. To date the available accounts are of a narrative-type, attempting to provide what a recent study called 'a relatively simple schematic story which takes account of these main elements'.[5] What constitutes 'these main elements' is very much dependent upon the interpretative framework invoked for purposes of organising the material. An interpretative framework engaging the difficult task of deciphering the relationship between changing policy regimes and their impact on economic activity must contend with a number of different dimensions of the problems, three of which we address in this section. This account is clearly not meant to be comprehensive, but rather to illustrate a number of problems associated with this issue.

There is, firstly, the identification of the contributing factors that account for the recent growth of the Irish economy. The obvious starting point here is an appeal to economic theory, but as already noted there is no single theory available to provide a comprehensive and unified account of the growth process. Commentators, of necessity, have adopted an eclectic approach where a number of different areas of economic theory are explored for possible sources of insight into the economic growth process. In particular, these include the new growth theory literature with its emphasis on the role of human capital accumulation and physical infrastructure. Complementing this, and of specific interest in Ireland's case, is the literature on spatial development theory or economic geography.[6] This latter corpus of literature addresses the complex agenda of the spatial allocation of economic activity and, in particular, the conditions for economic growth in peripheral locations such as Ireland. While these different areas of economic theory provide key insights into the role of important, long-term contributing factors, of central concern to the problem is how these different factors are handled within the short to medium term. An overarching condition, therefore, for the successful pursuit of economic growth is the achievement of a stable macroeconomic environment, which highlights the issue of short-term stabilisation to facilitate long-term economic growth.

Secondly, there is the issue of the relative contribution of internal and external influences. The extent to which these factors combine and coincide to mutually reinforce their cumulative effects on the economy, either positively or negatively, is crucially important in any analysis of economic policy. The distinction between internal and external is extremely significant in Irish circumstances. Not for the first time in the post-independence period have our economic fortunes been shaped by the interaction of internal and external influences. In an economy like Ireland's, characterised by extreme openness to international influences, our capacity to ignore such influences or to flaunt the rules or norms of international competitiveness cannot be indulged, except at the expense of enormous economic and social costs.

The major shift in policy, which was undertaken over thirty years ago when the experiment in economic nationalism based on extensive protection was abandoned, represents an earlier example of the influence of both internal and external developments converging to subvert a major policy experiment. This led to a radical reconfiguration of the economic policy environment and the adoption of a strategy of export-led growth.[7] Similarly, the more recent changes in our economic policies are also the result of converging influences from both domestic and external sources. Domestically, the depth of the fiscal crisis of the 1980s provoked sharp and focused corrective action, which was a pivotal factor in the short-term stabilisation of the economy. Externally, rapidly changing economic circumstances, from globalisation and rapid technological change to the creation of the Single Market within the European Union, forced a reconsideration of our policy stance. The influence of these external developments in reinforcing the move towards domestic policy reform should not be underestimated. An interpretative framework in this domain must therefore engage the complex, subtle, and powerful interactions between domestic and external influences and, in particular, their mutually reinforcing effects.

There is, finally, the time dimension over which the different contributing factors, whether domestic or external, combine to generate powerful impulses for change in the economy. The basic distinction made in this chapter is between the short-term concern to achieve stabilisation of the macroeconomic environment, which preoccupied policy makers from the late 1980s, and the influences of longer-term policies implemented earlier and over a longer period. The positive influence of longer-term policies, such as industrial, educational and infrastructural policies, may be overshadowed if not seriously undermined by the negative impact of short-term policies in the fiscal, monetary and exchange rate domains. This is the case if the latter violate the requirements of good economic management and lead to high inflation, high interest rates and unsuitable exchange rate regimes.

There is a delicate balance between the positive and negative impacts of both short and long-term policy measures. A necessary, if not a sufficient, condition to generate the kind of economic growth currently being experienced in Ireland is the convergence of the positive effects of such measures. This convergence, or lack of it, is arguably one of the central considerations in the analysis of the contribution of economic policy to economic performance. An interpretative framework addressing the complex relationships between economic policy and economic performance must therefore engage, among other things: (a) the underlying influences (contributing factors); (b) the sources of the contributing factors (domestic or external), and (c) the pattern of convergence, or divergence, between policies of different time horizons (short, medium or long term).

EMERGENCE OF THE FISCAL CRISIS: CONTEXT AND CAUSES

There is general agreement among commentators that the year 1987 marked a crucial turning point in the redirection of short-term macroeconomic strategy. While lacking the historical significance of such events as our entry into the European Economic Community (EEC) in 1973 or our membership of the European Monetary System (EMS) in 1979, the year 1987 nevertheless marks a clear division between a period of crisis which preceded it and a unique period of economic growth which followed. The period of crisis can be identified with the years 1979 to 1987. To appreciate the significance of the stabilisation that was achieved after 1987, it is useful to contextualise the circumstances prevailing prior to 1987. Table 1.1 summarises the performance of the Irish economy since 1960, divided into a number of subperiods by reference to a number of key economic indicators. These data are contained in a major publication by the Central Statistics Office entitled *Revised Economic Indicators since 1960*, published in September 1996.

Table 1.1: Macroeconomic Performance 1960–1996

	1960–1973	*1973–1979*	*1979–1987*	*1987–1996**
GNP	4.2	3.5	–0.3	[illegible]
GDP	4.1	4.3	1.5	5.0
GDP	3.4	2.7	4.5	5.0
Inflation	5.9	15.0	10.7	2.6
Employment	12,000	78,000	–55,000	172,000
Employment (% annual change)	0.1	1.2	–0.6	1.6
Unemployment	2,000	23,000	45,000	–54,000

Source: CSO (1996), NESC (1996), Table 1.1, p. 5.
*1995–96 Figures are provisional.

The differential pattern of economic growth is immediately evident between the subperiods contained in Table 1.1. The period 1960–1973 represented the results of the shift in economic strategy from protectionism to trade liberalisation culminating in entry to the EEC in 1973. Over this period the real growth rate averaged over 4% per annum which was the highest rate of growth achieved up to that time. The per capita gross domestic product (GDP) also increased at an average rate of 3.4% between 1960–1973, compared with 2.2% for the previous decade.[8] The economic growth achieved over this period reflected the high growth rates which then prevailed both in Europe and in the developed world as represented by the Organisation for Economic Co-operation and Development (OECD) Member States. It was also the consequence of changes in the domestic economy arising from the redirection of economic policies, which included trade liberalisation and the attraction of direct foreign investment, along with major changes in the sectoral patterns of production and employment.

The 1970s, as reflected in the period 1973–1979, brought a series of major economic events, both positive and negative. On the positive side there was Ireland's membership of the EEC in 1973 and of the EMS in 1979. These developments were paralleled by the negative impacts of the two oil crises, also of 1973 and 1979 respectively. Notwithstanding the world-wide recessions that followed the first oil crisis of 1973, Ireland's economic growth performance was sustained and real GDP grew at an annual average rate of over 4%, which maintained a comparable performance with the previous period. However, this growth was based on increased government spending, which was increasingly financed by borrowing. This was the beginning of what was to be a central component of the crisis which dominated public policy through the 1970s and 1980s.

The current budget deficit of central government as a percentage of GDP, which from 1960 to 1973 never exceeded 1%, jumped from a value of 0.4% in 1973 to 3% in 1974 and to 6.8% in 1975. While it decreased to 4.4% and 3.6% in 1976 and 1977 respectively, it increased again to 6.1% in 1979 and back to 6.8% in 1979. Over the period 1973 to 1979 the average annual current budget deficit was 5%, and it was not until 1990 that it again fell below the 1% level, thereby regaining its 1973 level. These figures, while reflecting accurately the emergence of the serious deterioration in public finances, could easily appear to understate the depth of the fiscal crisis which would preoccupy public policy through the course of the 1970s and 1980s.

The impact of the oil crisis was quickly reflected in both the general price level and the balance of international payments. From the late 1960s and early 1970s, Ireland, in common with most other European countries, experienced an acceleration in the rate of inflation, but the oil crisis was to greatly exacerbate this trend. Over the period 1973–1979, inflation averaged 15%, which was moving towards a three-fold increase in the average annual rate of inflation recorded between 1960 and 1973. The impact of international inflation arising from the oil crisis was reflected in the deterioration in the terms of trade, which in turn adversely affected the balance of payments on the current account. It was a trend that remained throughout the 1970s and 1980s. While the economic growth rate was sustained, mainly due to increased government borrowing and expenditure, it also led to an improvement in employment compared with the previous period.

Total employment over the period 1973–1979 increased by 78,000, but this was outstripped by the increase in the labour supply which rose by 101,000 over the same period. By the end of the period the unemployment figures had reached almost 90,000. In 1979, Ireland joined the European Monetary System, breaking a link with sterling that had lasted 150 years. The primary motivation for joining the EMS was to join the low inflation currencies of Europe dominated by the Deutschmark. The impact on inflation was not particularly dramatic and inflation fell rather slowly in the early 1980s with the result that interest rates remained high. Later a devaluation became necessary to restore Ireland's competitive position.[9]

The period 1979–1987 was one of economic stagnation and extremely poor economic performance in most areas of economic activity. Economic growth, as measured by annual GDP, fell to almost a third of the previous period, averaging 1.5% as compared with 4.3% between 1973–1979, while the average annual GNP growth was negative (–0.3). This reflected the increase in net factor overflows arising from, among other factors, the increase in profit repatriation by the new multinationals establishing in Ireland. The most distinguishing feature of this period, and the aspect of economic policy which received most of the media attention, was the deterioration in the public finances. The increase in government debt, which began to rise in the early 1970s, occurred largely due to the recession which followed the 1973 oil crisis. The accompanying rising unemployment accelerated overall during this period. In 1972, immediately prior to the oil crisis, there was an explicit commitment to deficit budgeting by the Minister of Finance. The current budget deficit, which amounted to 0.3% of GNP in 1972, rose to 6.8% in 1979 and to 7.9% in 1986, the latter figure representing a twenty-six fold increase.

The Exchequer Borrowing Requirement (EBR), which represents the total amount of money that the central government must borrow to cover the excess of expenditure over revenue on both its current and capital budgets, stood at 6% of GNP in 1972, and averaged 13% over the period 1979–1987. The government debt, or national debt as it is more commonly referred to, is measured by taking the total government debt as a ratio or percentage of GNP. It is a critical ratio in monitoring the dynamics of national debt. This ratio, which stood at 54.7% in 1972 had increased to 85.7% in 1979 and reached 125% in 1987. In addition to the stock of debt that was accumulated over this period, there was also the problem of servicing the debt. The payment of interest on the national debt was greatly aggravated by the rise in real interest rates during this period, with the result that debt service as a percentage of GNP rose from 4.3% in 1972 to 6.7% in 1979 and peaked at 12.5% in 1985.

The national debt comprises two components – a domestic part arising from government borrowing within the state, and an external component arising from the foreign borrowings of government, mainly from consortia of foreign banks. The repayments of the domestic debt, and particularly the interest charges on this component, can be argued to remain within the country and thereby contribute to domestic economic activity. The external component of the debt and interest repayments are direct payments to non-residents and therefore represent a net loss of financial resources to the country, which reduces the volume of resources available to the economy. Interest repayments as a proportion of GNP rose from 0.3% in 1972 to 1.4% in 1979 and within the period 1979–1987 reached a peak of 4.9% in 1985.[10]

The serious deterioration in public finances and the escalation in the national debt were not unique to Ireland in this period. Following the second oil crisis of 1979, the oil-exporting countries accumulated extremely large surpluses of foreign exchange through surpluses in their balance of payments. Many of these countries deposited these surpluses in European and North American banks, who in turn were eager to find borrowers for these large surplus funds. There was no shortage of borrowers, particularly in Eastern Europe, Africa and Latin America. Within a short period of time however, both the volume of borrowing involved and domestic circumstances within the debtor countries began to put pressure on their capacity to meet their interest repayments. This process culminated in August 1982 when Mexico announced its intention to cancel its interest repayments on its outstanding debt. It quickly became evident that many other countries were about to default or threatened to do so, including several in Eastern Europe, Africa and Latin America.

The stability of the global banking system, certainly the western financial system, was deemed to be under threat. The 1980s became preoccupied with the process and economic implications of debt rescheduling, an agenda which remains at the centre of international affairs. While the official position in Ireland never contemplated defaulting, this country unquestionably experienced a serious fiscal crisis and came very close to undergoing a major debt crisis. While the fiscal and national debt crises dominated the attention of commentators and the media, it should be noted that in addition there was stagnation in per capita disposable income, huge balance of payments deficits emerged, unemployment increased from 88,000 in 1979 to 232,000 by 1987, and the industrial relations situation deteriorated. The stabilisation of this difficult economic situation became the overarching national priority and the year 1987 marked the critical turning point.[11]

FROM CRISIS TO STABILISATION: ACHIEVING FISCAL CONSOLIDATION

The formation of a minority Fianna Fáil government in January 1987 did not bode well for the future of economic policy given the economic circumstances, the state of public finances and external developments in the European Union.[12] In opposition, Fianna Fáil relentlessly accused the coalition government of Fine Gael and Labour of 'monetarist' or 'Thacherite' policies and campaigned on a platform of increased government expenditure. It was a politically inconsistent stance given that, during the general election campaign of November 1982 all the major political parties, including Fianna Fáil, recognised the seriousness of the fiscal crisis facing the country. The coalition government of Fine Gael and Labour, which held office between June 1981 and March 1982, attempted to correct the deteriorating fiscal situation inherited from the previous Fianna Fáil government which had been in office from 1977 to 1981.

The strategy that had been pursued by this Fianna Fáil government, based on high government expenditure and the reduction of the burden of taxation (the abolition of rates on private houses being the most spectacular example), went badly wrong following the second oil crisis of 1979 and the failure of economic growth to materialise. This led to reduced tax buoyancy and, combined with large government expenditure, generated the momentum for expanding fiscal deficits and rising national debt. The new coalition government, following the general election in June 1981, introduced a mini-budget in July 1981 which identified the strategy of increasing taxes rather than cutting expenditure as the most effective way of addressing the fiscal situation. This set the strategic thrust of the coalition government, but due to the absence of any tax buoyancy given the poor economic growth, the budget deficit actually increased and with it the public sector borrowing requirement, which in 1981 stood at 20.3% of GNP, the highest ever recorded.

The fiscal and economic crisis continued to deepen during 1981 and 1982 and the balance of payments deficit deteriorated. This was also a period of political instability as reflected in the fact that there were three general elections within the space of eighteen months. Notwithstanding enormous foreign borrowing, unemployment continued to spiral upwards, increasing by 38% between 1980 and 1981 and by an additional 17% the following year. By the time of the general election of November 1982, all the main political parties recognised the seriousness of the fiscal crisis and the priority that it would have to receive as a policy objective, even at the expense of competing policies. Perhaps the only point of disagreement was the length of time which would be involved in eliminating the current budget deficit and achieving the appropriate balance between taxation and expenditure in order to achieve this objective.

The coalition government (Fine Gael/Labour) of 1982–1987, attempted to address the problem by raising taxation and reducing current expenditure. As part of a strategy to curb expenditure, the government imposed a ban on public sector recruitment. It did not, however, succeed in controlling the public sector wage bill, nor was it successful in controlling current expenditure in general. Unemployment continued to rise, as did the national debt which was further exacerbated by increases in interest rates. Higher tax rates failed to generate the increased revenue in the absence of economic growth. When the government produced a major policy document, *Building on Reality 1985–87*, in late 1984, it actually switched its main target of attention from the elimination of the current budget deficit to the stabilisation of the debt/GNP ratio.

The switch of policy objective could be decoded as one of a certain admission of failure with respect to the feasibility of eliminating the current budget deficit. In the event, over the course of this government's term of office, little was achieved. The current budget deficit increased from 7.1% to 8.3% and the debt/GNP ratio went from 105% to 128% between 1983 and 1986. The situation deteriorated further with increasing loss of confidence, rising interest rates, increasing unemployment and renewed emigration, increasing tax evasion and the continued relocation of financial capital to more hospitable tax environments. By 1986 it was clear that the strategy of adjustment to the fiscal crisis through increased levels of taxation in the absence of economic growth and the failure to curb current expenditure was not working. The coalition collapsed precisely on this issue, when the Minister for Finance, Mr John Bruton, proposed cuts in current expenditure proved politically unacceptable to the Labour Party.[13]

When the minority Fianna Fáil government succeeded the coalition government in March 1987, it immediately engaged the task of tackling the fiscal crisis. This was facilitated by the support of the main opposition parties as articulated by Alan Dukes, who had succeeded Dr Garret

Fitzgerald as leader of Fine Gael, in what became known as the 'Tallaght Strategy' (which referred to a speech delivered by Dukes in Tallaght). The critical switch on the part of the new government, implemented by the Minister for Finance, Mr Ray McSharry, was away from increases in the level of taxation to reductions in expenditure. In his first budget in 1987, McSharry reduced current government spending below the level that had been proposed by Fine Gael.

Once launched, the momentum for expenditure cuts gathered pace and further reductions were implemented in 1988 and 1989. Measured in constant prices, current government spending fell by 11% between 1987 and 1989. The adjustments following from the switch in strategy from the use of taxation to expenditure reductions were quickly evident. The current budget deficit decreased from a peak of 8.3% of GNP in 1986 to 1.7% in 1988 and by 1990 had been reduced to a low of 0.7%. Similarly, the EBR fell from a high of 12.8% of GNP in 1986 to 3.3% in 1988, and to a low of 2.0% in 1990. Similar orders of reduction were recorded in the Public Sector Borrowing Requirement (PSBR). At the same time economic growth reemerged, and it is the attempt to explain the growth performance of the Irish economy after 1987, and more particularly since 1994, that has become the centre of analytical attention.

ECONOMIC CROWTH AFTER 1987: THE SEARCH FOR EXPLANATIONS

The growth which emerged at this time went from a negative rate of –1.6% in real GNP in 1985 to 4.4% in 1987 and in 1990 reached a level of 8.3%. While growth faltered somewhat between 1991–93, by 1994 the current high rates emerged and have continued. In a recently published study, which presents the 'reflections of a group of Irish economists on the process that led to this success', it is noted that while there is 'widespread agreement' by now on the factors that have a role to play in the story, 'the emphasis placed on the various components will differ as always with the storyteller'.[14]

The European Commission identified the basis of the current period of strong economic growth in the decisive change of economic policy after 1987. Starting in that year, the Commission argued that 'a new broadly based macroeconomic strategy was adopted involving three main components; fiscal consolidation, enhanced exchange rate stability and a broad based social consensus agreement which included a competitiveness oriented wage agreement'.[15] These factors were also invoked by Leddin and Walsh to explain the achievement of the stabilisation of the economy, and by implication provided the facilitating environment that contributed to the economic growth that was to follow.[16] This perspective contains a mixture of domestic and external factors, the latter contributing in a particularly important manner during the course of the 1980s. These external influences included the collapse of world oil prices in 1986, the availability of higher farm prices and the acceleration of economic growth in the UK economy arising from the policies pursued by Nigel Lawson, Chancellor of the Exchequer, in the late 1980s.[17] In addition, the devaluation of the Irish punt in 1986, arising from a wider realignment of currencies, greatly enhanced Ireland's foreign competitive position. There was also the general downward trend in interest rates, which greatly relieved foreign debt interest repayments in addition to stimulating domestic growth.

The impressive performance of the Irish economy post 1987 quickly caught the attention of the international academic community. The uniqueness of the Irish experience was perceived as a striking example of a more general relationship between the dynamics of government expenditure and economic growth, which was termed the 'expansionary fiscal contraction' hypothesis.[18] According to this hypothesis, the reduction in government expenditure, such as implemented after 1987 in Ireland, led to an increase in overall economic activity. Central to this hypothesis is the behavioural assumption that private sector expenditures, both consumption and investment, will increase by more than the reduction in government expenditure and thereby lead to a net increase in aggregate demand. The plausibility of this hypothesis lies in the argument that reductions in government spending and borrowing lead to a reduction in interest rates, thereby stimulating increases in private consumption and investment spending. In the circumstances of Ireland in the 1980s, such was the extent of the fiscal crisis that confidence in the government's commitment to restore order to the public finances had been seriously damaged. This sparked large outflows of private funds, not only seeking higher returns but also to evade taxation, which was deemed to be punitive and had arisen from the spending and borrowing requirements of the government. Therefore, if this hypothesis possessed a degree of plausibility, it arose from the reduction in interest rates and the restoration of confidence in the government's commitment to restoring balance in the public finances.

It has also been suggested that additional support for this hypothesis comes from the impact on the expectations of households, who perceive that as balance is restored to the public finances, the burden of taxation in the form of future tax liabilities may be anticipated to actually decrease, thereby influencing expenditure patterns. A more substantive issue which emerges from the ready acceptance of this hypothesis is the extent to which it could be used to demonstrate the redundancy of Keynesian economics and its implications for a reduced role for the state in economic matters.

In the event, when subjected to a more systematic interrogation, the expansionary fiscal contraction hypothesis rapidly loses a good deal of its plausibility. When detailed econometric analysis was undertaken, serious doubts were cast on the validity of the expansionary hypothesis in the case of Ireland. Alternative explanations for Ireland's economic growth were sought, particularly in the period 1987–89, based largely on external factors. These were felt to be important influences on economic growth.[19] From a short-term perspective, the role of exchange rate policy, or more specifically the influence of a series of devaluations of the Irish punt in 1986 and 1993, provided an important competitive advantage.[20] These devaluations provided a major impetus to the growth of exports, which have contributed significantly to the recent growth performance of the Irish economy. The competitive advantages imparted from the devaluations of 1986 and 1993 were significant influences in facilitating economic growth. More generally, for some commentators, the conduct of Irish exchange rate policy was a source of stabilisation during the 1980s. The pursuit of an overvalued exchange rate policy was avoided, first by breaking the link with sterling in 1979, and then by the successive devaluations of 1986 and 1993 within the Exchange Rate Mechanism of the EMS. This is the argument adopted by Walsh[21] and Leddin and Walsh.[22] The role of exchange rate policy in the stabilisation process has, however, been disputed by Honahan.[23]

Commentators will continue to deliberate on this particular issue. However, for those subscribing to the Leddin and Walsh interpretation of the role of exchange rate policy, then Ireland's entry into the EMU and the single currency arrangement was a serious policy mistake which has removed this instrument of economic policy. From a longer-term perspective, however, opposition to EMU entry was not justified on the basis of this line of argument divorced from a consideration of a number of other long-term issues.

The role of centralised wage bargaining, adopted after 1987, is now widely invoked as an important contributing factor to Ireland's stabilisation. During the 1970s a number of National Wage Agreements and National Understandings were negotiated, but between 1981 and 1987 there were no centralised wage bargaining arrangements in place. Increasingly, during the 1980s, the rising unemployment and the concern to maintain international competitiveness gave rise to the need for moderation in wage costs. A new series of national pay agreements were negotiated after 1987, which included *Programme for National Recovery (1987–90)*, *Programme for Economic and Social Progress (1991–93)*, *Programme for Competitiveness and Work (1994–1997)*, and *Partnership 2000: Employment, Competitiveness and Inclusion (1997–2000)*. The central thrust of these agreements has been that, in return for low nominal wage demands, the government committed itself to deliver reductions in income taxation, improvements in social benefits and an extended array of other agreed measures.

Between 1987 and 1997, gross industrial earnings increased in real terms by almost 15%, while the increase in after-tax earnings rose by a further 9%. The reductions in tax rates accounted for almost 33% of the increase in real net income. The reductions in the tax rates are reflected in the decrease in the standard rate from 35% in 1988 to 25% in 1997, while the higher rate has decreased from 57% in 1988 to 48% in 1997. The contribution of this centralised or corporatist model of wage bargaining is reflected in the extent to which domestic inflationary impulses, relative to 'foreign competitors' are deemed to 'have been largely subdued'.[24] It was a source of some disappointment that, notwithstanding the degree of wage moderation achieved under these agreements, the level of unemployment remained extremely high. It is only in the very recent period that real improvements in the reduction of unemployment have been achieved, even allowing for the various training and temporary work schemes that exist within the Irish labour market. Clearly the degree of wage moderation achieved through centralised wage bargaining, along with the fiscal corrections pursued after 1987, have been major contributing factors in achieving stabilisation.

During the course of the 1980s the external environment underwent rapid changes. Within the world economy the forces of globalisation were exerting an increasing influence at all levels of economic activity. In Europe, there were major efforts to revitalise the movement towards greater European integration, instigated by Jacques Delors, President of the European Commission. The launching of the project to complete the Single Market by 1992 as a necessary condition for the more ambitious project of European Monetary Union (EMU) was the direct result of increasing global competitiveness and the perception that Europe was in danger of being seriously outpaced, both economically and technologically, by the United States and the Asian-Pacific economies centred on Japan.[25] The culmination of this process was reached when the Maastricht Treaty was adopted in 1992 and this specified the criteria for entry into the EMU by 1999.

Even if corrective measures had not been taken domestically from 1987, the convergence criteria specified in the Maastricht Treaty would have ensured radical readjustments in Irish economic policy if Ireland was to be considered for membership of the EMU. The driving force of these developments was the centrality given to the competitiveness of the economy. Any resistance to the necessary measures to restore stabilisation and reestablish the economy on a competitive basis would not have been easily countenanced. The government, for a variety of reasons, not least being the allure of the transitional financial arrangements in the guise of the Structural and Cohesion Funds, committed Ireland to being among the first entrants to the single currency area.

Whatever the relative merits of these various factors in the short term, and they all made important contributions, accounting for economic growth in the specific circumstances of an individual country is a difficult undertaking and the Irish case is no exception. Precisely for this reason, a number of commentators have adopted a longer-term perspective in an attempt to capture the accumulated impact of policy changes implemented over a thirty-year period.[26] The critical turning point here was the decision to abandon the protectionist strategy of import substitution industrialisation which had been pursued from the early 1930s. The reorientation of economic policy in the late 1950s and early 1960s, a development which was driven by a powerful combination of both internal and external influences, had a number of different dimensions.

First, there was the decision to abandon the protectionist strategy in favour of an export led strategy of development. This arose from the stagnation and ensuing crises of the 1950s and the rapidly changing external environment, which in the post-war world was dominated by trade liberalisation. Even if this was not the full blown model of free trade, it was clearly a second-best version that would see the world economy reorganise its trading arrangements on the basis of major trading blocs.[27] The emergence of the European Economic Community (EEC) and the European Free Trade Area (EFTA) in the late 1950s represented this development at the European level. Faced with these developments and their economic ramifications, Ireland committed itself to dismantling its protectionist policies and progressed rapidly towards a free trade position. The landmark developments marking this progression included the signing of the Anglo-Irish Free Trade Agreement (AIFTA) in 1965, entry into the EEC in 1973, membership of the ERM in 1979 and the Single European Market in 1992. This process has culminated in Ireland's inclusion among the first group of Member States to participate in the single currency programme.

Secondly, and arising directly from the new export led strategy of development, was the government's attempts to attract foreign direct investment into the country. This became a central pillar of industrial development policy. It was legitimised on the basis of the direct benefits that such investment could bring, including employment, income generation, new technologies and innovative management techniques. It was also recognised that indigenous industry was incapable, in the short to medium term at least, of providing a competitively viable basis for an export led strategy of development, so a compensating and substitute alternative had to be found. An elaborate array of measures, including tax concessions on export sales, grants, accelerated depreciation allowances and advanced factories, were put in place to achieve the objective of attracting foreign direct investment. There can be little doubt that the policy has been successful. There are currently over 1,000 foreign-owned manufacturing and services companies located in Ireland. They account for 55% of manufacturing output and up to 70% of industrial exports. In 1995 they employed 107,000 people which amounted to 46% of the manufacturing workforce.[28] The expanding population of these foreign companies, which are generally technologically advanced operations, is perceived as being the major factor in the modernisation of the industrial base of the economy that accounts for the rise in productivity.

Thirdly, there have been major expansions in the educational system, which is now considered to have been an important factor in the economic growth process. Free secondary education was introduced in the late 1960s, the school-leaving age raised and the range of third-level institutions extended. The latter development included the creation of the Regional Technical Colleges (recently upgraded to Institutes of Technology), which were expressly established to meet the technological demands of the new industries. In addition, the existing universities were expanded and two new universities created. The investment in human capital was substantial. Over three-quarters of those entering second-level education now complete the process, while up to two-thirds of second-level school-leavers proceed to higher education, further education or training programmes.[29]

Fourthly, there has been the contribution of European Union grants and subsidies since Ireland's entry in 1973. Initially they were dominated by the inflows to the agricultural sector, arising from the guaranteed prices under the Common Agricultural Policy (CAP). Later additional funds became available from the Social Fund and the European Regional Development Fund (ERDF). More recently, and amounting to very considerable additional flows, have been the transfers from the Structural and Cohesion Funds, under the terms of the agreement of movement towards the SEM. Measured relative to GNP, these net transfers to Ireland have been extremely substantial. Initially, during the early 1970s they averaged about 2% of GNP, but by 1979 they represented up to 6%, and by 1991 had reached 7% of GNP. Over the period since 1973 they have averaged around 5% of GNP. Net transfers such as these, which in essence amount to the equivalent of foreign aid, need not of course necessarily contribute to long-term economic growth, depending on their distribution and final use. However, there is little doubt that the more recent transfers from the Structural and Cohesion Funds within the framework of the National

Development Plans have contributed positively to economic growth, both in their direct impact and in their enhancement of the productive capacity of the economy.[30]

The above considerations sit comfortably with the insights provided by modern growth theory, which are more general in nature and less specific in character than the extended menu of factors currently under consideration in the context of Irish circumstances. Modern growth theory will identify the role of savings and investment, particularly the latter, in promoting economic growth.[31] Ireland's investment ratio was over 30% by the end of the 1970s, which was exceptionally high by international standards. It fell sharply during the 1980s, especially in the second half of that decade, and up to the mid-1990s was closer to 15% of GDP. This presented Ireland as something of an anomaly in that the period of highest growth was associated with a declining investment ratio. This evoked the phenomenon of 'investmentless growth' that replaced an earlier paradox of 'jobless growth', that had characterised the 1980s. However, the paradox of 'investmentless growth' can be partly explained by the changing composition of the manufacturing sector under the influence of the high technology multinationals locating here and the upgrading of technology in indigenous industry. This, combined with a more productive public sector investment programme under the National Development Plans since 1989, has reduced the capital-output ratio in production.[32]

Consistent with modern growth theory, the new emphasis is on human capital investment, along with research and development intensive activities, as the new motive forces of economic growth. The emphasis on education in general and technological education in particular, which has occupied a central role in Irish development policy, has been justified by both the insights of modern growth theory and the findings of recent empirical research.[33] A recent attempt to analyse the factors that have contributed to the recent economic growth within a medium-to-long-term perspective, identified five such factors: the changing demographic structure; the deepening and extension of the human capital base of the economy; the openness of the economy; the recent investment in infrastructure, and the domestic macroeconomic environment.[34] While the effort of establishing the relative contribution of various factors, both short term and long-term, will continue for a considerable period into the future, the identification of difficulties, potential problems and the position of vulnerable groups within the economy remain major issues of concern.

THE FUTURE: 'UNDER THE BELLY OF THE TIGER'[35]

The centrality of competitiveness, against the background of intensified global rivalry, has been the dominant influence since the 1980s. Ireland, in common with most other European countries, has witnessed the emergence of the new forces of restructuring, privatisation, deregulation and the demand for new flexibilities in the operation of labour markets. Ireland, however, did not embrace an unreconstructed market model for wage determination, opting instead for a revamped and extended model of centralised wage bargaining.[36] This represented a continuity with the corporatist arrangements that characterised the 1970s. While it may appear at first sight to be inconsistent with the ideology of free market price and wage determination, it was enthusiastically embraced by the corporate sector and their representatives. And rightly so. It has served their purposes well and it is the trade union movement that is now voicing reservations about the wisdom of future commitments to this model.[37]

Economically, the functional distribution of income between aggregate profit and wage shares moved in favour of profits, facilitated by the acceptance and implementation of the centralised wage bargaining within the arrangements of social partnership. One of the interesting results that will emerge when the last ten years are subjected to systematic research, is the movement in favour of the aggregate profit share relative to the aggregate wage share. Though lauded as a major contributing factor to both stabilisation and economic growth over the last decade, the full implications of this process remains to be more thoroughly interrogated and researched.

More recently a new critical literature addressing various aspects of the 'celtic tiger' and its achievements, has emerged. The very concept of a 'tiger' economy, and also the comparisons with the Asian tiger economies, have been called into question in the work of Denis O'Hearn.[38] He argues that the comparisons, from the point of view of the time dimensions involved, are not valid in that the Asian tiger economies have experienced their spectacularly high growth rates over a thirty-year period, while in Ireland we are talking about a mere five years of high growth rates. Of even more fundamental interest is O'Hearn's very recent work where he explores the meaning of economic 'tigerhood'.[39] His conclusions are salutary reminders of the potential vulnerabilities of the recent growth experience. Irish tigerhood, he argues, is 'characterised by a rather strange set of contradictory results: high growth of TNC production and exports without correspondingly high investments or job creation in manufacturing; concentration of employment growth in services without correspondingly rapid growth of service provision; and rapid overall economic growth with stagnant investment, sluggish or spotty consumption growth, and rising inequality'.[40]

Others have also analysed the growing dependence on the foreign investment sector and have quantified the imbalance and increasing dependence on an extremely narrow base of foreign companies. Murphy, for example, has shown that selected MNCs, in five sectors of production, accounted for 43% of total net output in manufacturing industry in 1993, while accounting for a mere 11% of manufacturing employment. By 1995, in the same five sectors of productions, selected foreign companies accounted for 52% of total net output, with only 13% of manufacturing employment. The same analysis has demonstrated that between 1990 and 1996, if exports from the 'high tech' MNCs are deducted, the growth of GDP over this period drops from 55% to 23%. Murphy has argued that a more appropriate metaphor to that of the 'Celtic Tiger' would be the US 'High Tech Tiger with a Celtic Face'.[41]

For many, the most disconcerting aspect of recent developments in the Irish economy has been the failure to redress the persistence of poverty and social exclusion. Between 1987 and 1994 there was a modest increase in the percentage of persons below the 50% line, and a more pronounced increase, of the order of 3–4 percentage points, below the 60% line. The 50% line in this context is defined as being somewhat above the minimum social welfare payment derived from the Supplementary Welfare Allowance scheme, while the 60% cut-off was above the highest social welfare payment, namely the Old Age Contributory Pension rate.[42] While different indices measure different aspects of the problem of poverty and inequality and may indicate differential trends in the overall direction of poverty, there is general recognition that tackling poverty and social exclusion is now one of the major challenges facing Irish society.[43] It remains painfully disconcerting that, notwithstanding the economic gains of the 'Celtic Tiger', a Minister for Finance could refer to the existence of a 'poverty industry' which appears to have an assured existence for the foreseeable future.

CHAPTER 2

Negotiated Governance and the Irish Polity

GEORGE TAYLOR

INTRODUCTION

Competitiveness, innovation and flexible labour markets. Product diversification, polyvalent structures and lifelong learning. This is the future envisaged by many, an information rich age in which an entrepreneurial spirit is given free reign. It is perhaps symbolised in the iMac, an icon now synonymous with the principle that design and consumer choice will succeed in niche markets. But they are also concepts that pervade the language of contemporary Irish politics. From sources as disparate as the speeches of the Taoiseach, Bertie Ahern, to conversations in the pub, they are the common currency of political debate.[1] It may well be that the meaning of some phrases eludes us, but we may rest reassured that their widespread use ensures that precise details are often unimportant. As far as the accompanying political rhetoric is concerned, we have an intuitive feel not for what it is, but most certainly for what it is not. It is not a political project characterised by the claustrophobic embrace of state led modernisation typified in the formation of Team Aer Lingus. This is an altogether different exercise, one which promotes the 'gospels of globalisation' in order to ensure that multinational capital will seek to reside in Ireland.

Amid the clamour to celebrate the central tenets of this new era, then, it appears that convention among political scientists now dictates that macro forms of political bargaining be consigned to their rightful place; the media vaults of the 1970s or the memories of longstanding veteran politicians. It is not just that this form of bargaining appears to have fallen out of fashion but rather, the argument runs, that they belong to a bygone political age and are no longer compatible with the prevailing structures of global capitalism.[2] That such political bargaining should have been jettisoned so readily by conservatives should surprise few. The political legacy of a decade or more of Thatcherism, Reaganism and Kohlism has, it seems, irreparably tarnished the image of institutionalised interest intermediation.

However, even more surprising has been the ease with which such arguments have found favour in social democratic circles. Here it has been argued that capitalism has moved firmly into a new, dynamic phase in which the flexibility in personnel and organisational strategy is paramount. Under such circumstances business can no longer be expected to sustain the level of economic growth upon which both the welfare state and trade union influence over public policy were predicated. Put simply, macro-political bargaining procedures are viewed as increasingly anachronistic structures within an era of flexible specialisation.[3]

And yet, in Ireland, macro-political bargaining has formed the cornerstone of government policy for over a decade. Indeed, among high ranking officials in the EU, it is now commonplace to attribute the success of the 'Celtic Tiger' to the national level agreements constructed during this period. Certainly, as a small, open economy located on the periphery of western Europe, the need to respond quickly to changes in international markets is particularly pressing. Rigidities that emerge as a result of national level bargaining would compound the perceived economic costs of peripheral location and relative underdevelopment.

The real problem with those who casually dismiss a role for macro-political bargaining in the new global economy is not just that they tend to over-emphasise the level of rigidity within these institutionalised agreements but, in so doing, ignore the extent to which such agreements develop as responses to economic and political crises. It is not simply a question of being misled by the rhetorical assurances of Thatcherism, Reaganism or Kohlism. Rather, they appear to have been seduced by neo-conservative interpretations of alleged administrative failure which state that the real problem facing western European capitalism has been an explosion in the institutional impediments to economic growth.[4]

This chapter presents theoretical arguments and empirical data which contest the prevailing political orthodoxy on three counts. First, it challenges the inclination to view macro-political bargaining as inherently rigid and argues that such a limited focus is compounded by the tendency to portray decentralised forms of negotiation in a more favourable light, as if there is a natural complementarity between such forms of negotiation and the new, emerging structures of global capitalism. In other words, it contends that such an approach assumes *a priori* that these forms of negotiation are somehow better suited to the current 'needs' of capital.[5] Second, it argues that such an approach often ignores the complexity of the managerial function and is inclined to conflate the interests of individual businesses with business in general or, alternatively, to restrict the parameters of the managerial function simply to the issue of pay. Finally, the chapter avoids the temptation to view macro-political bargaining purely in terms of its function to set wage rates in public and private sector industry. Instead it examines the innovative role that recent national agreements have played in introducing flexibility into the provision of public services.

MACRO-POLITICAL BARGAINING: SOME THEORETICAL ISSUES

A useful starting point from which to discuss the efficacy of macro-political bargaining lies in Goldthorpe's view that it is possible to identify at least two forms of institutional practices or tendencies that form part of the state's response to crisis.[6] The first, corporatism, refers to a set of institutionalised negotiations between interest associations or social partners on public policy (an inclusionary response). The second, dualism, is associated with measures designed to exclude major interest organisations and expand the use of market forces in the provision of public policy (an exclusionary response).[7] The former clearly implies some form of macro-level concertation while the latter, which does not necessarily entail a calculated assault upon organised interests, envisages an expansion in the use of market based instruments in public policy.[8] In general terms, Goldthorpe envisages an expansion in market based instruments that may act as the basis from which to alleviate 'rigidities that prevail elsewhere'.[9]

In a similar vein, Streeck has questioned any viable role for macro-political bargaining in the new, emerging global economic order. While he was willing to concede that moderation in working-class wage demands under corporatist agreements was beneficial to capital, he now views such institutional forms as inflexible, constraining the adaptive response of business to market contingencies. Streeck's principal point, and it is a persuasive one, is that:

> some sort of effective Keynesian expansionist capacity seems indispensable for the kind of corporatist concertation and social contract bargaining that was to stabilise non-American capitalisms of the 1970s. As much as these systems may otherwise have differed, under the rules of corporatist bargaining a state that cannot with any reasonable prospect of success promise to apply its fiscal and monetary tools to alleviate unemployment cannot possibly hope to gain concessions from unions or to influence settlements between unions and employers by, for example, offering to improve the terms of the bargain through corresponding economic policy.[10]

In Streeck's opinion, this decay in neo-corporatism can be attributed to a qualitative change in an economic and social structure which served to undermine the structural and cultural foundations of corporatism.[11] The simple dichotomy between capital and labour, the central pivot on which neo-corporatist negotiations were secured, has become increasingly untenable in the new global economy. Volatile international markets, advances made in technology and new political cleavages have usurped the basis upon which the alliance between social democracy and the trade unions had been forged.[12] In other words, for both Goldthorpe and Streeck, macro-political bargaining arrangements impose rigid, uniform standards on business which have become unacceptable in a period in which a flexible response in product range, technology and social organisation is essential.[13]

Such themes are also resonant in the work of Lash and Urry who view corporatism largely as 'a matter for compromise between social classes in very much a national context of resource distribution'.[14] In their view, the penetration of global capital has dislocated national economies, making an assessment of what is an 'appropriate sacrifice' in the national interest a precarious exercise.[15] The internationalisation of capital markets and a corresponding shift towards 'disorganised capitalism' has manifest itself in a widespread decline in national level collective agreements and a corresponding increase in company and plant level bargaining.[16] The transformation in production techniques, the growth of the service sector and the internationalisation of production have all impacted detrimentally upon those areas of the economy that formed the basis for the centralised bargain of neo-corporatism.[17]

There are clearly discernible similarities between the respective positions of Goldthorpe, Streeck and Lash and Urry. All emphasise the importance to management of being released from the constraints imposed by macro-political bargaining structures, the deregulation of national and international labour markets, the internationalisation of capital and the corresponding shift in the composition of workforces. However, there should be some reservations in their respective positions, particularly with regard to the premise that decentralised forms of bargaining offer a more flexible response to the *rigidities* imposed by corporatist tendencies.

The problem lies in the way in which rigidity as a concept is used. More often than not it is only applied to corporatist tendencies and presumably, therefore, denotes problems that are not experienced in a dualist or market based responses to crisis. As such, the term becomes laden with *negative* connotations.[18] A more useful distinction, and one which does not carry the assumptions of efficiency implicit within the metaphors of rigidity/flexibility, would be to argue that both corporatist *and* dualist responses to crisis offer *opportunities* and *constraints.* Formulated in such a manner, the framework does not assume *a priori* that dualism is more flexible than corporatism as a response to crisis. In turn, research should, therefore, focus upon establishing the particular configuration of a dualist or corporatist response to crisis through an examination of the specific political and historical conjuncture.[19]

In this vein it is more preferable to see dualist tendencies as offering both *opportunities* and *constraints*. It may well be the case that a reduction in the size of the public sector offers the state an opportunity to depoliticise any programme of restructuring and avoid undue conflict in vulnerable areas. However, it should also be acknowledged that, in the process of relinquishing responsibility, the state may also lose strategic control in certain key sectors. This may be compounded by a reduction in the state's capacity to provide collective goods which are in the long-term interest of the economy but which may not emerge from the rational decisions of individual firms in a free market.[20]

A further problem implicit in the work of Streeck, Goldthorpe and Lash and Urry is the tendency to assume that decentralised forms of wage bargaining are necessarily more efficient in responding to the needs of business. This is exacerbated by the fact that such authors not only perceive this form of bargaining to be inherently more beneficial but that it is recognised uniformly as such by management. There is, needless to say, little evidence in the UK to support such a sweeping conclusion.[21] During the 1980s, for example, the UK experienced a radical overhaul of pay negotiations as companies sought to move toward decentralised agreements.[22] In managerial parlance, such moves were often justified on the grounds that there were gains to be made from the flexible deployment of manpower, enabling management to establish a closer link between pay, performance and the local labour market.[23]

However, Walsh's research indicates that decentralised forms of bargaining agreements present management with alternative problems and should not, therefore, be seen as inherently more 'efficient'. In particular, she argues that decentralised wage bargaining procedures may actually generate intrafirm bargaining pressures and as a consequence impede employers from securing productivity gains. Moreover, where productivity is determined by interdependent technologies as opposed to employee performance, management may encounter obstacles to the introduction of individual incentive schemes.[24]

A further area of controversy often raised in debates about macropolitical bargaining is associated with its alleged propensity to promote rigidities in the economy. Here, neo-liberals have been particularly vociferous in their condemnation of macro-level interest intermediation, attributing to it at least three fatal flaws. The first relates to 'obligations' which tend to accompany national level agreements. Here, critics of organised interest intermediation present a stark contrast between, on the one hand, governments who face pressure from trade unions to defend jobs and, on the other hand, managers who need to be released from their political masters to make 'tough economic decisions' in order to restructure companies. On this matter, it often took little more than the 'drop of a hat' for Mrs Thatcher to rehearse her grievance with the post-war welfare state which, she argued, had *allowed* management to 'fudge on the major issues'. In her opinion, successive governments had, during periods of difficulty, resorted to using the 'open cheque book of public finance' to assuage those union leaders who had gained access to the corridors of political power. The New Right's response, euphemistically referred to as a process in which the Conservative government would 'make you free' (whether you wanted it or not), invariably offered little more than a political justification to challenge the political and economic role of trade unions.[25]

In the Irish context it has also been argued that social partnership contributes to high levels of unemployment because the unemployed cannot perform the 'task' of 'wage undercutting'. However, as O'Donnell observes, without national agreements 'income determination will remain a non-competitive, highly collectivised process with tendencies to monopoly power on both sides of industry'.[26]

In a subtle and far more persuasive fashion, neo-liberals have also argued that it was not just that public sector industries suffered from poor management/union relations, but that the state imposed a series of institutional rigidities that are a burden upon *any* industry operating within an internationally competitive environment. Such a difficulty is compounded by the demands of a new global economic order where management is required to enact decisions in a shorter time frame, a function which cannot be performed within the straitjacket of political dialogue. A further theme, one mentioned only occasionally in the accompanying political rhetoric, was that involvement in macro-level negotiations allowed unions to secure wage increases above the market level, a situation that reinforced a 'rates for the job' consciousness and prevented management from reducing job demarcations.[27]

This antipathy toward the political access granted to trade unions is based on the assumption that wage rigidities are generated by trade union activity. Evidence to support this, however, is far from convincing. Despite a vast programme of legislation in the UK which sought to diminish the political and economic role of trade unions, wages during the 1980s consistently outstripped the rate of inflation.[28] Moreover, it is by no means clear that the unions' ability to secure better working conditions and pay are as detrimental to productivity as neo-liberals would have us believe. On this issue, for example, Dore has observed that measures that seek to improve employment security (a significant source of labour market rigidity) may actually motivate firms to adapt to market change through intra-company diversification. In addition, it may also serve to stimulate employers to pursue retraining programmes. Within such working environs, Dore believes that employees may be more receptive to the introduction of new technology and changing work practices.[29]

It is a position with which Streeck largely concurs when he points out that negotiations which keep wages higher than the market would otherwise dictate may actually *encourage* firms to diversify and invest in training and retraining.[30] In Streeck's opinion, a developed internal labour market with high and rigid wages and stable employment seems better suited to serving volatile and diversified high quality markets, a scenario confirmed by Rubery's research which shows that, in the British case at least, most firms benefit from 'continuous, stable relationships with committed workers'.[31]

This is a theme addressed more recently by Rhodes who has questioned the purported 'benefits' of a neo-liberal approach to labour market regulation. While conceding that the UK has been successful in its move away from a 'cluster of southern European states with rigid labour markets', Rhodes is unwilling to accept that this has transformed the productive fortunes of the British economy.[32] It is certainly plausible to suggest that greater external flexibility (the hiring and firing of workers) has been achieved and that the breakdown of union control over the workplace may have induced more internal flexibility. However, Rhodes warns that such gains have been achieved without a corresponding increase in 'levels of trust (except in inward investing Japanese firms which, in some sectors, have revolutionised work organisation)'. Neither, has the associated fragmentation of employers and trade unions assisted in the 'provision of collective goods such as an effective training system', hampering any concerted move away from a 'low skill equilibrium'. The consequence is that while the relationship between external flexibility and internal flexibility has been altered, the UK's regime is still a 'price based' rather than 'quality based' productive structure.[33] In general terms, then, neo-liberals accuse macro-political bargaining of granting unions inordinate political power and fostering institutional impediments which undermine an entrepreneurial culture.

A second flaw identified by the neo-liberal critique of the state intervention relates to the changing nature of citizenship in the post-war period. Here, objections primarily focus on the increase of citizenship rights which have altered the level of security assumed under the auspices of an expanded welfare state.[34] It is not simply a question of the level of entitlements to which neo-liberals object, but rather it is the very structure of those entitlements. The charge against the welfare state is that the very presence of benefits increases the level of wage rigidity in the economy and fosters a culture of dependency.[35] It is an argument which critics of the New Right have found difficult to resolve. Dore, for example, has conceded that welfare schemes have impacted detrimentally upon the take-up of low paid jobs, thereby increasing rigidity in the labour market. The solution, in his considered opinion, rests on ensuring specified levels of employment through national agreements, thereby reducing the impact of unproductive rigidities (such as income maintenance schemes).[36]

Streeck remains less circumspect. In a more novel and interesting fashion he has suggested that rigidity and flexibility are not always mutually exclusive and that the presence of some forms of rigidity need not present an insurmountable problem, providing that there is a reduction in productive rigidities. In countries like the United States and Britain, for example, they have had a trade-off between flexible access to the external labour market (hiring and firing workers to change the size and composition of their workforce) and strong 'rigidities' with respect to internal deployment, redeployment and retraining.[37] It is a position that contrasts sharply with that of Germany and Sweden where unions have managed to secure rigid entitlements to long-term employment in exchange for high levels of internal shop-floor flexibility.[38]

It is worth noting that both Dore and Streeck concede that a pattern of high wages and rigid job entitlements is unlikely to result from the enlightening forces of the free market.[39] In such circumstances, social peace, worker commitment and high and flexible qualifications tend to be undersupplied if left to the rational decisions of individual firms. In other words, certain rigidities (collective goods which are in the long-term interest of the economy) are important prerequisites to the development of an arena in which enterprising firms are able to respond and diversify in quality competitive markets.[40]

This is an interesting argument which has an important bearing upon this chapter. In particular, it raises the crucial question of why certain rigidities imposed upon management 'force' innovation but others do not? At least initially, Streeck was prepared to concede that certain forms of political regulation could be beneficial. Indeed, he went as far as to suggest that 'political regulation not only need not be detrimental to economic success, but may constitute a central precondition for it'.[41] This is certainly a position which fits comfortably with his original stance that rigidity and flexibility are not mutually exclusive. However, he seems reluctant to acknowledge that macro-political bargaining could have such a beneficial impact. This apparent discrepancy is intelligible only when we realise that for Streeck, political regulation is beneficial *only* if it is directed toward the *supply* side of the economy, a role which he feels macro-political bargaining cannot perform. As far as Streeck is concerned, macro-political bargaining remains circumscribed by its function as a tool for demand side change and is, therefore, ill-suited to engineer a restructuring of the supply side of the economy. It is a position which can be further teased out in the language he attributes to the forms of political regulation deemed beneficial (employment protection and training), where the vocabulary is effused with terms such as 'stimulate', 'encourage' or 'innovate', all of which are imbued with dynamic, positive connotations. It is also worth noting that they are positive, 'possessive' categories and, as such, fit comfortably within the current policy paradigm of reconstructed social democracy (the third way). Here, the rejection of macro-political bargaining (and a partial acceptance of the neo-liberal critique of the welfare state) presents a new dichotomy between passive and active policy paradigms. The policy recommendations of this new, active paradigm find their leitmotif in the persistent call for an overhaul of an archaic, passive, universal welfare regime.

In a subtle, but nonetheless crucial fashion, the view of reconstructed social democracy distinguishes itself from the neo-liberal critique of welfare in the fact that we are no longer exclusively concerned with the role of individual self-responsibility. A policy paradigm which attributes the *cause* of unemployment to the failings of individuals (and subsequently constructs a neo-liberal safety net) has been supplanted with one that creates 'opportunities' and generates 'incentives' for individuals who 'possess' the capacity to actively respond to their predicament. This is a policy paradigm populated not by individuals *per se*, but by categories of individuals whose membership is defined by their particular circumstance and experience of unemployment (lone parents, the young unemployed or absent fathers). We no longer have a 'catch all' experience of unemployment (or receipt of welfare) and consequently the policy response can no longer be universal. Rather, we have a series of unemployment experiences in which policy is tailored to categories of individuals. Unemployment is no longer ascribed to the failure of individuals, but neither does responsibility lie at the doorstep of the state. The active dimension to this welfare regime resides in the tension that exists between state support and individual responsibility. The state functions to create opportunities from which to assist those individuals who wish to respond to their predicament (this is the possessive dimension).

The intention here is to highlight the fact that macro-political bargaining tends to be (mistakenly) equated with economic demand management strategies (and/or a passive welfare state). One should not downplay the importance of pressures emanating from the global economy which pose significant problems for Ireland's negotiated form of governance. Clearly, the increasing penetration of multinational companies in the Irish economy, and their capacity to rapidly relocate production in periods of volatile market conditions, raises difficulties for successful macro-level concertation (and any co-ordination of policy response). It would also be naïve to assume that in such circumstances international capital will not seek more flexibility in the search for an optimal balance in labour market regulation. However, there is danger in the current tendency to view a neo-liberal approach to labour market regulation as necessarily 'better suited' to the prevailing conditions of global capitalism. It may, in the short-term, deliver greater external flexibility but that is far short of providing either political and economic stability or the collective goods (training and education) from which to pursue that most elusive prize; a high tech, high wage economy.

The case study below returns to these themes at an empirical level. It addresses at least two key arguments. First, that the rigidities normally attributed to macro-political bargaining agreements are not necessarily an inherent feature and that, far from being a constraint upon management, macro-political bargaining agreements in Ireland have been invaluable in the restructuring of the supply side of the economy. Second, that analyses to date have focused predominantly on the role of macro-political bargaining in setting wage rates in both the public and private sectors. This approach ignores the fact that in the Irish case, particularly with regard to the latest agreement *Partnership 2000*, macro-political bargaining has not only assisted management in the restructuring of the supply side of the economy (both private and public sector industry) but has also been at the forefront of recent moves to introduce flexibility into public sector service provision.

MACRO-POLITICAL BARGAINING IN IRELAND: FROM THE *PROGRAMME FOR NATIONAL ECONOMIC RECOVERY* TO *PARTNERSHIP 2000*

If the sentiments expressed recently by the Taoiseach, Bertie Ahern, are any indication of the likely trajectory of policy, then Ireland will continue to pursue the type of negotiated agreements that have taken place over the last decade.[42] There can be little room for doubt that, even if elements of its academe remain sceptical, those in political and media circles remain impressed by the contribution made by macro-political bargaining in creating and sustaining Ireland as an investment haven. It is hardly surprising that few politicians are willing to dismiss the foundations upon which Ireland's 'bewildering' economic success has been generated. As O'Donnell observes, economic growth between 1986–96 has averaged 4.6% against an EU average of 2.4%. Total employment, which had fallen by an average of 0.82% per annum between 1980–87, has since expanded by 1.8% per annum. Irish national output has risen by 7.5% and employment an astonishing 4.0%.[43] The figures certainly justify the tag of 'Celtic Tiger'. Neither have commentators in the media been slow to link economic growth with national level agreements. A recent *Irish Time*s editorial, for example, commented that:

> far too frequently, there is a public acceptance of glib criticism that economic and social planning is something that happens elsewhere and that our development has been almost accidental. This is not the case . . . the strategy reports on inter-related policy measures have provided the framework for . . . national agreements between government and the social partners. This is the bedrock on which our economic growth has been based.[44]

Such sentiments have also been voiced by senior figures in Brussels who have talked in glowing terms of the role macro-political bargaining has played in creating the 'Celtic Tiger'.

Such negotiated institutional arrangements were first mooted as a response to the industrial conflict which emerged in the late 1960s. To many inside government, the debilitating experiences of such industrial strife could be attributed to the particularities of Irish trade union organisation, multi-union representation and a relatively weak level of centralisation. In a concerted attempt to restore stability to wage negotiations and subsequently reduce the incidence of strikes, the government prompted a series of national level wage agreements and National Understandings with employers and trade unions during the 1970s. These agreements, which lasted between 1970 and 1980, involved negotiations over pay between employers and unions and a series of non-pay negotiations between unions and government.[45]

During the 1970s the national wage agreements assumed an increasingly more structured format. Largely at the behest of SIPTU, one of the largest trade unions, the unions sought to develop a structure in which future negotiations would attempt to pursue social and economic policies in a more integrated fashion. In particular, as O'Riordan has noted, unions were extremely conscious of the fact that an absence of structures in which they could influence government economic policy meant that wage restraint would not necessarily translate into additional employment opportunities.[46] Similarly, any success the unions may have enjoyed in securing higher wages could easily be lost in budgetary policies which placed an unfair burden upon employees.

By the end of the decade the objective was to restructure the nature of pay negotiations, placing them within an integrated setting which would take full cognisance of tax reforms and job creation. Although it was to become more successful in later agreements, the strategy was severely hampered in the early 1980s as the combination of political instability and economic crisis led governments to abandon negotiations with the trade union movement. That management had become disenchanted with national level agreements was apparent in its concerted campaign to decentralise wage negotiations, tying pay increases to local labour market conditions and the profitability of individual firms. However, the emergence of the *Programme for National Recovery* (PNR) in 1987 and the *Programme for Economic and Social Progress* (PESP) in 1990 signalled a renewed enthusiasm for national level negotiations.

The PNR had been negotiated amid a crisis in public finances with government debt peaking at 117% of GDP. As such, a large part of its remit was directed toward reducing the debt/GDP ratio to 96.5% by 1990.[47] The success of the partnership approach to public finance provided a significant element to a prolonged period of economic growth which has earned the Irish economy the tag of the 'Celtic Tiger'. Annual growth rates since 1987 have, to many economists, been nothing short of astonishing. Moreover, in contrast to the preceding seven-year period of declining employment growth, the period of the PNR provided a welcome boost to job creation. Similarly, the programme also delivered higher living standards for employees as modest wage increases were coupled with tax reforms. The success of the PNR led to negotiations for its successor, the PESP. By 1992, as Table 2.1 illustrates, the success of these programmes had ensured that national level wage negotiations, particularly in the manual and clerical sectors, were the norm.

Table 2.1: At What Level is Basic Pay Determined?

	Managerial	*Professional*	*Clerical*	*Manual*
National/Industry collective bargaining	33.3	39.9	55.1	71.0
Regional collective bargaining	0	2.2	6.5	8.0
Company/Division	27.5	23.9	24.6	18.1
Establishment/Site	15.2	17.4	17.4	13.0
Individual	39.9	31.2	16.7	5.8

Source: Industrial Relations News (IRN) 38, 1992.

The success of PESP can be attributed to a number of innovations that contrast with its predecessors.[48] In general terms, it involved a redirection of policy around the 'restructuring' of the supply side of the economy with the intention of enhancing flexibility in negotiations between management and unions. Here, the most important innovation developed was the introduction of a local bargaining clause (Clause 3) which allowed management to tie negotiations to local labour market conditions while successfully retaining moderation in wage demands at a macro-level.[49] Table 2.2, for example, shows clearly that Clause 3 of PESP was a significant contributory factor in management's ability to extract concessions in a wide range of operating areas. As the study undertaken by the *Industrial Relations News* (IRN) noted, management was successful in gaining significant concessions in almost half (48%) of the ninety-six local bargaining deals recorded at the beginning of 1991.[50]

The findings of the IRN study largely concur with the general thrust of an internal research analysis conducted by SIPTU.[51] However, unlike the SIPTU report, the analysis by the IRN made an important distinction between items such as 'agreements to cooperate with on-going change or the tightening up on tea breaks' with agreements on cashless pay, increased productivity or major reorganisation/rationalisation. However, what is of more significance is the fact that when both of these broad categories (significant and minor trade-offs) are put together, the overall figure for companies where concessions were agreed in return for Clause 3 came to a total of 79%.[52]

Table 2.2: Breakdown of Clause 3 Agreements

3% with 'significant' trade-offs	48.0%
3% with 'minor' trade-offs	25.0%
3% *without* trade-offs	14.6%
3% plus/radical change	6.2%
Less than 3%	4.1%
Other	2.0%
Total	*100%*

Source: IRN, 37, 1st Oct. 1992.

The figures provided by a survey undertaken by the Department of Enterprise and Employment also concur with these findings. This study monitored the outcome of negotiations on the local bargaining clause in 427 private and public sector firms, comprising over 121,000 employees. Successful negotiations were reached in 77% of the enterprises monitored.[53] Further confirmation of this trend can be deduced from the annual report of the Labour Relations Commission which pointed out that, while a large proportion of the conciliation service was called upon to resolve disputes about conditions of employment and pay, it was also heavily involved in protracted disputes about reorganisation, rationalisation and redundancy.[54]

A sample list of type of changes agreed by unions in a trade-off for payment of Clause 3 could be made up of the following: productivity improvements; rationalisation/reorganisation; regrading; co-operation with new technology/new machinery; introduction of 'just in time' working practices (JIT), and of course the all-encompassing 'co-operation with on-going change'.[55] In its annual report in 1993, the Labour Relations Commission noted that 300 cases referred to the commission involved Clause 3. However, of more relevance to the arguments here was that fact that an additional 200 cases presented involved disputes about company rationalisation programmes, periodic lay-offs and short-time working. In its analysis of these developments the Commission remarked that the majority of the cases involved 'disagreements about how the 3% trade-off could be handled'.[56] In other words, Clause 3 was not simply a local pay bargaining clause. While it clearly introduced an element of flexibility in macro-level negotiations (allowing management some latitude on pay), it also formed the basis from which discussions could take place on the introduction of new technology, changing work practices and job demarcations. It seems plausible to suggest that political regulation in the form of Clause 3 stimulated an exchange between unions and management about changes to the supply side of the economy. In other words, it engineered a situation which demanded consultation, negotiation and compromise. It realigned discussion away from the simple parameters of pay (increases) toward issues surrounding the introduction of new technology and working practices.

In a more novel fashion, the agreement not only allowed Clause 3 to be paid in phases but also ensured that delays could be sought in 'periods of financial stricture'. This latter element to the agreement was subject to approval from both the Labour Court and the Labour Relations Commission on the financial state of the individual firm. It is an interesting feature of the agreement since it allowed a 'breathing space' to emerge during volatile market conditions and a delay for those who may have experienced difficulties during a currency crisis. Although the data here are more limited, Table 2.3 indicates that while the majority of companies (55.5%) paid Clause 3 in a single phase, a phased payment was made in 27% of cases, a process which became more prevalent as 1992 progressed.

More revealing is the breakdown of changes provided in Table 2.4. This table highlights two important themes. First, despite the predominance of macro-political bargaining structures, management in Ireland has been extremely successful in altering working practices among core employees. Second, many of the changes which have taken place relate specifically to the status of employees. As column 1 of Table 2.4 shows, the type of response associated with flexible strategies designed to increase an organisation's ability to adapt to volatile market conditions has altered radically.

The use of part-time employees, temporary or casual workers, fixed-term contracts and subcontractors has increased significantly.[57]

Table 2.3: How the 3% was Applied

Full 3% (starting date, phase II of PESP)	53 (55.5%)
Full 3% on a phased basis (starting date, phase II of PESP)	26 (27%)
Full 3% (starting date before phase II)	5 (5.2%)
Full 3% (starting date after phase II)	3 (3.0%)
Deals in excess of 3%	6 (6.2%)
Interim deals	3 (3.0%)
Total	*96 (100%)*

Table 2.4: Changes in the Use of the Various Arrangements over the Period 1989–1992

	More	*Same*	*Less*	*Not used*	*Don't know*
Weekend work	14.5	50.7	14.5	14.5	5.8
Shift work	15.2	54.3	8.0	15.9	6.5
Overtime	23.2	34.1	34.1	2.9	5.8
Annual hours contract	4.3	17.4	9.4	50.0	1.4
Part-time work	31.2	26.8	4.3	26.1	11.6
Temporary	37.7	36.2	8.7	6.5	0.7
Fixed-term contract	37.7	29.0	4.3	19.6	0.7
Home based work	1.4	4.3	—	70.3	0.7
Govt training scheme	13.0	29.0	—	36.2	2.2
Subcontracting	36.2	29.7	3.6	20.3	0.7

Source: IRN, 38, Oct. 1992.

On this issue Morley, Gunningle and Heraty remain more circumspect. They suggest that while management in Ireland has pursued a strategy aimed at ensuring a more flexible response between labour inputs and the market environment, it has been a gradual rather than radical departure.[58] What remains far more important is that changes to employee status have occurred in a period in which management has *apparently* been denied the autonomy afforded by decentralised bargaining to exploit local labour market conditions and initiate change. Clearly, the incidence of such change reveals a significant disparity between the rhetoric of national level employer organisations, which allude to the restrictive nature of macro-political bargaining agreements, and the experience of such negotiations. A more considered appraisal highlights the flexibility which macro-political bargaining structures have given to management in its attempts to implement new working practices and technology.

Table 2.5 provides a breakdown of the relationship between full-time employment and part-time employment from 1983 to 1992. These data show that while unemployment was increasing the level of part-time work remained fairly even until 1987. Thereafter, as Table 2.6 shows, part-time work showed a steady increase so that by 1996 almost twice as many people were in part-time employment than was the case in 1983. Once again, such data need to be treated with caution. It is important to recognise, for example, that such change cannot be isolated from the high levels of emigration and immigration Ireland experienced during the 1980s and 1990s.

Table 2.5: The Changing Nature of Employment

Economic status	*1983*	*1985*	*1987*	*1988*	*1992*
Full-time	1,067.7	1,030.6	1,029.6	1,024.6	1,056
Part-time, not underemployed	61.9	56.6	61.6	68.3	84.9
Part-time, underemployed	14.5	12.0	16.4	18.9	19.0

Source. Labour Force Survey, 1993.

Table 2.6: The Changing Nature of Employment

Economic status	*1993*	*1994*	*1995*	*1996*
Full-time	1,052	1077.9	1120	1165.4
Part-time, not underemployed	103.4	112.1	126.9	128.1
Part-time, underemployed	23.8	24.7	26.6	23.3

Source: Labour Force Survey, 1996.

An additional, (but nevertheless) crucial component to the success of macro-political bargaining in Ireland has been the institutional apparatus designed to resolve disputes between management and unions. As Tables 2.7, 2.8 and 2.9 show, there has been a substantial reduction in both the incidence of strikes, the level of unofficial strike activity and the number of days lost in disputes. Moreover, a comparison between the period 1982–7 and 1988–93 provides stark evidence of the success of the Programme for National Economic Policy (PNER) and PESP in reducing the level of strike activity in the economy.

While such data confirm the evident success of macro-political bargaining in reducing industrial conflict, it is important to recognise that conflict has not simply evaporated. Any success in macro-level concertation demands a conciliation service (accepted as legitimate by all parties) which provides an institutional setting in which antagonism may be resolved. Here, as Table 2.10 indicates, the combination of the Labour Court and the

Table 2.7: Number of Strikes and Work Days Lost During a Six Year Period of Decentralised Wage Bargaining (1982–87)

	Strikes	*Days lost*
1982	131	434,000
1983	154	319,000
1984	192	386,000
1985	116	418,000
1986	100	309,000
1987.	80	264,000
Total	*773*	*2,130,000*

Average number of days lost per annum 355,000

Number of Strikes and Work Days Lost During a Six Year Period of PNER/PESP (1988–93)

	Strikes	*Days lost*
1988	65	143,000
1989	38	50,000
1990	49	223,000
1991	54	86,000
1992	38	191,000
1993*	48	65,000
Total	*292*	*758,000*

Average number of days lost per annum 126,000

*Source: Central Statistics Office/*Department of Enterprise and Employment.*

Table 2.8. Number of Strikes which Commenced in Period of 1987–91

Year	*Total*	*Official*	*Unofficial*
1987	76	54 (71%)	22 (29%)
1988	72	46 (64%)	26 (36%)
1989	41	28 (68%)	13 (32%)
1990	51	35 (69%)	16 (31%)
1991	52	39 (75%)	13 (25%)

Source: Department of Labour Annual Report, 1991.

Table 2.9 Days Lost in the Period 1987–91

Year	*Total*	*Official*	*Unofficial*
1987	260,000	235,000 (90%)	25,000 (10%)
1988	130,000	123,500 (95%)	6,500 (5%)
1989	41,400	29,800 (72%)	11,600 (28%)
1990	203,700	196,000 (97%)	6,800 (3%)
1991	82,900	73,600 (89%)	9,300 (11%)

Source: Department of Labour Annual Report, 1991.

Labour Relations Commission has proved remarkably successful in resolving disputes between management and unions.

Most commentators were of the opinion that PESP had been an outstanding success, but the latter stages of this agreement coincided with a particularly unstable European economic climate and a national interest rate crisis during 1992–3. Although growth rates were significantly less than those achieved during the late 1980s and early 1990s, the picture was far from disastrous since the levels attained were still above the European average. Also, in contrast to other EU states, Ireland achieved modest growth in employment. However, the legacy of high rates of long-term unemployment coupled with an above average rate of expansion in the labour force meant that there was no rectification of the seemingly interminable problem of long-term structural unemployment. It was against this backdrop of uncertainty that the social partners embarked upon negotiations for a third tripartite agreement – the *Programme for Competitiveness and Work* (PCW).

Table 2.10: Settlement of Industrial Disputes in the Public and Private Sector

Year	*No. of referrals* *Private Sec*	*Public Sec*	*Total*	*Meetings*	*Settled*	*No. of workers*
1990	1,105	469	1,474	2,074	73%	N/A
1991	1,303	577	1,880	2,385	85%	254,000
1992	1,388	547	1,935	2,450	75%	364,000

In contrast with its predecessor, the PCW did not have the provision for local bargaining. The debilitating experience of currency instability in 1992–3 had a profound influence on the parameters struck for the PCW. As a result of the slowdown in economic growth, employers were reluctant to concede wage negotiation at a local level over and above that agreed for the national level.[59] Thus in terms of the basic pay negotiations the PCW involved a series of staged payments to be made over a three year period from 1994–6. Basic pay increases of 2% in 1994, 2.5% in 1995 and 2.5% in the first six months of 1996 were agreed. An additional 1% would be made in the remaining six months of 1996.

From the outset the main objectives of the PCW were alleviating the burden of taxation on workers with low incomes and raising the income threshold at which higher rates of taxation come into play. With regard to the first priority, the increase in the level of income exempt from tax as a result of the government's 1996 budget did give a real benefit to the very low paid. However, it did so only after an inadequate increase in the exemption limit in the previous budget. Not surprisingly, from the trade unions' perspective, the overall experience of the PCW was disappointing. Little real progress had been achieved in reducing the burden of taxation on the low paid. Indeed, as O'Riordan observes, the low paid worker was still caught in the tax net at the same level as 1993. By 1996 the single worker was still liable for the top rate of tax at four-fifths of average male industrial earnings while the married worker (spouse not working) became liable for the top rate of tax when earning just 1.5 times average male earnings.[60]

The principal reason for the Irish government's failure to meet its tax reform commitments resulted from its decision to overfulfil the PCW's agreed fiscal policy objective. All parties to the PCW had supported a policy of maintaining the government deficit within the Maastricht ceiling of 3% of GDP. By staying at 2.2% the Irish deficit met that condition by a wide margin. In addition, all parties to the PCW were in agreement with meeting the other Maastricht guideline in respect of fiscal policy, namely that of making satisfactory progress towards a debt/GDP ratio of 60%.[61] And yet, during the period of the PCW, the Irish economy experienced an unprecedented level of economic growth, averaging 6.5% between 1994–6. In addition, as Table 2.11 shows, in 1994 Ireland recorded its lowest level of industrial disputes with just 25,550 working days lost.

Table 2.11: Industrial Disputes: 1994–97

Year	*Number of disputes*	*Number of firms involved*	*Workers involved*	*Total days lost*
1993	48	48	12,789	61,312
1994	29	238	5,007	25,550
1995	34	34	31,653	130,300
1996	32	30	13,339	114,584
1997	28	N/A	5,364	74,508*

* *This period falls under the Partnership 2000. A significant element of this figure is attributed to the Irish Life Insurance Company dispute which accounted for 10,080 days.*
Source: Central Statistics Office.

During the period of the PCW the Labour Relations Commission observed that pay and conditions were no longer the primary source of industrial relations conflict. Issues such as poor human relations between shopfloor and line managers, the absence of communications or consultation and the introduction of major change were now the most significant issues of contention. Indeed, the Commission went on to conclude that significant and constant change was the order of the day and reflected the impact of new technology, deregulation in state industries, international competition and the changing nature of the workplace. Accordingly, its conciliation service was now increasingly concerned in disputes about new management or production techniques and changes in work practices, particularly in the public sector.[62]

Such evidence confirms, once again, that industrial relations issues extend beyond pay, which remains the simple preoccupation of neo-liberal economists in this field. What is more, the period had also been characterised by a low level of industrial disputes and a high level of settlements

Table 2.12: Conciliation Activity 1993–96

Year	*No of referrals*	*Meetings*	*Settled*
1993	1,844	2,379	71%
1994	1,551	2,055	66%
1995	1,692	2,072	70%
1996	1,487	1,999	81%

Source: Annual Reports, Labour Relations Commission, 1993–5.

achieved in the institutional mechanisms designed to alleviate antagonism (see Table 2.12).

What also remains patently clear is that under the terms of the PCW (which had been far more narrow than PESP), management was also able to pursue with continued vigour the restructuring of the supply side of the economy. On this matter it is important to recognise that while unions were seeking better terms for their members, they were also acutely aware of the need to pursue a strategy that endorsed investment in new technology and capital. They were certainly keen to avoid the experience of unions in the UK which had found themselves isolated from the wider decision-making agenda of public policy. In this sense, while the terms agreed under the PCW were less favourable than those achieved under PESP, the trade union movement was still a significant actor in the political decision-making environment.

Almost all parties to the negotiations concur that in the area of employment expansion the PCW has been a qualified success. What remains in doubt is the adequacy of this achievement given the inherited unemployment problem and the level of resources being used to tackle long-term unemployment.[63] Under the terms of the PCW the government was committed to establish a new community employment (CE) venture which would enable the unemployed to undertake work of public or social value while at the same time providing them with work experience and development training. The intention was to reduce any 'disincentive' to take up such opportunities and consequently the government agreed that secondary welfare benefits would be retained. The government became involved in a commitment to provide 40,000 places on a voluntary basis by 1994.

The PCW also required the government to have regard to the findings of the National Economic and Social Forum (NESF), a consultative body which embraced diverse interests such as the unemployed and women's groups. In June 1994 NESF issued a report on Ireland's long-term unemployed that called for the development of an employment service targeted at those registered as unemployed for more than six months. In January 1996 the government responded with four initiatives: 30,000 or 75% of CE places would be allocated to those over 21 and unemployed for at least twelve months; 10,000 CE places (25%) would be reserved for those over 35 and unemployed for three years or more; an additional 1,000 places would be provided on a pilot basis for those over 35 who had been unemployed for more than five years, and finally, the introduction of a new scheme aimed at those who had been unemployed for six months and who were likely to become long-term unemployed.[64] The attractiveness and subsequent success of this initiative resulted in a conflict between the government and unions. Although participation averaged 31,800, the figure of 40,000 had been surpassed by the end of the year, encouraging calls from some quarters for cutbacks. This was confirmed in the 1995 budget which forecast a reduction in these figures from around 40,500 to 35,000 by December 1995. As far as the unions were concerned, such programmes had been jeopardised by an over-zealous pursuit of fiscal rectitude.[65]

In many ways the trajectory of the PCW reflected the dilemmas facing the Irish economy as it sought to balance the political demands of the trade unions to increase the living standards of its members and the government's intention of creating an environment in which global capital would seek to reside. As such, the main tenets of the programme were designed to engineer a consensus around the need to embrace more fully the realistic economic strictures of the global market. In this sense, it represented a subtle, but nonetheless crucial, shift towards a more conservative economic outlook, one which had effectively abandoned any pretension to the social democratic ethos which may have permeated elements of PESP. If we avoid being seduced by the political rhetoric that surrounded the PCW, it remains patently clear that while it may have embraced the language of inclusion it did little to alleviate the vast inequalities that still persist in Ireland or contribute in any significant sense to address fundamental questions about industrial democracy.

Such matters were the subject of negotiations that formed the basis of the latest agreement, *Partnership 2000*. The backdrop to this scheme was very different from that of the PCW. The unions sought radical tax reform to provide tax relief for public sector workers, a new flexible pay agreement which would benefit the low paid and new initiatives designed to include profit sharing in companies. However, one of the more important and indeed novel aspirations of *Partnership 2000* was the manner in which pay negotiations in the public sector would be tied to the introduction of greater flexibility in public service provision. It is not that the agreement sought to appease the more conservative elements of the Irish media or its academe who had voiced continued opposition to the 'spiralling' public sector wage bill. Rather, the agreement acknowledged the 'imperative' to build upon measures which had induced change in the public sector.[66]

Reflecting the international trend towards the restructuring of civil services, emphasis has been accorded to improving the quality of service provision, flexibility in the deployment of resources and the use of performance measurement. On this matter the local pay bargaining element to *Partnership 2000* has been linked to 'ongoing' discussions about new and more flexible working arrangements. Indeed, the agreement explicitly stipulates that adjustments in pay (at the local level) will 'be conditional upon there having been verified progress to a satisfactory level on implementation of the modernisation programme set out in chapter ten of the agreement'.[67]

That issues about restructuring and downsizing have assumed greater prominence can be gleaned from the Labour Relations Commission's annual report of 1996 which found that 18% of disputes were linked to this area of industrial relations. What is more, it noted that while a relatively low level of disputes had been recorded on the disclosure of information and union recognition they had shown a 'notable increase'.[68] For the unions this is an important issue, one likely to assume greater political visibility. The recent dispute at Ryanair in 1999 is a case in point. The media saw it as a 'flashpoint' between two protagonists over flexible working arrangements and pay. However, the move by union members outside Ryanair to support the action of the Ryanair baggage handlers can only be understood in the context of an ongoing struggle to achieve trade union recognition, an issue which has not been resolved successfully under the terms of *Partnership 2000*. It was not simply about Ryanair, or its outspoken management, but it did make political 'sense' to stand against a high profile company such as Ryanair rather than a multinational located at a greenfield site.

The presence of these issues on the political agenda reveal the continued importance assigned to the 'political dimension' to bargaining. It is not simply a matter of pay or introducing flexibility. All too often the literature on globalisation or flexible specialisation has a tendency to impose upon management an illusory hierarchy of 'needs' for all business. It is as if management can be furnished with a checklist of priorities, the suitability of which can be deemed by the fact that they either increase or decrease the level of operating flexibility.[69] This is to simplify what is often an extremely complex task, one which necessarily involves an important political dimension. It is often possible, for example, to identify conflicting interests within the management structure itself. The existence of such divisions casts a long shadow over the rudimentary perception of management as a unified group, either within individual firms or between firms.[70] All too easily, then, contributors to the debate on managerial strategy have a tendency to jettison the political dimension, a move designed to persuade its audience that the managerial function can be made intelligible purely in terms of a series of rational economic criteria. In short, there is a crucial political dimension to managerial strategies which does not fit easily into the assumptions of some mythical pure market that underpin debates about rigidity and flexibility.

SOME CONCLUDING REMARKS

The arguments presented here suggest that despite the presence of macro-political bargaining arrangements in Ireland, management has been pro-active (and at least partially successful) in pursuing a programme of productive restructuring. Indeed, in contrast to neo-liberal criticisms of such forms of interest intermediation, this chapter has argued that the very presence of such arrangements may have assisted in engineering an environment more conducive to constructive negotiations on flexible work practices, employee status and social organisation.

Initially, at least, this would appear to suggest that the optimism embedded in Streeck's view, that flexibility and rigidity are not mutually exclusive, is not misplaced. The problem for Streeck (and he is not alone on this matter) lies in the failure to appreciate the role macro-political bargaining can play in restructuring the productive (supply side) of the economy. It is not simply that management in Ireland has been able to trade-off a particular clause of the wage agreement in exchange for the introduction of new working practices and technology (although this has clearly been an important element). Rather, such agreements have contributed positively to the creation of a stable environment in which management has been encouraged to innovate and seek change in productive techniques. Social peace, worker commitment and the recognition of the need to encourage long-term investment in new plant and technology are all a part of the political dimension to managerial strategies which are shaped by macro-political bargaining agreements.

A further element, and one which has attracted less attention, has been the willingness of unions to initiate and encourage greater levels of investment in training and new technology. Such developments should provide tangible reasons for caution in those who see macro-political bargaining in terms of rigid, static structures, populated by actors implacable to the changing circumstances of the global economy. Negotiated forms of governance should therefore be seen in more dynamic terms, recognising their capacity to change over time and in response to influences emanating from outside national borders. It is all the more imperative that we avoid the temptation to view any move which does not adhere to some arbitrary classification of flexibility in a negative light. On the contrary, while macro-political bargaining agreements *may* introduce constraints for management in some areas, they will also provide new opportunities (social peace, stability) for management to exploit. In short, attempts to draw the final curtain on macro-political bargaining may not only be theoretically misplaced but may also prove to be premature.

CHAPTER 3

The Welfare State in Ireland – Challenges and Opportunities

EAMON O'SHEA AND BRENDAN KENNELLY

INTRODUCTION

For many, participation is the key to the future evolution of the Irish Welfare State. The maximisation of individual potential through active, human-capital oriented policies of support for individuals is a strategy which makes sense in any knowledge-based society. It is in this context that this chapter examines the challenges and opportunities facing the welfare state in Ireland. As such, it concentrates on the main issues with respect to its evolution, development and status. This chapter argues that there is a need for new forms of social protection and social organisation to deal with the many social problems which still face some people living in this country, despite the acknowledged success of the economy in many areas. It is esential, therefore, that we move people beyond the dimension of the present moment into a future where they can realise their considerable individual potential and have a stake in the communities in which they live.

We must also recognise that many people will continue to depend on social welfare payments for a large proportion of their income. For these people effective participation in society requires that welfare payments allow them to participate in social and economic life. In the 1980s it was argued that Ireland did not possess the resources needed to reduce poverty and inequality. Whatever the merits of that argument in the past, it is clear that the resources to make society a more inclusive one are now available so the question of directing those resources in an appropriate way is one that Irish society can no longer hide from.

THE WELFARE STATE: AN EMPIRICAL OVERVIEW

While many definitions of the welfare state exist, the term is generally used to refer to the public mechanisms of support (in cash, in kind or through public services) against a catalogue of standard social risks: old-age, death of a supporting spouse, invalidity, sickness, maternity and unemployment.[1] In addition to this core, a number of other programmes have evolved, such as transfers and direct care for children and other persons in special need, minimum income schemes, labour market policies and measures aimed at social integration.[2] The EU has compiled a database that compares Social Protection Expenditure[3] across all the member states. In this section we use this database to briefly outline the stylised facts about the nature of the welfare state in Ireland and other EU countries.

Table 3.1 shows the percentage of GDP accounted for by social protection expenditure (SPE) in EU countries for selected years between 1970 and 1996 (the most recent year for which reliable data are available). In 1996, SPE averaged 28.7% of GDP in the fifteen countries of the EU ranging from 34.8% in Sweden to 18.9% in Ireland. As the table reveals, the 1970s witnessed a dramatic increase in the proportion of GDP accounted for by social expenditure in Ireland. Indeed, by 1985 SPE accounted for almost a quarter of GDP in Ireland and was within a couple of percentage points of the EU average. Since then the growth in SPE in Ireland has been lower than the growth in GDP so that by 1996 the SPE/GDP ratio in Ireland was lower than in any other EU country. However, it also true that between 1990 and 1995 the average annual increase in SPE was 6.7% in Ireland which was the third highest in the EU during that period.

Table 3.1: Social Protection Spending as % of GDP

Country	*1970*	*1980*	*1985*	*1990*	*1995*	*1996*
Belgium	18.7	28.0	29.3	26.8	29.7	30.0
Denmark	19.6	28.7	27.8	30.3	34.3	33.6
Germany	21.5	28.8	28.4	25.4	29.4	30.5
Greece	–	9.7	15.4	22.7	20.7	23.3
Spain	–	18.2	20.0	20.4	21.9	22.4
France	19.2	25.4	28.8	27.7	30.6	30.8
Ireland	13.2	20.6	23.6	19.1	19.9	18.9
Italy	17.4	19.4	22.6	24.1	24.6	24.8
Luxembourg	15.0	26.5	23.4	23.5	25.3	26.2
Netherlands	20.8	30.1	31.7	32.5	31.6	30.9
Portugal	–	12.9	14.2	15.5	20.7	21.6
UK	15.9	20.5	23.8	23.1	27.7	27.7
Austria	–	–	–	26.7	29.7	29.5
Finland	–	–	–	25.5	32.8	32.1
Sweden	–	–	–	25.4	28.4	28.7
EU Average	19.0	24.1	25.9	25.4	28.4	28.7

Note: The EU average in a particular year includes only those countries for which data is available for that year.
Source: European Commission, 1995; 1998. Eurostat Press Releases.

While the SPE grew in all EU countries between 1980 and 1994, increases have been most marked in relatively poor countries such as Portugal and Spain. The percentage increase in Ireland over this period was about 55%, an increase slightly higher than the EU-12 as a whole.[4] When per capita SPE is expressed in PPS[5] we find that there are still considerable differences between expenditure per capita in countries such as Denmark and countries such as Ireland and Portugal.

As Table 3.2 shows, the composition of SPE varies across countries. In 1995 expenditure on pensions in Ireland took up a smaller than average proportion of total expenditure, while expenditure on family benefits and payments to the unemployed took up a significantly higher share in Ireland than the EU average.

Table 3.2: Social Protection Benefits by Group of Functions as a % of the Total, 1980 and 1995

	Sickness/health/ disability		*Old age and survivors*		*Family and children*		*Unemployment/ employment promotion*	
	1980	*1995*	*1980*	*1995*	*1980*	*1995*	*1980*	*1995*
B	34.6	30.3	41.5	39.8	11.3	7.7	11.6	13.4
DK	35.8	27.6	35.7	36.6	10.8	12.0	12.9	14.3
D	40.3	36.5	42.6	40.8	10.1	7.2	4.5	8.8
G	26.2	24.5	66.1	68.8	3.6	1.2	2.7	2.7
E	37.2	36.7	41.0	44.1	4.4	1.8	15.7	13.9
F	35.6	33.0	43.9	40.7	12.7	8.5	5.1	7.8
IRL	43.4	38.4	31.4	24.9	11.5	11.2	8.8	16.6
I	34.9	27.4	55.1	62.7	7.5	3.4	2.3	2.1
L	40.4	36.2	47.5	43.2	10.0	12.8	0.9	2.9
NL	48.5	42.7	31.0	35.5	8.5	4.4	6.1	9.6
P	44.8	39.9	39.4	38.6	8.0	5.1	2.8	4.9
UK	32.9	36.3	42.8	38.0	13.1	8.7	9.6	5.7
A	–	32.3	–	46.7	–	11.0	–	5.4
FIN	–	35.1	–	31.8	–	12.9	–	13.9
S	–	33.5	–	36.6	–	11.2	–	11.0
EU average	37.5	34.4	43.3	42.4	10.5	7.3	6.4	8.1

Note: The EU average in a particular year includes only those countries for which data is available for that year. Data for Greece refers to 1994.
Sources: Eurostat, 1997a. European Commission, 1998.

A major question underlying these figures is whether changes in expenditure are due solely to changes in the number of beneficiaries or whether they are due to higher levels of payment. It is an issue which has attracted the attention of the European Commission.[6] Its analysis for two categories – old-age pensions and unemployment benefits – is reproduced in Tables 3.3 and 3.4. If we look at Ireland, we can see that the small decline in the share of GDP accounted for by old-age pensions between 1980 and 1990 was in fact the result of two factors working in opposite directions. There was quite a significant increase in the number of people claiming pensions (from 10.8% of the population to 12.4%) but this was offset by the fact that the pension relative to GDP per head declined significantly.

Table 3.3: Decomposition of Expenditure on Old-Age Pensions

		Old-age pensions (% GDP)	*People over retirement age (% total)*	*Early retirement (% total population)*	*Total retirement (% total population)*	*Expenditure per person (% GDP per head)*
Denmark	1980	10.0	12.5	2.3	14.7	57.7
	1990	10.6	13.7	3.0	16.7	63.6
	1993	11.0	13.7	3.1	16.7	65.6
Germany	1980	11.9	17.1	1.1	16.3	66.3
	1990	11.0	18.9	0.7	19.6	55.9
	1993	11.0	20.3	0.9	21.2	51.9
	1993*	12.1	19.9	1.1	21.8	56.6
Greece	1980	6.1	14.8	1.9	16.5	37.8
	1990	10.5	17.0	3.6	20.6	51.2
	1993	10.2	18.0	3.6	21.5	47.6
Ireland	1980	6.2	10.1	0.7	10.8	57.3
	1990	5.7	11.4	1.0	12.4	45.8
	1993	5.7	11.4	1.0	12.4	46.2
Italy	1980	9.9	18.1	1.5	19.5	50.9
	1990	13.6	23.7	1.8	25.4	53.6
	1993	15.4	24.7	1.9	26.6	57.8
Netherlands	1980	9.5	11.5	1.1	12.5	76.1
	1990	11.4	12.8	1.0	13.8	82.6
	1993	11.9	13.0	1.6	14.6	81.4
UK	1980	8.5	17.6	1.0	18.5	45.8
	1990	9.1	18.3	0.8	19.1	47.6
	1993	10.8	18.2	0.7	19.0	57.1
EUR12	1980	10.0	16.0	1.6	17.6	57.0
	1990	11.0	18.3	1.7	20.0	56.2
	1993	11.9	19.0	1.7	20.8	57.2

Note: Old-age includes survivors; Germany 1993* includes the new Länder.
Source: European Commission, 1995.

If we examine expenditure on unemployment benefits (Table 3.4) we see that the increase in spending on this category in Ireland between 1980 and 1993 was due entirely to the increase in the unemployment rate during this period. In fact, the average benefit paid to claimants declined relative to GDP per head.

Table 3.4: Decomposition of Expenditure on Unemployment Benefits

		Unemployment benefits (% GDP)	*Population 15–64 (% total)*	*Activity rate (%)*	*Unemployment rate (%)*	*Expenditure per person (% GDP per head)*
Denmark	1980	3.0	64.7	51.1	6.7	68.0
	1990	3.2	67.4	55.1	9.4	61.3
	1993	4.1	67.5	54.8	12.1	61.8
Germany	1980	0.9	66.3	45.3	3.2	58.7
	1990	1.1	69.5	48.0	6.2	36.0
	1993	1.6	68.6	47.7	7.3	45.0
	1993*	2.0	68.5	47.6	8.9	46.8
Greece	1980	0.3	64.0	35.2	1.1	64.9
	1990	0.4	66.9	38.0	3.6	32.6
	1993	0.5	67.4	37.5	4.5	31.1
Ireland	1980	1.6	58.9	36.8	8.1	51.9
	1990	2.3	61.5	38.7	16.5	35.8
	1993	3.0	62.9	40.4	20.4	35.8
Italy	1980	0.4	64.6	39.1	7.2	14.8
	1990	0.4	68.6	44.9	18.4	5.1
	1993	0.5	68.8	44.2	19.3	6.2
Netherlands	1980	1.8	66.2	39.3	5.4	83.5
	1990	2.6	68.9	44.1	5.4	107.5
	1993	2.9	68.6	46.1	5.9	108.5
UK	1980	1.5	64.1	47.9	5.9	53.2
	1990	0.8	65.3	49.5	5.8	28.8
	1993	1.6	64.9	48.1	10.4	32.6
EUR12	1980	1.2	64.5	42.6	5.9	48.1
	1990	1.3	67.3	45.4	9.6	29.8
	1993	1.9	67.1	44.9	12.0	34.9

Note: Expenditure includes social assistance paid to the unemployed as well as social insurance benefits; D 1993* includes the new Länder.
Source: European Commission, 1995.

Finally, a major issue in all EU countries is where does the money come from? Table 3.5 shows the trend in social protection receipts over this period. On average about two-thirds of receipts come from contributions by employers and protected persons (including employees and other protected persons). Ireland is one of only two countries (the other is Denmark) which rely on general contributions from government for the majority of social protection receipts.

Table 3.5: Social Protection Receipts by Type as % of the Total, 1980, 1994

	General government contributions		*Contributions by employees and employers*		*Other receipts*	
	1980	*1994*	*1980*	*1994*	*1980*	*1994*
B	34.0	20.6	62.3	69.6	3.8	9.8
DK	82.9	75.6	12.3	19.3	4.7	5.1
D	27.0	26.7	69.4	70.3	3.5	3.0
GR	4.7	19.2	89.0	72.3	6.2	8.5
E	16.1	29.6	82.4	68.3	1.5	2.1
F	17.3	21.5	79.8	76.7	2.9	2.0
IRL	63.3	61.0	35.8	38.2	1.0	0.8
I	23.8	35.0	69.8	62.8	2.4	2.2
L	32.8	42.6	58.8	51.3	8.4	6.1
NL	20.4	16.3	68.1	67.9	11.5	15.8
P	25.4	37.4	71.9	55.7	2.7	6.9
UK	43.2	43.9	48.0	41.7	8.7	14.4
EUR12	27.9		65.4		4.7	

Sources: *Eurostat*, 1996a; *Eurostat*, 1997a.

WELFARE STATE MODELS

The previous section illustrated that all EU countries have some kind of a welfare sector financed and/or provided by the state. It is much more difficult, however, to agree on a set of criteria for deciding when a country qualifies for the nomenclature 'welfare state' given the different levels of spending and provision across countries. Classification is important because it allows us to address important questions of scale, provision and convergence. We are interested in the evolution of the welfare state in different countries, the relationship between that development and capitalist production, and whether it is possible to describe welfare state coverage and provision in terms of one unifying model. For instance, can the welfare state be explained in terms of a model of social citizenship? If citizenship were used as the primary criterion to define the modern welfare state, then comparative analysis of welfare state provision in the EU would be confined to Scandinavian countries, since most other countries, including Ireland, would fail the test of universality. This would be a very dramatic result, contradicting most of our working hypotheses on the nature of welfare state provision. On the other hand, simplifying matters by using the ratio of social expenditure to GDP as an indicator of welfare state development is equally problematic. The aggregate nature of expenditure, together with differences in classification, is bound to conceal large differences in the mix of provision across countries. The choice of some arbitrary cut-off ratio to confer welfare state status is also likely to be unsatisfactory.

Alber attempts to sidestep some of these issues by examining the historical transformation of state activities. He points out the difficulties of the welfare state as a descriptive concept, given the large cross-sectional and historical variation in its definition and boundaries. According to Alber, welfare state development can either support existing modes of production and distribution or it can intervene in these processes.[7] Welfare state development in Western Europe began with the minimalist approach to intervention common in the nineteenth century, continued through the various stages of welfare state provision in this century, and has evolved into the current mix of welfare provision involving the state, the voluntary sector and private sources. Ploug and Kvist also define welfare state development as a prolonged historical process that is not yet finished.[8]

Historical schemata of this sort are a useful way of organising our thinking on the evolution of the welfare state. However, they have rarely been detailed enough to explain fully the relationship between the development of the welfare state and political, cultural and institutional processes within countries. Welfare regimes and their associated power structures have led to different forms of development at different times, and these are not always captured in aggregate schemes based on the historical transformation of state activities. Not all countries follow the same pattern of development.

More recently a basic distinction between residual and institutional welfare regimes has provided the framework to categorise welfare states. In residual models, the state assumes responsibility for welfare only in the event of market, or family, failure. The basis for intervention is need; coverage is restricted to marginal groups unable to provide for themselves and without the support of their families. In contrast, the institutional welfare regime is more universal in its application, even if it is sometimes confined to an industrial achievement model that complements the market economy. The residual-institutional dichotomy remains largely general. It has led to the development of more finely tuned ideal typologies that seek to locate welfare state provision within three, or four, fields, each one characterised by its own objectives, means, provision, financing and outcomes.[9]

The most influential work on the categorisation of welfare states has been that of Esping Andersen. He starts by trying to identify the level of decommodification provided by the different welfare states. Decommodification refers to 'the degree to which individuals or families can uphold a socially acceptable standard of living independently of market participation'. The level of decommodification depends on the stringency of eligibility rules, the level of income replacement and on the range of entitlements.[10] Within his schema he identifies three distinct welfare models – the Scandinavian model, the continental model and the Anglo-Saxon model.

The Scandinavian, or Social Democratic, model has a high degree of universality and institutionalisation and is financed to varying degrees by general taxation and social insurance contributions. The emphasis is on social rights, with the state the primary agency for ensuring citizenship. The welfare state is inclusive, covering workers in both market and non-market activities. The decommodification of social goods is, by and large, complete in this model. At the same time, however, the labour market continues to be the primary focus for participation. The state ensures participation through an emphasis on training and education and significant public intervention in the labour market. Typically, the state has been the employer of first resort, especially for women.

The second regime, the continental or state corporate model, is a selective welfare state financed mainly by the contributions of employers and employees through work-based social insurance schemes. The entitlement to social rights is based on an attachment to the paid labour force. People outside the labour market are left to depend on support from families, local governments, voluntary organisations and the Church.[11] The principle of subsidiarity underpins the selectivity implicit in this system, which has been described by Van Kesbergen as one of 'social capitalism'.[12] Because social protection is tied to employment status, the redistributive impact of the welfare state is weak. Esping-Andersen points to the preservation of status differentials as a fundamental aim of the selective welfare state.[13] Germany and Austria are examples of countries with strong conservative and selective traditions in welfare state provision.

The final regime identified by Esping-Andersen is the liberal, Anglo-Saxon model. The system is a combination of modest universality and extensive means-tested assistance. Here, the welfare state is a compensator of last resort. Need is the principle on which the state intervenes on a discretionary basis. Intervention is necessary in order to support people unable to insure themselves, either because they are not attached to the labour market or because they belong to a high risk group. Benefits paid by the state are usually flat rate and are financed out of general taxation. This model has been most associated with the United Kingdom. Ireland is usually regarded as being an example of this model. For instance, while social assistance expenditure accounts for over one-third of social security expenditure in both Ireland and the UK, it accounts for less than 12% in every other EU country.[14]

The main criticism of Esping-Andersen's work focuses on the difficulty of representing the myriad of social structures, both within and among countries, using only three distinct classifications. Mishra, for example, points to two different traditions in liberalism.[15] Classical liberalism is associated with a *laissez-faire* philosophy and is best illustrated by reference to the United States. An alternative liberal tradition is firmly rooted in the collectivist philosophies of Keynes and Beveridge. Both of these traditions have influenced the current mix of welfare provision in the United Kingdom. Social assistance, for example, may be characterised as neo-liberal while health care displays more social democratic traits. The tendency for some countries to fit into more than one regime is not confined to the United Kingdom. The Netherlands may also be characterised as providing both selective and comprehensive measures. Similarly, the welfare system in Ireland has elements of all three regimes: comprehensiveness (general taxation financing), corporatism (social partnerships, associated mainly with labour market participation) and residualism (means-tested, social assistance programmes). Differences also exist between countries normally included in the continental corporatist model, particularly between Germany, the Netherlands and Switzerland.[16]

Kemeny has criticised the absence of theories of power in Esping-Andersen's discussion of welfare state regimes. He claims that some of the ambiguity about the classification of social structures would be removed if more attention were paid to power relationships in different welfare societies. For Kemeny, working-class hegemony is the main determinant of the development of national welfare state systems.[17] Other criticisms of Esping-Andersen's work have focused on the male-centred definition of commodification, which tends to lead to a residual treatment of gender issues in welfare state classification.[18] This explains the absence of any treatment of social care provision, which is mainly the domain of women in Esping-Andersen's typology. Bonoli has also argued that comparative studies have concentrated almost exclusively on the 'how much' dimension of welfare provision and have almost totally neglected its 'how' dimension. He argues that the main problem of Esping-Andersen's model is that it ends up with a uni-dimensional measure of welfare states, which is overly reliant on the question of quantity.[19] Thus, in Esping-Andersen's typology, Denmark, a welfare state based on universal tax-financed provision, is placed in the same group as The Netherlands which is a welfare state based on social insurance. Consequently, Bonoli argues that we should pay equal attention to the question of the *source* of social protection expenditures.

These methodological problems have encouraged others to develop and extend Esping-Andersen's topological scheme. Leibfried[20] and Ferrera[21] have added a new category – the 'Latin Rim' countries – to Esping-Andersen's three worlds. In these countries (Italy, Spain, Portugal and Greece), the state does little to regulate employment or to redistribute income. The solution to traditional welfare state problems has been located primarily in civil society. The emphasis is on the family, the Church and private charity. Leibfried describes the Southern Europe welfare state as rudimentary but in the process of catching up, in that many of these countries have made promises towards a modern welfare state in their constitutions. In all of these countries, social expenditure has been increasing in recent years. Notwithstanding these changes, social protection in Southern Europe continues to be categorical and work-focused. For those who are covered, social protection can be generous but for those without protection, coverage is fragmented and weak. For instance, the Greek welfare system lacks any kind of universal minimum income support scheme, except for non-contributory benefits available to old-age pensioners.[22]

Bonoli proposes a two-dimensional model which is based on a distinction between Bismarckian and Beveridgean welfare states. The former is based on social insurance and is principally concerned with income maintenance for employees, while the latter aims at the prevention of poverty.[23] He uses the proportion of contribution financing as the best approximation of the size of the Bismarckian component in a welfare state and uses the ratio social expenditure to GDP as his measure of the quantity variable. He ends up with the following typology:

Figure 3.1: Bonoli's Classification of Welfare States

	Beveridgean	*Bismarckian*
High spending	Denmark, Norway, Finland, Sweden	Belgium, Luxembourg, Netherlands, Germany, France
Low spending	Ireland, UK	Italy, Greece, Portugal, Spain, Switzerland

Cousins has criticised the absence of a historical perspective in the typological approach, which in the case of Ireland leads to the absence of any consideration of the colonial experience. This is exacerbated by the absence of any explanation of the role of the state and the Catholic Church in the evolution and development of the Irish welfare state. The absence of a historical and cultural perspective makes it easier to understand Esping-Andersen's difficulty in classifying Ireland within the schemata described above. For Cousins, the Irish welfare state is not capable of being understood within the core-centric and modernist framework chosen by Esping-Andersen and others to classify welfare states. Instead, the heterogeneous and idiosyncratic nature of welfare state development demands that much more attention should be paid to the 'local-specific' over the 'homogeneous universal'. Political, cultural, and economic influences have all combined to make national welfare states into what they now are. In most cases, the combination of circumstances arising from the constellation of these forces is unique to each country.[24]

The search for general and universal classification systems has also narrowed the focus of welfare state analysis to social protection and social transfer payments. These areas are easier to classify and demand less in terms of rigorous examination of actual service provision in the various countries. However, for many people the welfare state is synonymous with social care and its interaction with family care and voluntary provision. For example, the care of children and the care of old people are mediated outside, as well as within, the market-state nexus.[25] Problems are resolved within families, between families and the voluntary sector, and between the market, state, family and voluntary sectors. There is, therefore, a much richer set of possibilities associated with social care provision than is covered by a simple comparative analysis of aggregate expenditure on social protection.

The diversity of social care provision and the complexity of organisation make it difficult, however, to develop typologies of care, as has been done with respect to social security. There are no comprehensive international data sets on social services provision, making it difficult to compare the various services across countries. Much of what goes under the general heading of social care is very difficult to quantify and, consequently, remains outside scrutiny and measurement.[26] In addition, countries tend to be idiosyncratic in the way social care services are described, making it difficult to compare like services with like.

Alber[27] explores the pattern of social care provision for old people in Europe in terms of regulatory structure, financial structure, the structure of supply and the degree of consumer power. Based on a detailed examination of social services in three countries, Germany, Denmark and The Netherlands, Alber identifies two crucial sets of relationships in social services provision: one between church and state, and the other between the centre and periphery. These relationships, rather than a theoretical perspective based on class cleavage or the power relations between capital and labour, should form the basis of any future analysis of variations in social care across Europe. This is potentially a much more interesting framework than traditional welfare state classifications, particularly for peripheral, post-colonial, countries like Ireland since it allows the complexity of the historical experience to be included in the analysis.

Anttonen and Sipila explore potential models for European social care services. Their starting point is that existing typologies of welfare state provision are too narrow, since too much attention is paid to the relationship between the state and the labour market. In particular, the focus on decommodification ignores the relationship between the state and the family, and the tendency to ignore the subordination, and dependence, of women within family relationships. Anttonen and Sipila identify four distinct groupings for two categories of social care consumers – children and older people (see Figure 3.2). Denmark and Portugal represent the two ends of the social care continuum in Europe – Denmark representing the highest level of provision, Portugal the lowest.[28]

Figure 3.2: Social Care in Europe

	Abundant (elderly)	*Scarce*
Abundant (children)	Denmark, Sweden, Finland	Belgium, France, Italy
Scarce	Netherlands, Norway, UK	Portugal, Greece, Spain, Ireland, Germany

There is some correspondence between the above groupings of social care provision and Leibfried's classification of income support systems.[29] In particular, it is possible to identify both a Scandinavian universalist model and a Latin-Rim family care model. Beyond these groupings, classification becomes more problematic. Subsidiarity plays an important role in care of the elderly in central Europe, particularly in Germany, but it is stretching credibility to talk in terms of a generalised continental model of elderly provision. Differences between the countries of continental Europe are even more pronounced in the area of services for children. It is possible, for instance, to identify both a residualist and family care orientation in the Irish social services mix. The welfare mix of social services provision may also change over time, as witnessed by the movement from a universalist system to a residual one in the UK in the past two decades.

HOW HAS THE IRISH WELFARE STATE PERFORMED?

A fundamental question in any discussion of the welfare state concerns its effectiveness in reducing inequality and poverty. Few would deny that there has been a considerable expansion of welfare provision in Ireland since the 1960s. Social citizenship rights have expanded enormously with more and more categories of people drawn into the state insurance system. Indeed, the welfare state now extends far beyond redistribution of income in an effort to mediate life choices. The state is involved in direct employment, in subsidising voluntary and private market activity, and in providing and financing education, health care and housing services.

O'Connell and Rottman argue that the state has been an important agent for change in Irish society, leading them to the view that a state-centred model is the most useful approach to understanding the expansion of social rights in this country in recent decades.[30] Alternative theories of the welfare state, which emphasise the 'logic of industrialism' or the 'social democratic model', are out of place in Ireland. The former is overly deterministic in its emphasis on the functional necessity of the welfare state to industrial development, while the social democratic model does not easily fit the fragmented and residual nature of class politics in this country.

If one accepts the plausibility of the state-centred model as the vehicle for exploring the expansion of social expenditure, the question arises as to how successful the state has been in improving the position and status of the less well-off in society. To what extent has inequality been reduced in Ireland as a result of state intervention, and do fewer people live in poverty now than in previous decades? If the expansion of the welfare state has not resulted in any diminution of measured inequality and poverty then the state, through its institutions, structures and provisions, may, perversely, be reinforcing market inequalities rather than serving to undermine the negative affects of the market system.

There is evidence that a pay-related welfare state has evolved with the middle classes gaining disproportionately.[31] This is particularly the case with respect to public and private pension provision. In Ireland, the pension system consists of three tiers. Under the first tier, pensions are provided under social insurance on a non-means tested basis to those who have sufficient contributions registered during their working life. People who do not qualify for a contributory social insurance pension may apply for an old-age pension under social assistance. Entitlement to the latter is subject to a means test. This constitutes the second tier of pension provision. The third tier is made up of the combination of occupational/private pensions with state contributory pensions. There has been a significant growth in the number of people covered by occupational pensions since the 1960s, particularly in the private sector. Over one half of the working population are now covered under occupational schemes, including membership of public sector schemes.[32]

The exchequer provides significant support to the accumulation of private and occupational pensions. Tax relief on approved pension schemes is equivalent to approximately one-fifth of total social expenditure on pensions. And yet, it should be recognised that tax expenditures of this kind are a redistribution in favour of those on higher incomes. Individuals covered by occupational pension schemes tend to have secure and reasonably well paid employment. In a study of 495 recently retired employees, Whelan and Whelan found that about 90% of people in managerial and professional jobs were members of occupational pension schemes, whereas less than 40% of manual workers were members of such schemes.[33] Typically, people who are not members of occupational pension schemes are part-time, temporary or contract employees, employees in the agricultural and fishing sectors and workers in small, recently established firms.

Women, particularly those in older age categories, tend not to be covered by occupational pension schemes. Here, Whelan and Whelan found that 57% of male retired employees receive occupational pensions compared to only 33% of females.[34] It seems clear that the public pension system, while contributing strongly to the extension of social rights experienced in Ireland in recent years, has not been a major catalyst for equalising life chances for the elderly. While basic rights have been extended, support for the better-off through significant tax expenditures continues to sustain market-based inequalities generated throughout the life cycle.

The least well-off sections of the community in Ireland have unimpeded financial access to public health services, both primary care and hospital care. The structure of eligibility has been defined such that people on lower incomes are not disadvantaged with respect to access to health care. Moreover, although the provision of health care is far from a publicly funded national health service, recent extensions to eligibility criteria mean that everyone in the country is now entitled to free hospital care in a public hospital. In general, the pattern of health care expenditure is concentrated on people towards the bottom of the income distribution. Nolan, for example, estimates that 30% of allocated state health care expenditure goes to the bottom quintile by equivalent income.[35] In contrast only 7.5% of expenditure goes to the top quintile. This data confirms estimates of the redistributive nature of allocated health care expenditure provided by Rottman and Reidy which showed similar, though not as strongly progressive redistributive, patterns.[36]

However this does not mean that regressive elements are absent from public spending on health care. The regressive element arises from the fact that people with higher incomes receive subsidies for private health care consumption and tax relief on the purchase of private insurance. Legislative changes under the Health (Amendment) Act 1991 have sought to define more clearly the distinction between private and public consumption, particularly in public hospitals. At one stage in the early 1980s, over half the cost of private care was being funded either directly or indirectly by the state.[37] The public subsidisation of private consumption was reduced somewhat during the 1980s by the discontinuation of public subventions for patients in private hospitals and by the increase in charges for private patients finding accommodation in public hospitals. The purpose of the 1991 legislation was to provide an even clearer distinction between public and private care, particularly in public hospitals. Private practice is now confined to designated beds in private and semi-private accommodation in public hospitals and full economic charges are levied on patients and their insurers. The intention was that the new legislation would effectively eliminate the cross-subsidisation of private patients in public hospitals.

The new arrangements for the public subsidisation of old people entering private long-stay homes, based on the Health (Nursing homes) Act, 1990, also seeks to establish a clear separation between public and private provision. Old people who are without means are, for the most part, to be confined to public provision. Means-tested criteria are also to be used, along with dependency criteria, to determine eligibility for public subvention in private nursing homes. The two systems are, for the most part, separate, with very little cross-over between the two, except that the public sector has regulatory control over both. The problem here is that if people on low incomes are allocated to one particular system then the potential exists for a dual system of care to eventually emerge. Facilities and quality of care in the private sector will respond to the more sensitive and more vocal level of demand in that sector. The public system is likely to lag behind, providing residual care for those who cannot afford to make any contribution to the cost of care. It is the inevitable outcome of any system which separates people on the basis of income.

Although efforts have been made to reduce the public subsidisation of private health care consumption, there is no evidence of any movement to abolish tax relief on health insurance premia paid to the Voluntary Health Insurance (VHI) and BUPA (Ireland). Membership of VHI and BUPA is voluntary and covers accommodation in private and semi-private wards as well as consultant fees and other health professional charges. Currently just over one-third of the population is covered by VHI. Many of those covered are entitled to free public care, so quite clearly health insurance in Ireland is playing a much wider role than simply filling the gap in public entitlements to hospital care.[38] VHI enrolment increased significantly during the 1980s, a time when public expenditure on health care was substantially reduced. Many people see VHI and BUPA as means of ensuring faster access to better quality care than is available to public patients. The equity case for the elimination of tax relief on voluntary insurance premia is strong since it is a subsidy directed mainly towards those on higher incomes. The Commission on Health Funding favoured the phasing-out of income tax relief on health insurance and on non-reimbursed medical expenses.[39] This is in line with the more general view of the Commission that no element of private consumption should be subsidised by the state.

The public subsidisation of private expenditure on health care is another example of the 'pay-related' welfare state referred to by O'Connell and Rottman.[40] The Irish state provides a comprehensive good quality health care system for public patients but then subsidises those with higher incomes who opt out of that system through the provision of exchequer financed subventions for private care and private insurance. While the system is successful in providing a minimum standard for all people, the support that the state provides for private consumers of health care undermines the ethos of equal access for equal need or outcome. It also provides ammunition for those who view the state as having a weak influence on the redistributive process in Irish society.

Similarly, the transformation of the welfare state since the early 1970s has not succeed in reducing poverty in Ireland. Both the incidence and risk of poverty increased significantly between 1973 and 1987.[41] The latter was the first study in Ireland to provide a measurement of poverty based on a range of relative poverty lines. The income thresholds used in the study are 40%, 50% and 60% of average disposable income. The latter is calculated, in this instance, using sample data collected and analysed at the level of households but standardised to take account of households with variable sizes and composition.

The major findings relate to the overall extent of poverty in 1987. The authors found that 'about 10% of persons are in households below the lowest threshold (i.e. 40% of average income), about 20% are below half of average income, and about 30% are below the highest, 60% threshold'.[42] The second key finding concerns the trend in poverty over time, in particular for the time periods 1973–80 and 1980–87. There was an increase in the number of people falling below each poverty line between 1973 and 1980. A similar trend was evident between 1980 and 1987, although there was variation at the 40% line depending on the equivalence scale used. Over the entire period 1973–87, the percentage of persons falling below each of the relative poverty lines rose, irrespective of the equivalence scale used. More sophisticated measures of poverty, which measured the intensity and depth of poverty as well as its incidence, were also calculated and confirmed a substantial increase between 1980 and 1987.

The groups most at risk of poverty were identified as follows: the long-term unemployed, small farm households, households with large families and people who were sick or disabled. The major trend with respect to 'at risk' categories was the increase in the predominance of households headed by an unemployed person below each poverty line. Indeed, the increase in the incidence of unemployment between 1980 and 1987 was identified as the main reason for the dramatic rise in family poverty. In contrast, the risk of poverty among the elderly declined significantly in the 1980s due mainly to a real increase in state pension provision and occupational pension maturity.

Data from the 1994 Living in Ireland Survey has been used by Callan *et al.* to analyse the changes in poverty between 1987 and 1994.[43] Compared with 1987, the proportion of people with incomes below the 40% line had fallen, or was stable (depending on the equivalence scale used). The proportion below the 50% line had risen slightly, while the proportion below the 60% line had risen by 3–4 percentage points. The 1994 survey constituted the first stage of a panel survey. A recent report for the government has analysed the results for 1997. The percentage of persons or households below each of the poverty lines was generally higher than in 1994.[44]

Summary measures that take into account not only the number of individuals or households below the lines but how *far* their incomes are below the lines, fell between 1987 and 1994 for all the income lines.[45] However, these distribution sensitive measures increased significantly between 1994 and 1997. The numbers below relative poverty lines and experiencing basic deprivation declined marginally between 1987 and 1994 and significantly between 1994 and 1997. For example, the percentage of households below the 50% poverty line and experiencing basic deprivation declined from 9.8% in 1987 to 8.9% in 1994 to just over 7% in 1997.[46] There was a good deal of continuity in terms of the groups in society likely to experience poverty, although the relative risk of poverty for single adult households, the elderly and households headed by someone in home duties had increased significantly between 1987 and 1994. Households with an unemployed head continued to face a higher risk of poverty than any other labour force category at all poverty lines. Even though unemployment has continued to fall since the survey was undertaken, those who remain in long-term unemployment continue to be vulnerable to poverty. Between 1994 and 1997 the risk of falling below the poverty line continued to rise for single-parent households.

The increase in relative poverty measures between 1994 and 1997 reflects the critical role that social welfare policy continues to have in determining the extent and depth of poverty. Since 1986 it has been heavily influenced by the recommendations of the Commission on Social Welfare, which were published in that year. The increases in various payments in the December 1998 budget meant that all social welfare payments reached the levels recommended by the Commission. However, the increase in relative poverty also mirrors the fact that increases in social welfare payments were generally lower than increases in market incomes during this period. Indeed, the ratio of social welfare expenditure to GDP has declined each year between 1995 and 1998. One way of ensuring that relative poverty does not continue to rise during the current period of unprecedented prosperity would be to link social welfare increases to increases in other incomes but so far the government has been slow to consider such a policy.

EMPLOYMENT, INCENTIVES AND SOCIAL POLICY

While the initial aims of social protection systems in Europe were wide-ranging and differed across countries, two objectives were common to most systems. The first concerned the alleviation of poverty and the support of people without any market resources whatsoever. There was strong support for the view that the poor in society deserved some form of institutional protection. The second objective was the provision of a secure income for workers subject to temporary financial contingencies due to unemployment, sickness or work injuries. In practice, social protection based on participation in the labour market was supported by the development of residual systems of non-contributory protection, covering people with little or no attachment to primary labour markets. That said, the foundations of social welfare in market economies were firmly rooted in the labour market. Moreover, although nearly all countries in the EU have initiated some changes to their social security programmes, the fundamental attachment of the welfare system to the labour market remains intact.[47]

Current debates about welfare reform reflect partly how economic circumstances have changed in recent decades, particularly in the sphere of industrial production and labour market outcomes. During the 1970s and 1980s major and prolonged international recessions led to high levels of long-term unemployment, thereby placing an immediate strain on systems of social protection. Social insurance was developed to deal with short-term contingencies. An increasing number of people were reliant upon social assistance for long-term protection, as eligibility for social insurance came to an end or was not available in the first instance. In addition, labour force participation rates have fallen in many countries, atypical work is more common and there is a more differentiated occupational structure than in the early years of the welfare state. People in secondary labour markets, engaged in low paid, temporary or part-time work, are usually not eligible for social insurance cover at all. These changes in the labour market have led to gaps appearing between the provisions of the social protection system and the needs of both the employed and the unemployed.

These changes have led many commentators to question the continued viability of the modern welfare state.[48] There are many diagnoses of the crisis besetting welfare states, but it is possible to identify two main areas of concern about efficiency.[49] First, in a world characterised by increasing international trade, globalisation and competitiveness, fears that countries in Europe have fallen behind competition from Asia and from the USA have added an urgency to debates about reform of the welfare state. Both the USA and the newly industrialising countries of Asia have far less developed systems of social protection than Europe. This has led some people to the view that poorer employment growth, and higher levels of unemployment in the European Union relative to its main competitors, have resulted from an overly-generous social protection system.

Second, some economists argue that the welfare state is a fundamental cause of unemployment.[50] Overly-generous levels of social protection discourage people to look for work, thereby destroying the incentive to support themselves and their families. Several overlapping arguments have been developed by economists on how replacement ratios affect unemployment. First of all, high replacement ratios reduce job search activity. This not only increases the duration of unemployment but also leads to an actual or perceived decline in job skills and work habits. Secondly, the insider–outsider theory of unemployment suggests that the loss of skills by unemployed workers means that they are no longer regarded as adequate replacements for the employed labour force. Both theories imply that the long-term unemployed do not exert a sufficient downward pressure on wages which a well-functioning labour market requires. A third suggestion is that income support systems serve as a wage floor below which wages cannot fall. The real wage flexibility in the USA where wage floors are not a problem is widely cited as the main reason why employment growth has been much higher there than in Europe. Lindbeck argues that the disincentive effects of the welfare state grow stronger over time as it takes a while for existing habits and social norms to break down. Serious benefit-dependency or 'learned helplessness' may, therefore, emerge only in a long-term perspective.[51]

For some people, the key issue in resolving these arguments is the empirical evidence on the relationship between unemployment and replacement ratios. The OECD constructed a variable 'benefit entitlements' model which takes into account replacement ratios and benefit duration. It concluded that there is considerable cross-country evidence that relative levels of benefit entitlement affect unemployment rates. Both benefit duration and replacement ratios were found to be significant causes of unemployment in another cross-country analysis by Layard, Nickell and Jackman.[52] Esping-Andersen agrees that there is considerable evidence in favour of the employment effect of wage flexibility. Employment growth in the 1980s was two to three times higher in the USA, Britain, Canada, New Zealand and Australia (all regarded as having relatively flexible labour markets) than in the rest of the OECD.[53]

However, other studies have proffered different conclusions. Atkinson, for example, while acknowledging that the welfare state and the taxes necessary to finance it may have adverse consequences for economic performance, warns that the extent of such disincentives should not be exaggerated.[54] He concludes his review of the evidence by stating that there are relatively few situations in which a disincentive effect has been clearly established and that, even where they have been established, the effects have been relatively small in size. Moreover, McLaughlin has pointed out that, while out-of-work benefits have some impact on the duration of unemployment spells, the effect tends to be small.[55] Similarly, an earlier review by Geary concluded that '. . . there are disincentive effects on labour supply associated with income support policies, but that . . . they are not very large'.[56] This is confirmed in a recent evaluation of social protection programmes in several European countries which concluded that there is little evidence that labour market flexibility is substantially affected by the presence of social protection programmes, nor is there evidence that the speed of labour market adjustment can be enhanced by limiting these programmes.[57]

Many recent studies in comparative growth theory have found 'a puzzling positive association between the size of transfer programs and the growth rate of the economy'.[58] Indeed, Sali-Martin proceeds to provide an economic model which explains this relationship, based on the idea that social transfers are a means to buy social peace and reduce social unrest (which in turn have positive effects on the productive efficiency of an economy). Overall, the theoretical basis for disincentive effects seems to be stronger than the results of empirical investigations of the presumed relationship.[59] Where disincentive effects exist they are likely to be weak and confined to certain well-defined categories of unemployed.[60] The danger is that in seeking to address the disincentive effect for the few, social protection for the many will be undermined and ultimately reduced. Many of these issues have come to the fore again in recent debates about the proper role of the European Union in the sphere of social policy and it is to this that we now turn.

SOCIAL POLICY AND THE EUROPEAN UNION

The primary objective of the Treaty of Rome was to create an economic union based on the free movement of goods, capital, labour and services among the member states. The original six member states were relatively homogeneous in terms of both economic development and institutional design, apart from the Italian Mezzogiorno. Consequently, disparities in either social conditions or social provision were not major issues. Not surprisingly, in the years following the Treaty of Rome, the main emphasis of social policy was on ways to enhance the freedom of movement of workers within the Community. This was followed in the 1970s by an emphasis on the improvement of living and working conditions, especially for women. The focus on women included the areas of equal pay, access to employment, training and promotion, and equality in respect of social security. During the first half of the 1980s support began to emerge for a more regulatory social policy at Community level, particularly from France. Concern about unemployment and social division, the existence of disparities in social protection across the member states of the growing Community, and the feeling that further integration in the political and economic spheres would require a social dimension, lay behind the increased interest in social policy.

Membership of the European Community played an important role in the expansion of the Irish welfare state, particularly in regard to the rights of women and workers. It is accepted that without membership of the European Community legislation on equal pay and equal treatment for women would not have reached the statute books when it did.[61] The Community was responsible for major advances for women such as the removal of the marriage bar in public employment, the introduction of maternity leave and greater equality in the social welfare system. Health and safety for workers in Ireland has also been considerably enhanced by membership of the European Community. This is not surprising given the fact that health and safety has been the main bulwark of European social policy mainly under the influence of member states from northern Europe. Irish workers have also benefited from the influence of the European Community in the areas of redundancy, work-time organisation and industrial democracy. Even if one believes that some of these positive developments for women and workers would have occurred anyway, membership of the European Community has undeniably accelerated progress in these areas and contributed significantlyto the development of the Irish welfare state.

The European Social Fund also funded both training and employment programmes for workers during periods of high unemployment in Ireland. There may also have been more intangible demonstration effects coming from Europe on the development of Irish social policy which both protected and enhanced social protection and provision in this country. This effect may have been particularly important during the 1980s when both the UK and the USA embarked upon an attempt to either reduce public spending or dismantle the welfare state. While demonstration effects are difficult to prove in that the purveyors of enlightened social policies are unlikely to want them attributed to sources outside the country, the influence of the European social model should not be underestimated.

For all of the influence of the European model, real or perceived, on the welfare state of individual member states, social policy at the European level remains underdeveloped. Opposition to the development of a social dimension in the EU arises from two main sources: those who hold the view that any form of interventionist social policy is undesirable since it undermines efficiency, and those who view a federalist social policy as unnecessary since disparities in social provision across member states represent genuine national differences in productivity and economic development.[62]

The conflict between those who want more Community involvement in social policy and those who want less was evident in the various controversies concerning the inclusion of a Social Charter on the rights of workers in a protocol to the Maastricht Treaty. In the lead up to the Treaty, social policy was treated very cautiously and conservatively. In truth, the prize of monetary union was too great for it to be threatened by a failure to agree a comprehensive integration package, including action on social policy.

The first major policy document on social policy emanating from the Commission post-Maastricht was a consultative Green Paper. Its main purpose was to seek views on how social policy might develop in the Union, given differences in both system objectives and institutional structures between the member states and between the social partners. This was followed a year later by the publication of a White Paper on European Social Policy. This document is much more explicit on the goals and objectives of European social policy. It is impossible not to be struck by how much of an influence the White Paper on Growth, Competitiveness and Employment[63] had on the White Paper on social policy. The key value in both documents is efficiency. The context is the competitiveness of the Union in an increasingly globalised economy.[64] What is at issue in both White Papers is a better balance between social protection, competitiveness and employment creation. The overriding concern is the need to improve job creation through greater flexibility in the labour market, thereby leading to greater equality of participation in the market economy.

The harmonisation of social policy across the Union is not an objective of the Commission. The emphasis is on minimum standards, reflecting the view that low social standards should not be used as an instrument of unfair economic competition. The social dumping argument is an old one, and reflects the concern that economies with low real wages and low social protection may have a competitive advantage over economies with higher wages and higher levels of social protection.[65] The main instruments for the implementation of a minimum standards approach are co-operation, co-ordination and information. There is no support in the White Paper for a wide-ranging programme of legislative reform. Co-ordination, rather than explicit harmonisation of legislation, is the favoured approach of the White Paper. If convergence is to happen it will be through voluntary means.

The reluctance of the White Paper to sanction a new wide-ranging programme of social legislation meant that it was inevitable that the Social Action Programme which followed would be conservative in its approach to Community intervention in the social field. There are two further reasons for the slowdown in social action in recent years. First, the social partners are now more closely involved in the formulation of any new legislative measures. The new Action Programme, through structures like the Forum on Social Policy, is also more participative than previous programmes and reflects a move towards wider consultation on the form and direction of social policy. This inevitably slows down the process of decision-making in the hope of making the implementation process easier later on, should agreement be reached between workers and employers. Second, the Commission is now paying much more attention to the application of existing European legislation at national level. The emphasis is now on the full implementation of proposals already agreed under existing legislation. In that regard, the European Court of Justice continues to play an important role in widening Community competencies in the area of social policy.[66]

Any assessment of current EU social policy must begin with a statement of what it is we expect social policy to achieve. T. H. Marshall defined social policy as the use of 'political power to supersede, supplement, or modify operations of the market system in order to achieve results which the economic system would not achieve on its own'.[67] Based on this definition, there is a social policy in the EU. Achievements in the areas of labour mobility and health and safety, the existence of an embryonic collective bargaining system, together with various market-making regulations are evidence of a supranational exercise of political power designed primarily to improve the operation of the market system. Yet, despite these successes, it is clear that social policy in the EU is not anywhere near as developed as social policy within individual member states. The three main treaties are largely characterised by a liberal economic philosophy; social policy remains the poor relation of economic, monetary and political union.[68] Intervention in the social sphere, where it has developed, is mainly a consequence of practical problem-solving stemming from market integration.

Heterogeneity in both social structures and provision across the member states remains the key constraint to the development of an elaborate common approach to social policy in the EU. The existing diversity of national welfare states, which is linked to differences in economic development among member states, makes harmonisation very difficult. In addition, the fragmentation of political institutions, allied to the multifaceted and complex nature of decision-making at EU level, makes it easier to sustain non-decisions than to agree on models for social progress.[69] Finally, the absence of social democratic hegemony makes it less likely that a balanced social corporatism will develop, thereby undermining the possibilities of an extension of social rights into areas opposed by capital. In this regard, Caporaso argues that whereas new transnational spaces have been created for capital, beyond the boundaries of the state, opposing forces of organised labour are not always as prevalent, and if they are present, they are not as organised or as strong as capital.[70] Finding space for labour and for those marginalised groups outside formal labour markets will be a major challenge for both national governments and European policy-makers in the years to come. In this regard Ireland may be better placed than most, given the strong support for social partnership agreements in the country and the current emphasis on widening partnership discussions to include representation from hitherto excluded sections of the community.

FUTURE PRIORITIES

Meaningful and fairly remunerated work continues to be the main bulwark against poverty and inequality. It is important, therefore, to maximise the degree of participation in the Irish labour market, in both market-oriented work and in community-based or socially-oriented work. This will involve support for many different kinds of work, as well as trying to secure an increase in the number of jobs in the economy. There are a number of different elements in the Irish social welfare system that contribute to both unemployment and poverty traps and prevent people from taking up meaningful work opportunities. Most of these are well known and have been commented on extensively.[71] While good progress has been made in reducing disincentives to work, more needs to be done if people are to make meaningful and unconstrained choices with respect to both the level and form of their involvement in the market economy. We need to focus attention beyond the simple dichotomy – employment or unemployment – to encompass more interesting issues concerning the availability of work, the type of work, the organisation of work and the worthiness of the training programmes put in place to support new forms of employment.

The concept of social participation might also be a useful way to approach the labour market potential of many in the 'economically inactive' segment of the labour force. The vast majority of persons in this sector are women engaged in home duties, receiving no paid income for services rendered to the economy. The issue of how to develop a range of socially necessary and productive activities in the social care field using a combination of part-time or temporary employment has been completely absent in policy discussions of the labour market. Yet many people classified as economically inactive are socially active, engaging in productive and valuable activities, such as caring and voluntary work. Legitimising some of these activities by bringing them into the social enterprise economy may be an important liberating experience for participants, particularly for carers, many of whom want to have their contribution to society more formally recognised by the state.[72] If handled properly so that the complex human dimension of much of this activity is respected, the transformation of the informal economy into a more commercial sphere could yield significant returns in the form of more care being made available to meet growing needs in the community.

Much attention has been given in recent years to the job creation potential of the social economy.[73] The National and Economic Social Forum (NESF) has defined the social economy as being 'concerned with meeting real demands which cannot be fully met by the market alone and are not provided by the public sector'.[74] The development of the social economy will, however, require significant public investment in training if its employment potential is to be fully realised. There is some evidence that the employment potential of the social economy in Ireland has been undermined by the rigid application of social welfare rules with respect to the payment of unemployment benefits.[75] Participants engaged in training programmes may lose their welfare entitlements as they are contravening a rule about being available for work while in receipt of benefits. However, solving the problem of participation will require more than a simple relaxation of the rules concerning availability for work and participation in training programmes. The social economy needs considerable support and nurturing from official sources. At present there is only fragmented support for social enterprise activity, with poor linkages between statutory providers of social care and embryonic commercial suppliers of social activities.

The final policy issue concerns the adequacy of social welfare payments. Even within a new framework, which emphasises social participation rather than income maintenance, many people will continue to depend on social welfare for their income. Improvements in the flexibility of social welfare payments are also important in providing a secure base for unemployed people seeking to enter both primary and secondary labour markets. Inadequate levels of payment constrain the ability of some unemployed people to manipulate potential economic opportunities, where taking up these opportunities leads to a withdrawal, or a reduction, in welfare payments in return for an uncertain future. Many unemployed people operate within very tight budgets, to such an extent that any shock to the stability of income sources may have catastrophic and immediate consequences for their standards of living. Even a short time period without adequate income may be too much for low income families to bear, resulting in a decision not to take up the job in the first place.

Concern about incentives, adequacy and passivity have led to calls in recent years for a more radical overhaul of the welfare state in the form of a basic income scheme to replace both social insurance and social assistance.[76] The attraction of basic income is the freedom it would give to individuals to take up whatever work is available consistent with their own preferences and lifestyle. The safety-net income provides a base on which to build, while eliminating both 'poverty traps' and 'unemployment traps'. The basic income scheme would be consistent with the development of the economy away from a situation where the norm is full-time work for an entire working life. It would facilitate atypical work patterns in the sense of people working for part of each week or leaving the paid labour force for part of their lives.[77]

The main problem with basic income schemes concerns the cost of introducing schemes that would provide an adequate income for recipients. Callan *et al.* estimate that a tax rate of the order of 62% would be required to finance a basic income scheme for Ireland, at a level close to the lowest welfare payments.[78] The response in official circles to such estimates has been stark and unambiguous: a full basic income system is not a viable option at this time.[79] (The present government's commitment to a Green Paper on basic income may signal a change in attitudes.) One way of reducing the cost of basic income schemes, thereby making them more acceptable, would be to link their introduction to a reform of the market system. For instance, Meade proposed a new partnership economy between capital and labour in which both capital owners and workers would have shares in enterprises that would be linked to basic income provision.[80] For all the concern about costs, basic income schemes remain the best means of facilitating the genuine work choices of individuals, provided they are backed up by public support for lifelong education and training for all citizens. It is also possible that the recent interest in the USA and other countries in flat-tax systems may precipitate more careful consideration of basic income schemes.

The key issue in formulating a new approach is the interconnectedness between participation as a economic strategy and participation as a social philosophy, an approach which would incorporate the values of efficiency, equity and solidarity. The intellectual basis for this model can be found in the work of Sen, and his characterisation of living as a combination of 'beings and doings'.[81] These 'beings and doings' are referred to by Sen as 'functionings', and range from elementary ones such as being adequately nourished, being in good health, etc., to more complex functionings such as achieving self-respect or being socially integrated. Achievement with respect to functionings is influenced by 'capabilities', reflecting the alternative combinations of functionings that a person can achieve. This implies that we should examine a person's potential, as well as her actual achievements. A difficult question posed by Sen is whether a person's position should be judged, positively, in terms of the level of achievement, or negatively, in terms of the shortfall *vis-à-vis* what she could have maximally achieved? Sen argues that, for some objectives at least, social arrangements should be organised so as to equalise the shortfall in the attainments of different individuals.[82]

Nowhere is the distinction between performance and potential more important than in the labour market, given the importance of work in affecting the broad range of individual 'functionings', particularly in the area of self-respect. Marshall argued that citizenship should be understood as a set of rights enjoyed equally by every member of society.[83] Perhaps it is now appropriate to revise the concept of social citizenship as entailing a right to lifelong learning and training, leading to meaningful participation in society.[84] This approach can be justified on several grounds, but it is primarily an equity enhancing measure. Given the increasing divisions between households where one or more members have secure, well-paying jobs and households subject to income insecurity, or having to rely on non-market income, the inclusion of training and education in the social welfare 'package' is an attempt to equalise individual choice sets.[85] Downward wage pressure in the labour market is mainly directed at the unskilled. Lifelong learning and social investment strategies offer a positive-sum solution to the trade-off between jobs and equality. A dynamic commitment to equality implies a social policy more explicitly designed to optimise the self-reliant capacities of individuals. The key to progress may be the replacement of the guarantee of social protection with a new guarantee of social participation, which is linked to the introduction of a basic income guarantee for all people.

Finally, we have noted several times how changes in economic and social conditions have affected the evolution of the welfare state. It is reasonable to expect that these changes will also affect the attitudes that citizens adopt towards the welfare state which in turn affect the potential of the welfare state to meet its objectives. Le Grand has analysed the changes in welfare state policies in Britain as being based in part on a shift in beliefs about human nature.[86] Recent policies are based on rational self-interested model behaviour as being the norm, whereas earlier policies were based on altruism among taxpayers and passive acceptance by recipients. By contrast other Western and Northern European countries are more likely to place emphasis on developing and maintaining values and norms of solidarity. Sometimes there is a presumption among commentators and policy-makers in Ireland that the only country we need to look at is the UK and that it reveals why economic objectives should take precedence over social objectives. An important goal of comparative social research should be to critically evaluate these presumptions.

CHAPTER 4

Environmental Policy in Ireland

GEORGE TAYLOR AND CATHI MURPHY

INTRODUCTION

To both politicians and environmentalists alike, the arrival of the environmental protection agency (EPA) in 1992 was welcomed as a breath of fresh air on the tarnished landscape of environmental regulation in Ireland. To its supporters, of which there were many, the creation of an independent national agency with greater powers of enforcement provided reassurance that Ireland's environment would not be jeopardised in the inexorable quest for economic growth.

Taking its lead from the influential Culliton group, the rhetoric that pervaded much of the accompanying debate maintained that a negative trade-off between stringent environmental regulation and economic growth was no longer inevitable. Indeed, the group's final report ebulliently declared that 'Irish industry should be positioning itself to cope with more stringent regulation'.[1] Amid such political confidence it is hardly surprising that in some quarters the EPA should be seen as the manifestation of a new ecological awareness in Ireland. However, the EPA's positive reception has been due less to its perceived role than to the fact that the Irish polity has proven a fertile ground for post-modern political rhetoric. It certainly accords with the fashionable idea that Ireland is now an emerging, cosmopolitan state which has successfully thrown off the shackles of Catholic orthodoxy and economic backwardness.

However, this view should be challenged. The EPA is not, as some would have us believe, the outcome of an emerging ecological modernisation within the Irish polity. Rather, it represents an institutional response to a succession of environmental conflicts that have threatened to undermine the interests of the agricultural and business lobbies. Put simply, environmental policy debate in Ireland is concerned no longer with the extent of ecological degradation, environmental justice, the quality of the environment or encouraging environmental sensitivity, but with the complicated process of organising consent around new definitions of the extent to which pollution can be justified.[2]

That this new agency offered an invaluable opportunity to restructure environmental regulation in Ireland is undeniable. Nor should we lose sight of the positive contribution that new legislation has performed. However, on a more disappointing note, what has patently failed to emerge has been any serious attempt to overhaul Ireland's environmental regulatory style. The consequence is that it has left the Irish courts inundated with environmental litigation. Luggala in Wicklow and Mullaghmore in Clare may have appeal to the more discerning among us who choose to cycle tandems around Ireland. However, the fact that such names are indelibly stamped upon the Irish political landscape is a serious indictment of the inability of environmental policy to respond to the challenges that were presented in the 1990s.

ENVIRONMENTAL POLICY IN THE 1970S AND 1980S

Despite an explosion in environmental directives emanating from the EU during the 1970s and 1980s, Ireland's environmental regulatory regime remained largely intact. The Department of the Environment was largely responsible for policy direction while the implementation of legislation lay at the doorstep of the local authorities. Change, where necessary, was slow, incremental and largely undertaken through the incorporation of EU Directives into Irish law, a situation that may have eased its passage but left it ineffectual.[3] This was by no means the only identifiable problem in this regulatory regime. For some time the environmental lobby had expressed disquiet about the regulatory role of local authorities, the lack of statutory powers and the need to ensure more stringent enforcement.[4]

While the legislation may have left much to be desired, it was with the enforcement of regulations that the principal source of difficulty lay. In most areas, if not all, sufficient legislative powers certainly existed. The Local Government (Water Pollution) Act 1977, for example, gave the Minister the requisite powers to compel a local authority to create water quality management plans and set standards for sewage discharge. However, it will surprise few familiar with environmental issues during this period to find that no Minister ever undertook such a task.[5]

Given the extended role performed by local authorities it is hardly surprising that they should receive intense scrutiny from the environmental lobby. And yet it is difficult to ignore the observation that a significant number of problems in their regulatory role could be traced back to the failure on the part of central government to provide adequate finance. In circumstances of such financial stricture, many local authorities had to rely on outside expertise in the more complex areas of regulation and did not possess either the resources or expertise to apply the control measures for which they were responsible.[6]

As if to complicate matters further, local authorities were, on the one hand, charged with monitoring and regulating the environment and yet, on the other hand, were in competition with one another to court the investment of multinational companies.[7] The 'politicised' nature of this role intensified during the 1980s amid concern that further enforcement of pollution regulation in the multinational sector could destabilise Ireland's 'climate for investment'.[8] As Leonard notes, such concerns had an important bearing upon the role of local authorities who were faced with the prospect of balancing the demand for jobs with the need to ensure adequate environmental regulation.[9] It was, in the opinion of one chief planning officer, a dilemma which the multinationals were fully aware. Indeed, he went as far as to suggest that:

> [there] must be a manual that US industrialists use to deal with local authorities when they want to get the plant to clean up the muck. First, make some veiled threats to close. Then get the workers and unions involved. Then just sit back and let concern about jobs and the economy divide public opinion enough to immobilise local officials.[10]

A further source of tension within the environmental regulatory regime lay in the pervading influence of the agricultural and business lobbies. Traditionally, the approach of the Department of Agriculture, Fisheries and Food (DAFF) was amicable with the agricultural lobby realising that the most effective way of influencing policy was to establish both formal and informal contacts.[11] However, as far as the environmental lobby was concerned, more concrete evidence of this 'influence' lay in the Department's persistent refusal to remove the 'good defence' clause in the Water Pollution Act, 1977, which prevented the prosecution of farmers for water pollution as long as they were in accordance with 'good agricultural practice'. As the environmental lobby was only too well aware, what constituted 'good agricultural practice' was, of course, defined by DAFF and not by those consigned to prevent water pollution.[12]

A further problem that served to undermine the confidence in Ireland's environmental regulatory regime during this period relates to the critical role the industrial development agency (IDA) performed in Ireland's quest for economic modernisation. Its function was to encourage and co-ordinate investment projects and throughout the 1960s, 1970s and 1980s it had a virtually free hand with industrial development.[13] Initially, policy was geared towards attracting labour intensive industries with the intention of reducing unemployment. However, recognising that such forms of production were vulnerable to competition from third world countries exploiting cheap labour, the IDA revised its strategy in the late 1970s and shifted its focus towards the chemical industry which, it felt, could generate skilled employment.[14] To some extent the success of this strategy can be gauged by the number of pharmaceutical companies which later chose to locate in Ireland.[15] Initial optimism, however, soon gave way to circumspection as the environmental track record of the multinationals came under the scrutiny of the environmental lobby. While environmentalists were willing to concede that skilled employment had been secured, they were alarmed that most of the companies that finally located in Ireland chose to develop the most hazardous aspect of their production process.[16]

Almost inevitably, the ensuing debate raised the spectre of the IDA marketing Ireland as a pollution haven. While this may have fallen well short of being a deliberate aim of policy it did little to sustain confidence in Ireland's environmental record. The perception among many environmentalists was that Ireland was unlikely to jeopardise potential investment through stringent environmental controls, a view partially confirmed in the candid remarks of one director of a pharmaceutical company who stated that 'we wanted a place with a similar infrastructure to the home country *without so many government restrictions*'.[17]

A considerable element in the IDA's success could be attributed to the 'one stop shop' nature of its service. Prospective multinationals wishing to locate in Ireland entered into negotiations with a single organisation, avoiding the complications of overlapping agendas, parallel power structures and bureaucratic inertia.[18] Once 'on board', the IDA acted effectively as an agent of the multinational companies, assisting in the creation of opportunities, smoothing over difficulties with other government agencies and helping to construct defences against the imposition of rigorous pollution control.[19] However, as in so many other instances, its strength was also its Achilles' heel. As far as the environmental lobby was concerned, the IDA operated a cosy cartel in which its principal function was to impose political leverage on local authorities. This is confirmed in Leonard's research which shows that the IDA was certainly not averse to impressing upon local authorities the need to relax environmental controls in order to secure 'a competitive advantage over other "potential" locations'.[20]

Critics of the IDA suggest that while its policy may have stopped short of deliberately creating a pollution haven, it was nevertheless implicit to its overall aim.[21] While there may be sympathy with the general thrust of such arguments, these approaches tend to ignore the complicated task addressed by the IDA. Indeed, it is important to exercise caution in promulgating the simplistic view that it was involved in some form of duplicitous act designed to conceal the environmental impact of new investment.

Controversial views such as these may well secure 'air time' in media debate but that does little to enhance our understanding of the complexity of environmental regulation during this period. Too often the IDA's critics lapse into little more than conspiracy theory, accusing it of a myopic disregard for Ireland's environment. It is as if the cumulative effect of the IDA's endeavours over the last twenty years have amounted to little more than a deliberate attempt to create some form of post-industrial landscape more commonly associated with the 'Mad Max' movies.

All too often such arguments conveniently ignore the changing political terrain upon which the IDA operated. There was no predetermined or absolute standard from which to judge the policy response. As such, we need to acknowledge the fact that the IDA did not act in some political vacuum, unaware of the political pressures arising from increased unemployment and emigration. Its role, as an integral element in a closed industrial policy community where access was privileged, was to develop a strategy that reconciled the tension between economic growth and environmental regulation. It was a policy community populated by other prominent political actors such as the Federation of Irish Chemical Industries (FICI), the Irish Business and Employers' Confederation (IBEC) and the Institute for Industrial Research and Standards (IIRS),[22] whose challenge was to present an 'alternative vision' of environmental regulation to that offered by the increasingly politicised environmental lobby. In contrast to the conspiratorial tone of its critics, therefore, the IDA was engaged in a far more subtle and complicated process of engineering consent around new levels of 'acceptable pollution'.

Few would deny that this task had become increasingly difficult to manage in the late 1980s as the IDA became embroiled in a protracted political struggle with the environmental lobby. The roles of both the planning system and local authorities were also subject to increasingly hostile criticism during this period. In February 1989, for example, the Gardaí launched a major investigation into allegations of bribery and corruption in the planning system following claims by a major Dublin builder that he had to make payments to a senior planning official in order to secure planning permission. At least six other figures were implicated, among them a senior local authority figure (linked by marriage to another builder), a Dublin Fianna Fáil backbencher and another high ranking planning official. According to the *Irish Times*, senior Gardaí 'expressed astonishment at the extent and pervasive nature of the alleged corruption now being uncovered'.[23]

The integrity of the planning system in Dublin was also undermined by the interaction between developers and Dublin corporation officials which was revealed to be significantly closer than would 'inspire confidence' in the ability of the corporation to discharge its responsibilities in an impartial manner. At the Bord Pleanála hearing into one particular planning application, An Taisce maintained that the manner in which it dealt with the proposed scheme had so compromised the corporation that it had effectively set aside the requirements in the planning acts that the views of third parties be taken into account.[24]

Public disquiet, however, undoubtedly reached its zenith in the controversy surrounding Merrell Dow. This dispute served to focus the public's gaze on the relationship between the chemical companies and state agencies.[25] The prevailing mood of this period was captured by an editorial of the *Irish Times* which declared that the IDA had not succeeded:

> in securing the trust of the people . . . that the highest standards of environmental control would be maintained and enforced. There is a growing conviction . . . that the provision for policing such controls are less than adequate, and that the industries are, in effect, left to police themselves. If this perception is not faced up to – rapidly – there is no telling how many others will go the way of Merrell Dow.[26]

By the late 1980s it was clear that environmental regulation had become effectively hamstrung by inadequate enforcement and a lack of coherence, flaws which ultimately precipitated a 'crisis of confidence' in the state's determination to protect the environment. The extent of cross-party support for change indicated the pressing political need to replace a myriad of confusing legislative arrangements with a single agency to provide a co-ordinated, integrated and fully transparent approach to environmental regulation. It was this struggle that provided the political backdrop to the formation of the EPA.

ENVIRONMENTAL POLICY IN THE 1990S

To its supporters, the admirably ambitious remit of the EPA reflected the increasing prominence green issues had assumed on the Irish political agenda.[27] The thrust of the legislation was to develop coherence and integration where previously indecision and incoherence had reigned. Indeed, with her finger firmly on the pulse of the electorate's sympathy toward green issues, the Minister for the Environment, Mary Harney, confidently predicted that the EPA would play a vital role in restoring Ireland's green credentials. Her neo-liberal political instincts were betrayed, however, in her determination to allay any fears on the part of business that it would strangle economic enterprise. Indeed, she was insistent that the agency would not be hijacked by the environmental lobby as part of some evangelical crusade against multinational companies.[28]

The most important part of the new legislation undoubtedly lay in the introduction of integrated pollution control (IPC) licensing, a move designed to restore public confidence in the regulatory framework. Above all else it revealed a shift in policy, conceding that the previous regime had been overly bureaucratic and had singularly failed to regulate industry. The novelty of IPC lay in the manner in which it would address 'managerial perceptions' toward environmental protection. In the process of securing (and retaining) an IPC licence it was envisaged that the traditional 'managerial outlook' would be altered, encouraging a more 'forward thinking' approach to environmental issues. Prior to IPC most firms would have been unfamiliar with either continuous release monitoring or the public disclosure of potentially polluting activities. However, it was anticipated that the advent of IPC would herald a new departure, one in which the dissemination of environmental information would restrict the capacity for companies to 'cut corners' and simultaneously encourage a new, more holistic managerial approach to environmental protection.

It was not a move that had been welcomed in the UK, where IPC licensing had been introduced in 1990. There was consternation in business circles at the prospect of environmental information being used by pressure groups to initiate private prosecutions. Indeed, the more sceptical elements had warned of an endless stream of prosecutions 'which would allow the green nutters to get on parade and have a field day of litigation against industry on entirely inconsequential grounds'.[29] Similar sentiments toward more stringent regulation have also been echoed in Ireland. In the aftermath of Lancefort's challenge to Treasury Holdings, for example, developers were 'apoplectic' at the prospect of being submerged by vexatious or frivolous appeals. Indeed, one developer was moved to remark that, if appeal fees were increased in relation to the size of the proposed development, 'objections to large developments would come from housing associations rather than from any person on every street corner'.[30]

Under the IPC regime introduced in the EPA Act the onus to improve environmental performance shifted toward the operator who would be obliged to justify and defend environmental practices. This vision was encapsulated in one of its fundamental aims – that it would eliminate or minimise the risk of harm to the environment by preventing the emission of potentially polluting substances wherever practicable or minimising such emissions where not practicable.[31] Its operating rationale was underpinned by the adoption of 'best available technology not entailing excessive cost' (BATNEEC). As the EPA's guidelines inform us, the technology (which extends to production techniques) would be 'best at preventing pollution, and available in the sense that it is procurable by the operator of the activity concerned'. 'Not entailing excessive cost' would set out the 'balance between environmental benefit and financial cost'.[32] The decision to adopt BATNEEC represented a subtle, but nonetheless crucial, shift away from the principle of precaution which had been mooted in the Environment Action Plan launched with much fanfare during Ireland's 'green' European Presidency. The declaration was greeted with dismay by environmentalists who saw this as further confirmation of the failure of Irish environmental policy to evolve in a more ecologically conscious manner. Indeed, critics of the EPA Act saw BATNEEC as simply a variant upon its discredited predecessor, 'best practicable environmental option' (BPEO).[33]

That the principle of BATNEEC provides the best direction for environmental policy is clearly a contentious issue. Critics of this policy instrument have argued that what constitutes 'best available technology' or 'excessive' cost is open to considerable debate. In particular, its critics have sought to ask whether judgements on these matters measure the external costs of investment or the external costs of not adopting the best available technology. It has certainly provided a fertile ground for debate between the EPA and licensees who object to more stringent licence conditions on the grounds of cost. The most politically controversial case has been that of Aughinish Alumina in Limerick where the EPA decided to relax elements of the IPC licence. The company had appealed the proposed conditions allowing it to discharge pollutants associated with production on the grounds of cost. It claimed that the recommended changes were financially prohibitive and estimated that it would increase costs by $40 million. The company also pointed out that the proposed regulations had threatened the viability of a plant which 'has always been very precarious in financial terms'.[34]

The EPA Act also anticipated that the IPC regime would secure both a continuing reduction in pollution and the adoption of cleaner technologies. In addition, it also explicitly stated that the regime's success would ultimately hinge upon the collation and dissemination of environmental information. The critical role to be performed by greater access to environmental data had been acknowledged earlier in the UK where the Department of the Environment's first set of guidelines had observed that the increased availability of environmental information on public registers would aid confidence in the system and facilitate public participation.[35] In the Irish case, the EPA was adamant that important environmental information, from compliance and release monitoring data to detailed justifications of business practices, would, for the first time, be placed in the public domain. Public registers would be the forum in which transparency was secured and oral hearings the arena in which disputes or challenges would be enacted.[36]

In practice, however, these aims have been partially undermined by the EPA's reliance upon self-monitoring among licensees. Its preferred option is to rely on voluntary compliance and, where necessary, encourage more environmental awareness. To its critics, this has been compounded by the agency's determination to avoid punitive action, pursuing this line only as a last resort.[37] On a more positive note, it should be recognised that the EPA has made important strides in the dissemination of environmental information. Thus, in marked contrast to its counterpart in the UK, the EPA has significantly increased access to information on licence applications, reviews and compliance monitoring results.[38] The registers also contain information regarding enforcement notices and improvement programmes which perform a critical role in authorisations under BATNEEC.

The purpose of improvement programmes is to place a legal duty on the operator to implement improvements over a set time period. It is invaluable information that should reveal the extent to which the IPC regime effects a change in managerial philosophy and enables pressure groups to assess the performance of the EPA.[39] The presence of such data on the public registers should also prevent the occurrence of the sort of problems that surfaced in the UK where, despite the stipulation in the process guidance notes that operators should provide upgrading plans with their applications, most failed to do so, and most post-authorisation improvement reports were not submitted.[40] Environmental information was the linchpin to the legislation. The collation and dissemination of environmental data provides an invaluable resource in the attempt to persuade industry to voluntarily adopt eco-friendly work practices and utilise cleaner technologies.

The EPA's success in this area can be seen in the introduction of a series of innovative methods of gathering environmental information. Most notably, this has included the adoption of annual environmental reports (AER), pollution emission registers (PER) and environmental audits. The aim has been to improve environmental 'accounting' in firms, a move which should enable a 'snapshot' of a company's environmental performance. Novel though this may appear, the record to date leaves room for considerable improvement. During 1997, only ten AERs and thirty-seven environmental performance reports (their precursor) were received from a total of 387 licensees.[41] These methods of data collation are complemented by inspections and audits undertaken by the EPA. In 1997, for example, the EPA carried out 1,439 visits (889 for sample emissions and 550 for auditing and inspection). However, of 387 licensees only sixty were audited, revealing a disturbing pattern of non-compliance (forty-eight of the sixty). The EPA's annual report painted a depressing picture of persistent levels of 'procedural irregularities' and lapses in documentation control. More disturbing was the report's view that in some facilities 'procedures were lacking for the operation of pollution abatement equipment' and that 'many facilities had no corrective action procedure to investigate and correct instances of non-compliance'.[42] Such candid remarks do not augur well for the ability of the current regime to change managerial perceptions of the vital role of environmental protection.

In light of its performance to date, it is hardly surprising that the EPA should have lost the confidence of the environmental lobby. It is not the EPA's use of new technology, innovative policy instruments or new practices that have been derided, since in many ways they have been innovative. The problem stems not so much from design but execution. Its operating ethos is to persuade, cajole and encourage the adoption of new eco-friendly approaches rather than impose stringent environmental regulations. It is this 'throwback' to the regime of the 1980s which has incurred the ire of the environmental lobby. There are also a number of other key areas of the EPA's operations which have been subject to criticism. These include its relationship with local authorities, the level of independence the agency enjoys, the voluntarist nature of its legislative powers and the manner in which its environmental discourse is shaped by a fundamental belief in the ability to provide.

While local authorities retain many of their environmental responsibilities under the 1992 legislation, the EPA had been assigned a monitoring role. This was a legislative response that acknowledged the extent of disenchantment over the regulatory role of local authorities. Many new clauses were designed to increase the powers of the EPA to request information and, where necessary, demand action. The Act stipulates, for example, that the agency has the power to fix criteria for the management of sewage treatment plants and landfill sites, and to perform a general supervisory role in the area of the quality of drinking water. Moreover, in cases where the EPA believes that a local authority has failed in its statutory obligations, or where it feels that these responsibilities have been carried out in an unsatisfactory manner, the agency *may* request a report from the local authority. If the local authority fails to respond adequately the EPA possesses the requisite powers to implement the necessary changes and impose the costs on the local authority.

A brief glance at the legislation would appear to confirm that it is sufficiently robust to ensure that local authorities will finally face up to their environmental responsibilities. Appearances, however, can be deceptive and on closer inspection it is evident that serious flaws remain. There is, for example, no compulsory obligation on the part of the EPA to request environmental reports from local authorities. In addition, the Act allows local authorities the opportunity to provide convoluted excuses for inaction, a flaw that curtails any serious endeavour to sustain pollution abatement. But more damning is the clause that allows local authorities to ignore any directive from the EPA if it has 'insufficient funds' with which to comply. This clause effectively provides local authorities with an excuse to 'do nothing'.

In the political discussion which accompanied the proposed legislation the government was adamant that the agency would be both fully independent and sufficiently resourced. On both these issues, however, the government was subject to hostile criticism. There was, for example, a discernible drift on its commitment to create a genuinely independent agency during the drafting of the legislation. The government's green credentials were further tarnished by its failure to establish definite funding levels. In addition, the environmental lobby also raised questions about the lack of an appeals structure for third party objectors and was alarmed at the level of government control over the agency's advisory committee. The role of this committee is to select a list of candidates from which the director general and four directors of the agency would be selected. However, the Act stipulates that a number of bodies should have permanent representation; the IDA, the Irish Congress of Trade Unions (ICTU), the Council for the Status of Women and An Taisce. The environmental lobby were apoplectic, arguing that the decision to allow the IDA to have permanent representation on the advisory committee was indefensible. On this matter the Democratic Left TD, Eamon Gilmore, observed:

> despite all the talk of achieving balance between environmental and economic issues in the composition of the advisory committee, it is worth noting that the same degree of balance was not reflected in the review body established by the Minister for Industry and Commerce on industrial policy. Not a single member of that body is representative of what we would call environmental interests.[43]

The Minister remained undeterred. In her considered opinion, the choice of the IDA seemed more apposite than an arbitrary decision between the Confederation of Irish Industry, the Federation of Irish Chemical Industries and the Federation of Irish Employers.[44] More revealing, perhaps, was the government's determination to assuage the agricultural and industrial policy communities that the EPA would not become an agency controlled by 'environmental radicals'. It was a message that found support among the Labour opposition who argued that the 300,000 unemployed would 'thank us in no small way' when the government talked in terms of technology being 'bad in the most luddite of terms'.[45]

From the outset the government's stance was clear; the EPA was an agency that would possess a strong managerial ethos. While this would not *necessarily* impose any undue constraints upon its environmental priorities, especially its scientific and research output, it would ensure that the agency's primary focus would be upon *managing* rather than *conserving* the environment.[46] As Harney pointed out to the Dáil:

> What we are doing is choosing a Director General and a full-time board of Directors who will be given a very important role and function in relation to the way the agency will operate . . . some of them will have to have particular expertise. In addition, they will need management skills and be capable of making decisions.[47]

The composition of the advisory committee was a crucial concern to the environmental lobby since, presumably, the general operational ethos and political will of the EPA would take its shape from this body. It was particularly anxious that any decision to undertake a survey of politically contentious areas would be clouded by the conservative composition of its advisory committee and the discretionary nature of the tasks set out in the legislation.[48] A further source of consternation was the omission within the legislation of a formal structure through which environmental protest could be accommodated. This has been exacerbated by the tendency within the EPA to accentuate the 'technocratic' dimension in any response to environmental protest. This follows a well worn path taken by a number of environmental agencies in Western Europe where there has been discernible inclination to rely upon scientific expertise to enhance the legitimacy of their decisions, rather than making them more accessible to the lay public. Debate becomes mired in obscure scientific issues, a move hindered further by the tendency among scientists to adopt risk analysis in defence of their arguments. In the short term it may enforce the illusion of scientific rigour, but it has done little to enhance the public's confidence in the regulatory regime. It should come as little surprise that decisions once adjudicated upon by civil servants and public officials have now become a source of intense public debate and conflict. It is a political 'hot potato' likely to increase in prominence as waste management assumes a higher profile in the EPA's activities.

In resolving the type of political protest likely to ensue on subjects such as landfills, public hearings, in whatever guise, have become a mainstay of measures designed to increase the participative nature of decision-making and ease fears among environmentalists that regulation has become the preserve of epistemic elites. Consequently, hearings tend to be loosely structured, open forums where members of the public hear government proposals and have the opportunity to respond, typically in a format set by the agency. Indeed, the EPA Act stipulates that where an objection has been lodged, the agency shall have *absolute discretion* to hold an oral hearing which shall be conducted by a person appointed by the agency.[49]

One of the more common objections to oral hearings is that they rarely provide citizens with an opportunity to participate on a equal footing since the agency defines the agenda and establishes the format. Furthermore, hearings provide limited time for citizens to grasp technical issues and offer a substantive element to discussions. This difficulty is compounded by the fact that while the legislation is strong on procedural regulatory (with a range of stipulations regarding time periods for the submission of written evidence, the decision to hold an oral hearing and the notification of decisions taken by the agency), it remains far more opaque on issues such as the dissemination of the information which enabled the agency to make a decision. The notification of a decision is a far cry from an explanation of 'how and why' a particular decision was taken.[50]

There are large parts of the legislation that hardly pretend to enhance the democratic nature of the decision-making process. It appears that its principal aim is simply to ensure that a decision is made quickly so that, if the application should fail, business can move on. This is evident in the fact that the legislation is replete with clauses that define the legal standing of a 'valid objection', revealing an overwhelming preoccupation with procedural regulatory at the expense of environmental justice. It is also endorsed in the EPA's guidance notes. These follow the line taken in the Local Government and Planning Act (1992) where a 'valid objection' should contain all the 'necessary documentation' since the agency will not consider 'further submissions'.[51] Indeed, the EPA's guidance notes would appear to enforce more stringent conditions than those offered by the Local Government and Planning Act (1992) when it stipulates that 'a person or body which has made a submission may not elaborate on it or submit a further submission, *even if this is done within the prescribed time period*'.[52]

At first, these may seem rather innocuous parts to the legislation. Their inception certainly attracted scant attention in wider political and media circles. However, given the changing nature of environmental regulation with its propensity to rely upon complex scientific argument to defend cases, clauses designed to impose time limits or prevent further submissions being made have a substantial and detrimental effect upon environmental democracy in Ireland.[53] It is also worth noting that the EPA's stance with regard to third party objectors differs markedly from that it takes towards *applicants* for licences where it is willing to go 'as far as possible to assist industry' and to 'provide pre-application clarification facilities where necessary'.[54]

The final issue raised in the political exchanges over the agency's independence relates to the thorny issue of finance. During the early stages of the passage of the legislation, the government estimated that the agency would need around £8 million. However, its funding has operated at nowhere near this level. In 1994, the agency's funding stood at £4.4 million.[55] In the following year the Minister declared that its available funds would be £3.6 million for current spending and £750,000 capital spending, with an expected fee income of £1.4 million.[56] It was a figure that fell considerably short of the original £8 million.

The issue of funding raised a chorus of disapproval from the opposition parties. As the Democratic Left TD Gilmore noted, there was a significant amount of legislation on the statute books and a number of environmental bodies in existence. The problem was that government had starved the latter of the finances necessary to implement and enforce the former. On a more sombre note, he pointed out that the EPA's precursor, An Foras Forbartha, had 'come a cropper' because government 'had decided it did not want an independent agency to deal with environmental issues'.[57] During the course of the Dáil debate it became clear that while the government's political rhetoric was willing to embrace the 'green issue', it was reticent about offering additional funds. Indeed, the funding of the agency, which has been steadily eroded over recent years, has been transferred from other areas or raised by the agency itself.

The creation of an independent agency was countenanced by the need to ensure that there was sufficient political accountability. Here, even the government's most vocal critics were concerned that there existed a danger in setting up an agency that effectively became a committee of experts divorced from democratic accountability and public participation.[58] As Garland noted, if the institution was separated from the responsibility of the Minister it would be impossible for the Dáil to scrutinise and reveal issues which were of public concern. Here, Deputy Garland, among others, noted that many of the provisions contained in the Act would be brought about through ministerial action but would not be subject to debate in the Oireachtas. Further, no time limit was placed on ministerial action in this area. Thus, with regard to large portions of the Act, once passed they were effectively removed from the public arena. Nowhere is this more evident than in the regulations that control access to environmental information. These allow the Minister to delay the introduction of the EU Directive on access to information and mean that, as with other ministerial regulations, no debate will be carried out on the matter in the Oireachta).[59]

IRELAND'S AGRI-ENVIRONMENTAL POLICY IN THE 1990S

The Rural Environmental Protection Scheme (REPS) is a prominent feature of Ireland's agri-environmental policy. It forms part of a wider package of reforms that operate in tandem with the common agricultural policy (CAP). Pre-reform CAP, with its price control mechanisms, had fulfilled a key objective of the Treaty of Rome – providing adequate food supplies at reasonable prices. Policy was formulated around the use of incentives to increase production but this had a largely unanticipated and significantly deleterious effect upon the environment. Both wildlife habitats and water quality were impaired as intensive agriculture increased its use of fertilisers and pesticides. By the mid to late 1980s the level of opposition to this system had become formidable as a range of political groups argued that the CAP was in need of serious reform.[60] The response from within the agricultural lobby to calls for reform was to reconstruct the farmer as both producer and custodian of the countryside.[61]

REPS, to a large extent, is the policy expression of this duality in the farming function, serving to reconcile the need to maintain income transfers to farmers and yet assuage the demands of the environmental lobby for greater regulation of the environment. It was intended that under the auspices of an 'environmental conservation' programme, government would be able to effect a reduction in the burden of agriculture, a move made all the more meaningful when placed against the backdrop of a political climate in Europe which was increasingly hostile to agricultural support. REPS has three principal objectives. First, to establish farming and controlled production practices which reflect more closely a concern with conservation, landscape protection and wider environmental degradation. Second, to protect wildlife habitats and endangered species of flora and fauna. Finally, it aims to promote quality food production in an environmentally friendly way.

The nutrient management plan (NMP) is pivotal to REPS. Its aim is to ensure that nutrients are used in a more effective, environmentally conscious manner by employing new measures for the collection, management and disposal of farm wastes. However, its design reveals a number of flaws which mitigate against its success as an effective form of environmental protection. In particular, payments are made for areas only up to forty hectares, which acts as a disincentive for the larger, more intensive farmers. And yet, perversely, it is these latter operations that need to embrace new agri-environmental practices. Further, although aid is available for additional conservation measures, payment for only one measure is allowed. There is little incentive, therefore, for farmers to develop a range of environmentally sound working practices. And, as in so many other instances of agri-environmental policy, participation in the scheme remains entirely voluntary.

From its inception REPS has been beset with problems. Initially, DAFF predicted a participation level of about 40,000 farmers, covering about 1.3 million hectares.[62] At the close of 1996, however, agricultural consultants declared that participation would have to double for the scheme to reach this target.[63] Such a low level of participation undermined the potential success of the scheme since, as Regan has commented, the potential contribution of REPS can be realised only if there is a good response to the scheme among qualifying farmers.[64]

The level of inspection of participants in REPS also cast doubt on its credibility as a *bona fide* pollution control programme. In 1996, all cases were being checked for compliance and the Minister for Agriculture, Food and Forestry declared that such an inspection rate was in the best interests of Irish farmers. Not surprisingly, the farming lobby opposed what it saw as stringent regulation. Its response was to call upon the Minister to halve the rate of inspection in order to speed up the payments to farmers, a request he dutifully performed within a month.[65]

Another key problem that has undermined the credibility of REPS as part of an integrated environmental protection package is that it sends out conflicting signals to farmers. Under the CAP, farmers are encouraged to maintain or intensify farming operations by price supports and annual payments. The ewe premium scheme in Ireland is typical of this initiative. It is a payment on the unit of livestock rather than by hectare, which makes overgrazing financially beneficial to certain farmers. The principal problem facing REPS, therefore, is that it is largely viewed as one of a number of competing programmes of income transfer rather than as an environmental protection scheme.

As an environmental protection scheme REPS also has an interface with the programme for the protection of Natural Heritage Areas (NHAs). This scheme, which comes under the jurisdiction of the Department of Arts, Culture and the Gaeltacht (DACG), stipulates specific conditions which farms must operate under to qualify for payments. At first, the conditions drawn up for participants provoked a strong reaction from the farming lobby, particularly on the issue of stocking densities. After negotiations with the Minister for Arts, Culture and the Gaeltacht, the severity of the rules relating to the stocking densities were reduced.[66]

The above analysis of REPS illustrates how an agri-environmental scheme interacts with other policies in the environmental sector in such a way that the environmental element in agricultural policy-making remains significantly reduced. This failing is compounded by the conspicuous lack of a fully integrated approach to environmental policy that is most evident in the controls on afforestation and the debacle surrounding the collapse of the Control of Farmyard Pollution scheme (CFYPS). The Minister of State at DAFF declared to the Dáil in January 1995 that environmental considerations would not be forgotten in the state's afforestation programme and that a review of planning controls on large-scale forestry projects would be carried out in co-operation with the DoE.[67] Details of this co-operation were made public in May 1996. The environmental dimension to this policy focused largely on changes to planning permission where new controls would reduce the threshold for which planning permission and EIAs were required from 200 hectares to seventy hectares.[68] From May 1996, it stipulated that Coillte must notify local authorities of any application for grant aid for projects over twenty-five hectares and consider the views of the local authority in any application for grant aid. Furthermore, local authorities would designate areas considered sensitive to forestry development. While the reduction in the threshold at which planning permission and EIAs were necessary was a welcome step in environmental control, difficulties with regulation are still evident, particularly given the poor record of local authorities in the environmental arena.

From the point of view of environmental policy, the forestry sector is riven with ambiguities, displayed by the low level of integration between departments. Thus, for example, it is by no means clear what the respective regulatory responsibilities of DAFF and DoE are in this area. The Minister for the Environment has informed the Dáil that any decision on the type of trees planted was primarily a matter for DAFF, while the environmental impact and planning requirements were in the jurisdiction of DoE.[69] In response, the Minister of State at DAFF, when asked who would be responsible for environmental impact and planning controls of forestry, declared that the Forestry Department would be responsible for *all matters* affecting the forestry programme. When it was pointed out that the Minister of the Environment had seen certain aspects of the forestry programme falling within the remit of DoE, the Minister stated that 'our Department will be responsible for *all matters that we deem affect the implementation of our programme*'.[70] Such a failure to achieve co-ordination between departments should come as little surprise to those conversant with the processes of Irish politics where political prestige is lauded upon those who successfully secure or defend the territory of their respective departments.

The reaction of the DoE to the collapse of the CFYPS further attests to the lack of any genuine spirit of institutional integration on environmental policy. The CFYPS was a central part of the government's effort to address agricultural pollution and its subsequent failure had a deleterious effect on REPS. When questioned about the collapse of the CFYPS, the Minister for the Environment claimed that questions in this regard should be addressed to DAFF and that they had 'no implications for my department'.[71] The position held by DAFF was markedly different. As far as the Minister for Agriculture, Food and Forestry was concerned, the collapse of the CFYPS would impact upon the ability of farmers to reduce pollution. In the absence of any direction from the DoE he stated that it was his intention to exert the power of DAFF on local authorities, inhibiting them from taking prosecutions against farmers for water pollution offences. Clearly, while the Minister for the Environment claimed that the collapse of the CFYPS did not come within his remit and therefore did not require comment, it is evident that the sentiments of the Minister for Agriculture, Food and Forestry were rather different.

CONCLUSION

It is apparent that the institutional structure of environmental regulation in Ireland has undergone change in recent years. But what remains a far more important source of consternation for many environmentalists in Ireland is not so much the inadequacy of any individual element to the legislation as the failure to overhaul a regulatory style which has often made significant concessions to the agricultural and business lobbies. If we are to understand the nature of the institutions which have emerged, and the failure to alter their policy style, then it is imperative we comprehend the dynamics which lay behind such change.

At the heart of the EPA's conception was more than a simple realisation on the part of the Irish state that its environmental regulatory regime was inadequate. Indeed, as its institutional structure and operating rationale suggest, the motivation which lay behind the formation of the EPA was not one exclusively concerned with protecting the environment. By the end of the 1980s the agricultural and industrial policy communities had come under increasing pressure from the environmental lobby and government recognised that if it was to depoliticise the environmental policy domain it had to revamp its regulatory framework. There were two critical elements to this overall strategy. First, if the public's perception that industry was not being adequately controlled was to be dispelled then the agency's independence would have to be at the forefront of the political debate. Second, the legislative powers of the EPA would have to reflect a significant shift from previous environmental regimes. The principal dilemma facing the agricultural and industrial policy communities was not the institutional configuration of the agency, but rather the need to establish a new environmental discourse which fully appreciated the crucial implications that further regulation held for the economic performance of the Celtic Tiger.

The government's most pressing task was therefore to assuage the environmental lobby by diffusing potential areas of conflict and resistance and removing from the public realm important questions about the relationship between economic growth and the environment. A protracted upsurge in environmental protest enveloped the Irish state in a struggle to construct a political discourse on the environment which was concerned not with embracing ideas about environmental degradation, justice, or democracy but with the complicated task of constructing a consensus around an *acceptable level of environmental pollution.* That policy has singularly failed to effect a successful overhaul of environmental regulation in Ireland can be seen in the resurgence of environmental protests in recent years. For the protests of Merrell Dow or Raybestos Manhatten in the 1980s read Aughinish Alumina or Mullaghmore in the 1990s. The participants to this unfolding drama may have changed, the stage upon which it has been enacted transformed, but it is the familiarity of the script which remains the more perturbing.

Silence and the Golden Years: Older People and Public Policy in Ireland

R. EDMONDSON[1]

INTRODUCTION

> The Irish Republic fully recognises the necessity of abolishing the present odious, degrading and foreign Poor Law System, substituting therefore a sympathetic native scheme for the care of the Nation's aged and infirm, who shall not be regarded as a burden, but rather entitled to the Nation's gratitude and consideration.[2]

A society's policy towards ageing and older people embodies its collective stance on being human during the dynamics of a life course. This policy – in effect the result of converging sets of policies – expresses assumptions and establishes parameters that lay down what lives in a society are for and what they can be thought of as aiming at. Is living a life about creative and positive co-operation, for example, or about self-development in relative privacy, or chiefly about not causing trouble?

In former times, moral and public reflection incorporated ideas about lifetime, such as the expectations depicted in discussion of 'the seven ages of man' or such as discussions of the experiences required to achieve maturity.[3] Moral and political aspirations could be expressed by showing their relation to the kind of old age that embodies the fruits of a life well lived. In contrast, contemporary debate about policy on older people in Ireland, as in most other European countries, generally evades such reflections.[4] Not only that, its existence *as* public policy automatically creates a group in society, that of 'older people', in competition for scarce resources with other groups.[5] In this setting, without reflection on the meaning of ageing, policy decisions will fail to make sense or will become destructive. It is apparent in a number of areas – from arrangements about the earning and payment of pensions to the whole conception of 'care' for older people and who is to provide it – that policy for older people is suffering markedly from this overall lack of direction. Such a lack cannot be attributed solely to official policy-makers, however. Public policy does not influence society purely in a 'top-down' direction, and there is room for considerable input from a variety of social actors here – including, especially, older people themselves.

Ireland at the beginning of the twenty-first century has undergone a transition in relation both to the public standing of older people and to the accepted functions of public policy. The immediacy of the personal power of older people over the lives of family members has waned with the declining economic significance of smallholdings. In this sense, family dynamics and lifecourse development have been tied to the industrialising trajectory taken by the entire social structure. At the same time it has become taken for granted that state interventions should impinge in blanket fashion wherever parts of society are held to be weak – areas which have uncontroversially been taken to include older people. This vast extent of expenditure in itself affects the nature of debate on public policy because it makes it impossible for the state to be non-committal about the nature of ageing, however much it might prefer to remain so: both instituting policy and refraining from doing so communicate official attitudes and views. However, expensive public policy does not necessarily indicate as general a benevolence as might first appear. In Ireland, as elsewhere in Europe, the idea of older people commands extensive allegiance, in principle; but in terms of social influence and meaning, older generations remain very much contained. Policy interventions are residualist in their implications in the sense that provisions are intended for when older people can be found to be poor, ill or 'lonely'. In an economy where older people have retreated from the area of production, there is no clear sense of a public policy that has the aim of enhancing older people's social power or elaborating possibilities for an excellent older age for citizens as such. Emerging groups of the 'active retired' and similar older people's associations will, it may be hoped, radically alter this situation in the future.

Given the radical changes in Ireland's social structure during the last fifty years, it may not be surprising that the status of older people has faltered – perhaps temporarily – while new ideas develop about what participating in society means. People in Ireland who were old during the first half of the twentieth century often held considerable family power through possession of property, especially land, which held the key to the survival of the next generation. Inheritance was largely concentrated in the time period when the giver reached old age or death. In this situation the position of older people was relatively strong, both economically and culturally, and this was reflected in the longevity of Irish people in the early decades of last century. Arensberg and Kimball remark that Ireland was 'in some ways an old person's country'.[6]

It seems that the past in general was respected, at least in theory; a respondent now in his nineties, talking to this author about his youth, said: 'We used always to be talking about the old people – about how we weren't a patch now on the ones that had lived long ago'. But Arensberg and Kimball[7] make it clear that this respect for age was directly linked to concrete forms of life in which older people had considerable practical roles to play. 'In the Irish case they live long because they have much to live for. In their own sphere of life, they are honored. They have power'.[8]

Still it is not clear that their status consistently protected older people in farming economies from harshness attendant on age. Hareven, pointing out that old age has always been insecure in rural societies, recalls that on the East Coast of America, trust between the generations was sufficiently insecure for it to be necessary that the owner of the farm, allowing his heir to take over, should make a legal contract stipulating his right to remain in his home for his lifetime.[9] This was common on the continent and Brown refers to the same arrangement in Ireland.[10] A similar lack of sentiment is reflected in the term from the West of Ireland for the niche thrown out near the fireplace where the old woman of the house would sleep: the 'cailleach', the witch or old hag. Similar terms can be found in rural settings abroad. Murphy's play *Bailegangáire* details conveniently untraceable ways of disposing of members of the older generation whose presence had become an insupportable inconvenience.[11] It is not the case, therefore, that ageing in the past was inevitably a comfortable experience. However, the fact that older people were expected to pass on inheritances towards the ends of their lives endowed them as a group with a certain amount of social leverage. In this setting, older people did not need to agitate for power and reflection on the meaning of life was in some ways part of ordinary living. Contemporary societies, in contrast, necessitate both a much more deliberate search for meaning on the parts of their participants and a more conscious defence of their interests by those who are not economically active. This is made all the more difficult in respect to ageing because the social role played by older people may not be less important than it used to be, but it is much less obvious. Now that participation in the labour force is tightly linked to educational credentials, heavy parental expenditure regularly begins much earlier in children's life-cycles. Though class influences on families' capacities for boosting the fates of their members have, if anything, increased, they exert their effects in less obvious ways.[12] In individual family terms, expenditure from older to younger members continues over average lifecourses to predominate over financial support the other way round, but this expenditure is tied in with the officially universalistic educational goals of public policy itself.[13] Not only is the personal power of older people not as apparent as it used to be but older people also now seldom appear to be credited with authority because of their age as such.

Indeed, older people in employment appear often to be viewed primarily as an unnecessary expense; they are more readily perceived as objects of charity than as creative contributors to society. In Ireland, what evidence is available suggests that intergenerational social commitment continues to be respected, if in a somewhat nebulous fashion. Yet the anodyne character of public discourse about older people tends to negate the effectiveness of this diffuse good will. It also conceals a number of profound problems, not only about older people and ageing but also about the nature of participation in society itself. On the one hand, public expenditure on older people has increased in Ireland since the 1970s in part via pensions whose real value has multiplied, and in part via health care whose cost, here as elsewhere, has burgeoned.[14] As far as pensions are concerned, the real value of social welfare pensions rose by about 17% between 1980 and 1987, for example, and by about 107% over the period between 1973 and 1987.[15] It is accepted that numbers of older people will increase considerably in Europe in the foreseeable future; in Ireland, which has a very young population in European terms, about 15% of the population is aged 60 and over. This is projected to increase to approximately 19% over the next thirty years.[16] This will mean that older people will form a large proportion of the electorate, and perhaps of the purchasing public, and these are potential sources of strong leverage.[17]

On the other hand, at least four crucial weaknesses attach to the position of older people. First, within the system of measures that are set out for older people, actual provision is irregular and often cosmetic.[18] Secondly, people who are ageing now are doing so without the generalised social status which older people used to possess. For example, occupational pensions are currently crucial in distinguishing between richer and poorer older people.[19] Not only are some people relatively ill-placed to acquire such pensions (offspring of manual labourers or the unemployed, and women in general), but both the experience of employment and the public regulation of pension provision are becoming increasingly fragmented and unpredictable. Thirdly, the status of all older people is damaged by the residualist implications of state policy. Provision is in effect arranged on the principle that the state should intervene in case of disaster, but otherwise leave older people to fend for themselves. Not only does this fail to endorse any positive model or image of the life course for society as whole, it repeatedly draws attention only to those older people who are ailing and in need, while at the same time stigmatising them as recipients of quasi-charitable arrangements. Older people are treated as different from the norm, even though as a worthy cause, and policy highlights those who are in difficulty and thus regarded as objects of care. There is little evidence of positive discourse about human life courses as evolving towards some desirable and worthwhile goal. Fourthly, but unsurprisingly given the foregoing, there is insufficient participation in the formulation and exercise of policy by older people themselves.[20]

All four of these problems can be summed up as a voicelessness which pervades the situation of older people, not only in terms of practical arrangements for ascertaining needs and views which can influence policy, but, much more insidiously, in the language which is currently available for debate. It appears that radical, positive measures for improving overall circumstances for the ageing of the population are not even imaginable in present circumstances: there is a dearth of terms in which to formulate and envisage them. Older people, therefore, urgently require a position from which participation in public life can take place, and also a language for self-defence and self-definition. If they do not acquire this, older age for Irish society in general will remain summed up in charitable terms. Of course such a language cannot be expected to be developed by sociological analysis. It will need to derive from the active participation of members of the society as they age – and those active in public policy will need to take care not to deaden it.

'Community care' is the keystone of official policy for older people, in Ireland as in most of Europe, and it provokes wide-ranging debate along at least two lines. First, does this care provide what is claimed for it, namely, dignified existence in or near home in which publicly financed care is dovetailed with that provided by community organisations and individuals? Or is it part of an attempt by governments to mitigate the increasing financial costs of health care of which older people consume considered portions though (according to Victor) perhaps not as considerable as politicians assume?[21] Secondly, do such attempts imply that in effect 'community care' is merely a euphemism for care at home by women? 'Community care' frequently takes for granted that there will be a person at home, usually a woman, to exercise much of the caring involved. Here the situation of women sharply underlines the importance of considering the nature of life courses as their social settings permit them to develop in different ways. Increasing emphasis on community care may mean that women have now reduced the numbers of their children only to find themselves in middle age taking on the care of their parents, not to mention household responsibilities and work outside the home as well. This is certainly a different type of maturing trajectory from that envisaged in debates on women's 'liberation' during recent decades. The significance of this trajectory emphasises the fact that public policy needs an approach to life course formation overall and not simply to old age, a period which, in any case, it is becoming more and more difficult to define.

In all this discussion, relatively little evidence is available about what policies people actually wish for as they get older. Nor is it a straightforward matter to ask them, since language tends to reflect present states of affairs rather than ideal ones and ageing involves more than making simple practical arrangements. It involves debates, disputes and decisions about the proper nature of human development and human obligations, and about the ways in which growing older can be related to goals which give social and political sense to life in society. Hence, constructing ageing means constructing living. It is not possible for social policy to remain neutral on such issues; both policy and the absence of policy have statements to make about underlying political values. For this reason a positive anticipation of ageing, developed with the participation of older people themselves, could invigorate social policy to the advantage of the whole society.

ARGUMENTATION AND POLICY ANALYSIS

Social policy does not just create or rule out the possibility of specific forms of action. It provides worlds of expectation and justification. A policy is not merely a practical arrangement, it is also a potent political message. It constructs, legitimises or denies courses of understanding and helps create the language that goes with them.[22] Hence new realms of practice emerge or fade as forms of behaviour – on the parts of the state, of groups, or of individuals become imaginable or lose their plausibility. For these reasons, policy on ageing can only be understood by means of a threefold method of analysis which responds to the creation by public policy of worlds of discourse which have powerful effects on social attitudes and behaviour, as well as direct impacts on those immediately affected.[23] This method is comprised of three major components: first, analysis of discourse creation in terms of argumentation and rhetoric; secondly, analysis of ageing in terms of a critical gerontological investigation of the ways in which older age is to a crucial degree constituted by social perceptions; and thirdly, an ethnographic approach to recording the phenomenology of the effects of social policy as they are actually experienced.

Analysis of policy in terms of argumentation derives from a classical rhetorical approach.[24] This both interrogates the processual components of communication and seeks to uncover underlying, socially sanctioned structures of legitimation which make arguments believable. People's surface views about what they feel they know are supported by several depths of unstated, often unnoticed, assumptions about what can validly be assumed and about what makes forms of reasoning seem coherent. These assumptions are often difficult to expose to view and can be deduced much less often by interrogating respondents directly on their reasons for their views than by examining the presuppositions and implications of what they feel, say and do. Berger points out the existence of 'plausibility structures' which allow some points of view to appear reasonable in given socio-political situations and rule out others. These structures may have definable relations to the forms of life within which they emerge.[25] Structures of reasoning and arguing change over time as forms of life change and forms of life are, in contemporary societies, heavily influenced by public policy – however assiduously policy formation may try to present itself as an information based, neutral process. Neither policy itself nor the views which people express about policy can be taken at face value. They are in part the products of the very social and political context on which they are commenting.[26] For reasons related to these, Frank Fischer points out that:

> In actual practice, policy analysts and planners do a great deal more than they have been given credit for doing. They scan a political environment as much as they locate facts, and they are involved with constructing senses of value even as they identify costs and benefits.[27]

Policy planners are often represented as justifying their views by reference to indisputable facts, or else universal but relatively non-specific values such as human dignity. The virtue of argumentational analysis is that it draws attention to the implications in terms of power and practicalities which given policies have, situating them in the context of the social settings in whose terms they have meaning. And it militates against the widespread and extremely destructive practice of presenting public policy in terms so neutral that they are positively deadening.

In relation specifically to older people, argumentational analysis can productively be combined with critical gerontology.[28] This approach stresses the effects of patterns of social, economic and political power on what older people are enabled to do or prevented from doing – on what it is practically like to be old in specific sections of time and society. Neugarten and Neugarten point out that age in itself has now become a poor predictor of people's health, work and family status, their interests and needs.[29] Despite this, people's expectations are still oriented to 'internalised social clocks' which indicate if they are 'on schedule' for whatever age they are at, but consensus about these schedules is declining.[30] Social settings continue to produce images of ageing that influence what is expected of older people and what they expect of themselves. However, these images are fragmenting under variable sociopolitical and economic pressures and they impinge differently on people who happen to reach older age at different times.[31] Both actual life course possibilities and expectations about their appropriate development will differ according to whether a person was born in the 1930s, say, and grew up in the relatively essentialist Ireland of protectionism, or whether he or she grew up in the 1960s, among almost diametrically opposed patterns of opportunities and constraints which relate directly to Irish participation in a global economic network.

Phillipson and Walker underline the role of public policy in augmenting the socio-political impacts of highly differential resources of power, money, and health.[32] Policy decisions, allocating these resources, create social landscapes in which it is possible to be one kind of person or another. For example, the impact of the old age pension (introduced in England and Ireland in 1908) has long been assumed to have created relative ease and security for many older people. But critical gerontologists argue that, given its context – a productivist, consumerist society – it has also contributed to a general assumption that older people stand outside the mainstream of real life, apart from the rest of society. This image has a clear potential to generate arguments that put older people at a disadvantage in the competition for resources between social groups thus lending this competition a generational turn. It already has taken a gendered turn, as women are more likely to be alone and poverty-stricken in old age than men are. This is partly because women live longer than men, at least in the twentieth century and for the first time, and partly because their command of material resources is consistently less than men's.

An emphasis on the social construction of ageing does not stress only economic resources; it also underlines the fact that what is socially accepted as appropriate in ageing affects what individuals can actually tolerate in themselves and in others. Social practice with regard to ageing changes our own views about our own ageing. It affects the phenomenology of ageing, shaping the ways in which ageing is experienced in any given social setting. Hence a sociological understanding of the social construction of ageing in a particular context needs to be extended by incorporating an ethnographic component to investigate more closely how public policy on ageing is felt, both by those who make it and by those who are affected by it. Ideally, these groups would overlap much more systematically than they now do: policy for older people would benefit from more input for older people and from a more effective language in which this input could be couched.

The practical difficulties involved in harnessing the views of older people for policy construction are many, though not all insuperable. It is a commonplace of contemporary work on ageing that older people should not be treated as a homogeneous group. It is also seen that there are as many differences between older individuals as between members of other age-bands, and that there are vital divisions between 'young old' and 'old old'. There are also difference between richer and poorer older people, and those of different class, genders, cultures and tastes as well as between the old in core cultures of the world and those in semi-peripheral ones. In Ireland, the country's recent and rapid social change has quickly produced changing cohorts of older people – generations who have been socialised at different times and whose contrasting life experiences may have given them different expectations about the process of ageing. Those born around or soon after the First World War grew up during a period when governments deliberately curtailed state interventions into citizens' lives, even positive ones. The Irish state and its policies only began to expand when they had reached late middle age themselves, and they may not have learned to expect much of public institutions; later cohorts may become more insistent. Moreover, rapid social change is associated with economic inequality and poor health in age is deeply dependent on social and economic structures.[33] Membership of a lower social class (as well, in Ireland, as of the travelling community) is associated with more illnesses of all kinds during ageing and with lower life expectancy.

Nonetheless, despite the significance of such distinctions, being the object of social policy in itself *constitutes* older people as in some sense a group. Social policy, even in attempting to support older people, has homogenising effects which may or may not be welcome or congenial to different groups of older people. This does not apply only on a national scale. Social workers who would in ideological terms defend the heterogeneity of older people can still be observed trying to make them coalesce in practice by urging mixing in residential homes between people who originate from different villages, or promoting regular social interaction between older people of such diverse class backgrounds that they would not voluntarily have mingled at earlier stages of their lives. Older people, for their part, are seldom organised to negotiate optimum responses to such national and local efforts to group them together. The changing nature of contemporary societies may mean that in future they will have little choice than to combine to develop practices allowing them to formulate views and strategies which influence policy in new ways.

POLICY IMPLICATIONS: PENSIONS AND NURSING HOMES

In the Western world today, the main source of social power and status is work and, in contrast to the Ireland of half a century ago, older people in today's Ireland are characteristically without work. This does not apply with such force to the farming community, where people often continue virtually indefinitely to regard themselves as working, and to be so regarded by others in their localities. There are a number of problems in relation to policy for older people which have been created by the fact that, in the non-rural world, the meaning of 'work' has come to attach exclusively to gainful employment outside the home. Argumentational analysis of policy, critical gerontology and ethnographic evidence all coincide in showing that older people in Ireland are vulnerable to being conceptualised as (a) doing nothing which is of interest to society in general and (b) without authority in debate about their roles and predicaments.

Colonisation of the world of work by capitalism has strong implications for ageing, but this does not imply that ageing policy is straightforwardly preferable in more rural settings. As we have suggested, conditions could be harsh for older people in rural societies who neither possessed property nor were able to contribute to farming life. Moreover, some highly industrialised societies, such as Germany, have retained cultural components (notably a regard for symbolically circumscribed sensuous pleasures – eating, drinking, walking, music and so on) and an appreciation of domestic creativity and craftwork which can be used to protect the status of older people and to link them to activities considered mainstream in the society as a whole.[34] Nonetheless it seems to be true in much of the Western world that the segregated notion of work, together with conventional state retirement policies, implicitly argue that older people do not belong in the area of society to which the highest status belongs. According to Phillipson, the concept of retirement and the existence of the old-age pension on the one hand helps create dependency in older age, and on the other it defines older people such that they *ought* not to be participating actively in the economy but should be receiving funds from state and other sources.[35] (In practice, the fact that they have earned these funds via earlier activities and financial contributions receives little attention.) In argumentative terms, this means that in any dispute about the social distribution of work as a resource, the debate is already constructed so that older people are expected to be excluded.

It is true that pension policy in Ireland can be described as having changed radically in the course of the last three or four decades, away from a 'poor law' or 'charitable' approach and towards an acceptance of the influence of social policy as a shaper of society.[36] But taking for granted that policy provisions for ageing are a public necessity, without modulating the argument with a strong input enhancing the status or authority of older people, adds weight to the assumption that older people should be supported by forms of public 'caring'. This situates them politically in a position that establishes their main source of well-being as in the hands of policy planners; certainly not in their own hands. In Europe, public debate about the future status of pensions structures the problem as one of dividing resources between those who are older and those who are not older. This is in itself indicative of attitudes to older people, since the division 'old/not old' is not equivalent to the division 'dependent/not dependent'. In fact, some older people may wish to work, and many people who are not older are absent from the workforce. Moreover, since more women now work than formerly, and since there are fewer children in Western populations than formerly, dependency ratios as such may now have peaked, a point which Fahey and Murray apply to Ireland.[37] In any case, since national productivity is not a straightforward function of numbers of people employed, it is not self-evident that a smaller number of workers necessarily constitutes an overall financial crisis. It *does* create a crisis in the meaning of work as a social category, but that is a separate issue.

State pensions now perform the residualist role of protecting older people against extremes of poverty, but it is *occupational* pensions that make the difference between relative penury and relative comfort in later life. Across the Western world the developing prominence of occupational pensions is accentuating a polarisation in life opportunities between wealthier and poorer older people. It is a division which carries within it others, in particular, class and gender divisions. Although the proportion of occupational pensions among older people in Ireland is increasing we should not assume that this necessarily heralds an era in which more and more people will build up occupational pension rights based on the steady accumulation of funds administered by their employers.[38]

On the one hand, employment security is becoming rarer and employment more sporadic, and on the other governments are seeking to withdraw from pension schemes.[39] Personal familiarity with the world of finance is becoming more crucial just as it is growing more complex and elusive. Individuals are expected to buy into pension plans at different times and with different resources. Occupants of a wide range of positions are now expected to make interventions in their own pension provisions which were formerly limited to occupants of middle-class professions with access to appropriate knowledge bases for defending their positions. Not only people working in the construction industry, for example, but also those in semi-state bodies such as Bord na Móna, the major part of whose time may be devoted to activities wholly unrelated to the world of pension finance, are expected to organise their own old age on the basis of expert knowledge whose status is disputed even by professionals in the business. (Continuing disputes in Britain on the implications of endowment mortgages have reached scandal proportions and are a case in point; both insurance companies and governments have been accused of deliberately concealing the information which would have been required to make suitable decisions.) Individuals are, moreover, expected to make these provisions at periods in their own life-cycles where other needs, such as those of providing for young children or for business expansion, may subjectively appear at once more pressing and more comprehensible. Occupational pensions have always been class-related in obvious ways; the fragmentation of the pension economy, as well as of that the workforce, compounds those class divisions and introduces further hazards and obstacles of unpredictable potency.

Moreover, the number of years required to amass pension rights is being increased in many areas at the same time as it is growing more difficult to acquire continuous work. In the next century, European women will no longer be expected to retire earlier than men, even while the notional benchmark of 65 for men is in practice dissolving. There is a wide dispersal of retirement ages in contemporary societies, and a strong tendency for official figures to disguise redundancy as retirement.[40] Whelan and Whelan point out in their research in Northern Ireland that only a quarter of their respondents actually had retired at precisely this age, and that the lower the social class, the less accurate is the notion that work will be continuous until retirement at 65.[41]

Women, moreover, standardly earn between two-thirds and three-quarters of men's wages and hence their occupational pensions (if any) are lower: the 'feminisation of poverty' extends into old age on a systematic basis. In addition to this, there arises the question of childcare. To receive a full occupational pension, retirees standardly need to have worked a statutory number of years – until recently, forty years in the traditionally women's worlds of teaching and nursing. In Ireland, occupational pensions do not include a statutory number of childcare years at home. This means, in effect, that if a woman wishes to obtain the full occupational pension which will make her older age more comfortable, it is virtually ruled out that she should stay at home during her children's formative years. It is impossible to reconcile this with the Irish Constitution's emphasis on the family and its stipulation that women should not be put under financial pressure to work outside the home.

According to the 1993 Eurobarometer, even though older people and the public regard the pension as the most important source of economic security in later life, in Ireland, the UK, Greece and Portugal more than one in four retired respondents said that they would have preferred to continue working full-time. Owing to the decontextualised methods of large-scale data collection, it is necessary to be circumspect about why this particular selection of countries are grouped together in this response, and about the possibly diverse messages which respondents are conveying about the status and meaning of work. It is far from safe to assume that going out to work is for most people a generally pleasant experience and these figures may in part reflect financial aspirations. Nonetheless, they do appear to indicate some anxiety among many older people that they should continue to play a meaningful role in public life in society. It is therefore pertinent to ask what 'work' actually means to different groups of people.

According to the Eurobarometer, many older people themselves do social work, for example, and there is some evidence that this is a significant source of enjoyment and satisfaction to them. However, this type of activity is not officially *termed* 'work' unless the person concerned possesses approved credentials and his or her contribution is regulated in some publicly ordered fashion. Moreover, there appears, as far as this can be inferred from large-scale sources, to be general approval for the right to work in some sense. The Eurobarometer shows that most people in the European Union favour the freedom to choose their own retirement age. Over two-thirds of Irish respondents disagreed slightly or strongly with the contention that people in their fifties should retire to make way for younger people. In four countries, including Ireland, a half or more respondents thought that older people should be permitted access to paid employment. Yet about three-quarters of European respondents believe that older people are discriminated against with regard to job recruitment, and more than half believe the same in relation to promotion. Though governments may want to keep people at work as long as possible, employers may be less willing to do so, as the popularity of early retirement schemes shows.[42]

A critical ethnography is urgently required to elicit attitudes to 'work' – work not in the official sense but in the sense of what is in practice accepted by different parts of the population as providing meaningful contributions to society. This itself would help to form a new language of work (or a return to the one in which 'work' was linked more directly to the creation of conditions for living than to being paid). The debates connected with working and age illustrate the need for critical ethnography because notions, such as that of the pension, have become so deeply ingrained in public consciousness that it has become difficult to regard them impartially. Both older people themselves and the public at large apparently take for granted the view that protection of older people should concentrate on pensions rather than on any positive contributions to their communities which older people may make. In effect the absence of a social policy enhancing the positive value of individuals at later life stages amounts to a policy in itself – a denial of argumentative authority to older people. If, under future circumstances, it becomes impossible for individuals to avoid dependence on public policy decisions in later life, this will constitute a considerable goad to social conformity. Policy on ageing, that is, could become an ominous source of social control.

NURSING HOME POLICY AND THE SILENT PUBLIC

If there is general silence in Ireland in relation to the timing of retirement and the effects of pension policy, there is not much more public debate on the question of nursing homes.[43] There are three aspects of this issue: first, official reticence on the difficulty of implementing the spirit, rather than merely the letter, of the (Health) Nursing Homes Act (1990), and the shortcomings of this Act in relation to the voicelessness of older people in residential homes in Ireland. Secondly, the silence expected from older people in residential homes, as expressed in their common design and location. Thirdly, public silence on the implications of property provisions for care in older age and for the socio-political meaning of lifetime in contemporary society. These three forms of silence point, in their different ways, to the fact that there is as yet no powerful public language with which to conceptualise later lifetime. Political movements (feminism and environmentalism are examples) have among their most significant functions the development of languages in whose terms new expectations can evolve and be legitimated. They stimulate the imagination, suggesting new courses for action, rather than composing new policies from old concepts. An appropriate public language is crucially instrumental in supplying a framework within which practical and theoretical possibilities can be experienced. Such a language need not always be strictly verbal. The language of architecture is a particularly eloquent expression of attitudes and beliefs about older people,[44] as are the symbolic implications of images of older people which accumulate from the mass media.[45] In the present situation, public language in relation to older people in Ireland tends to be characterised by aspirations, lacunae and condescensions which are, together, stifling.

Residential care is currently expanding in both public and private sectors, as are the associated costs and expenses.[46] To regulate this system the (Health) Nursing Homes Act (1990) was designed to enhance legal provisions affecting older people in residential institutions. There are, however, at least three major failings to this legislation. Its actual implementation is widely estimated to be too expensive to put into practice; secondly, the registration it requires is not equivalent to detailed supervision, nor does it guarantee quality in any detail. Finally, the Act does not stipulate genuine participation in as active a life as possible for residents in nursing homes. This may be compared with provisions in some parts of America, where patients are assigned social workers to protect their rights, or in

Germany, where each nursing home must have a residents' committee which liaises on a regular basis with equivalent committees from other homes. The image of the hospital, in which residents are cared for passively, prevails, especially in the West of Ireland, to the detriment of expectations of an active older age.

The form of life characteristic of many nursing homes in contemporary Ireland is itself eloquent of attitudes to ageing: little appears to be expected from residents or for them. In nursing homes and day centres around the country, inadequacies in stimulation are repeatedly revealed – partly as a result of low expectations on the parts of residents and nurses, and partly as a result of lack of staff. However dedicated and determined members of staff may be, it is not possible for two people actively to engage with forty very varied clients in the course of a few hours. A much more active model of retirement home life, perhaps following the model of Cheshire Homes, would argue that residents should contribute whatever they can to the life of their community, participating in running their own homes. Institutions in other countries are often comparatively proactive in informing older people of their rights and how to exercise them. It is mandatory for mechanisms to be in place whereby older people can complain to neutral parties if they have grievances, and for mechanisms to be installed which lay down some degree of participation in administering the home.

Here, not only the actual mechanisms put in place but also the language of defence provided by public policy is significant, permitting or depriving people of possible positions in effective social argumentation. Even in principle, the existence of the claim that older people should participate in their own institutions in certain specified ways provides a legitimate starting point for practical efforts to implement such ways of life. There is a significant strategic difference between living in a setting where there is at least official support for public participation and the remedying of faults, and living where there is no such formalised argumentative structure to provide a legitimating framework for action.

In relation to developing participative approaches to residential homes, the absence of a publicly accepted network of positive practices and expectations may cause difficulties. From an ethnographic standpoint it may also be difficult to interpret the forms of language that residents themselves use. In a home investigated in southern Germany, for instance, complaints by residents often appeared to concern relatively minor aspects of food preparation.[47] However, it would be cavalier to dismiss such matters as trivial. Views and feelings about extremely significant issues may be expressed in terms of basic household arrangements. In many or most aspects of behaviour affecting health and well-being, people express life orientations in phenomenologically immediate terms. In many surveys, inattention to the ethnographic interpretation of culturally specific language compounds the voicelessness of older people and makes it harder to understand how they experience residential homes and what their preferences are.

Interestingly, the Western Health Board document on policy on ageing, with the archaic title *Services for the Aged*, published in 1985, takes such exception to residential homes that it appears willing to abandon them as nearly completely as possible. It admits that organisations, by their very nature, incorporate a tendency for their own goals to take over from those of the residents. The document points to:

> the tendency of any institution, however small, to smother the personality of the individual through the requirement to conform to rules which are necessary for the institution's functioning.[48]

The individual's needs can become invisible, or become adversely labelled in an alien fashion. The document points to the importance of the 'sense of uniqueness which characterises the person in a more normal setting, even a substandard house in an isolated rural area'.[49] To preserve this 'uniqueness' the document therefore prefers visits by health nurses, or to day care by older people. For patients unable to live at home the 'next best option' may be boarding out or life in hostels or group homes, ordinary houses with a maximum of six older residents and two house parents. In conventional residential homes it may be:

> the common expectation that every need of the resident will be taken care of without effort by the resident or any great choice as to the manner and extent of meeting such need; there is also the tendency for the Home to expect that its requirements of, say, cleanliness and routine, will take precedence over the possibility that a resident's less material needs may be in conflict with same.[50]

If an older person needs more intensive nursing, then, in principle there should be small nursing units as close as possible to his or her home community. Large central locations have the considerable disadvantage of isolating older people from family and friends, according to the document.[51] If it could, it would apparently do away with nursing homes entirely.

In the absence of such a solution, the design and location of old people's homes are also eloquent expressions of expectations held about older people. The fact that they are frequently distant from centres of population, the scene of action for ordinary, active citizens, implies only too clearly that older people are 'out of it'. There are two aspects to the question of location; its relation to the real life activity of everyday participants in society, and its relation to community life as it is *conceptualised* by participants, which, in Ireland especially, has a very strong relationship to locality. Locating old people's homes in the open countryside may contribute to deracination in both senses, removing older people perhaps forty or fifty miles from the places and people they know and in terms of which their own identities and activities have meaning. A certain amount of dispute about the location of homes is apt to arise among administrative bodies. The following comment is taken from a combatant describing one of them:

> Young people think that old people's homes should be put in the country, on the tops of hills with beautiful views – but I think they should be in the centre of the town, next to the pub and the betting shop. I think older people should be encouraged to sin as they've always sinned.[52]

Various forms of housing scheme that combat the isolation of nursing homes have been established by the voluntary group Share in Cork. The language expressed by the architecture favoured by Share is quite different from that of the 'hospital model'. One example of their work, in the centre of Cork city, is a collection of self-contained flats constructed as a single building round a central courtyard in the fashion of medieval monasteries, universities and almshouses. These were places where architectural design was deliberately conducive both to stimulation and reflection, and the Cork example combines a harmonious overall form with ubiquitous visually or aurally intriguing features. Residents are generally in receipt of home helps to assist with housework and other aspects of daily living, and come and go as they wish during the day. It should be noted, though, that among many different forms of supported and 'sheltered' living, initiated by local government, voluntary organisations, business interests or private individuals, not all are administered in ways advantageous to the residents. There is no overall register capable of indicating to the intending resident what type or standard of care is provided. In one *cause célèbre*, residents in a business-run sheltered village have engaged in a long-running rent strike, countered by withdrawal of services and an atmosphere of remarkable acerbity.

The design of many old people's homes in Ireland – including all located in the West – follows the model of a set of bedrooms for the night-time, plus sitting-rooms in which the daytime period is spent communally.[53] The older person's bedroom may or may not be personalised by a few items of private property. He or she is expected to spend the day together with other residents, often watching television and on the whole engaged in little activity or interaction. This is a devastating scenario in which older people may deteriorate in alertness on entering such a home unless extensive counter-measures are taken, and scarce resources normally forbid such measures. This is in marked contrast to a model in which the older person lives in a self-contained bedsit, with washing and cooking facilities en suite. In this alternative, housework and catering are provided by the management and there are common rooms for eating, handwork and other activities provided. Participation in common life takes place on a voluntary basis; inhabiting his or her own mini-apartment, the older person is clearly in charge of his or her own style of life. The hospital model contrasts with the apartment model, and, particularly if homes on the apartment model remain small and village-based, it seems clear which more effectively supports a policy enhancing independence in older age.

The question of property disposition and nursing home residence is made trenchant by the fact that, in Ireland, about three-quarters of the population of older people own their own homes. This is a significant aspect of Irish society which the huge rise in house prices of the 1990s may have erased for ever. Not much more than a century ago, only 3% of Irish farmers owned the land they worked; both long-delayed land acquisition and the extreme attachment to locality of a rural community heightened the cultural significance of secure entitlement to live in a particular place. (The Irish for to live somewhere, 'bheith i do chonaí', has the implication that one cannot be moved on from the place concerned.) In Ireland it is still conventional for young married couples to assume that they will immediately occupy their own house. Here, less than anywhere in Western Europe, is home ownership a specifically bourgeois aspiration.

The political role of property ownership has been of perennial concern in theories of democracy. Since the initial discussions of nascent Western democracy in seventeenth-century England, the ownership of parcels of land has been connected with responsible participation in society. Recently, in Britain and elsewhere, property ownership has been encouraged in a perhaps confused attempt to solve the problem of social order. In Ireland, however, property ownership and social participation still retain some genuine interconnection. Home ownership and ageing, moreover, are specifically connected. The furnishings of the home provide a symbolic distillation of traditions and attitudes specific to the identity of the family concerned; in rural areas the west room belongs to the old couple and is the room where family photographs and other symbols are displayed. In rural societies especially, the home place locates members of the family on a social map which helps to confer on them membership of a community. The family home forms a focal point in which a couple's adult children, possibly scattered all over the globe, may gather. In rural societies, to live in a house near to which one's children have built their houses is a sign of having lived one's life well. Lastly, even though much of the economic support given by parents to children has been relocated to an earlier period in children's lives, financing education lacks the symbolic importance of the inheritance of house property or land. The latter are closely bound up with idea of continuance and permanence in family life; they incorporate ideas about social chronology and appropriate rhythms of lifetime and death.

In these circumstances, it is poignant in individual terms and contradictory in social ones that if an older person needs permanent care which cannot be paid for from his or her pension, the individual may be required to sell property, including house property, to pay for this care, keeping only a relatively small designated sum for the person's own use. This effectively unravels the most tangible evidence of the individual's life course construction. Note that residential care for a non-bedridden patient tends to cost at least three times the total of the basic pension. This means, in effect, that since their houses constitute the biggest form of saving for the majority of the population, patterns of inheritance, family continuity and provision for children are threatened, together with much of the social basis of the contemporary economy. This process, moreover, is taking place within families irrespective of the fact that middle-aged children may have spent years tending their parents as long as they could, only to be deprived of an inheritance at the end of this time. Moreover, the status of the older person is transformed by removal to a home; he or she no longer possesses 'a home to go to' but becomes the local equivalent of a stateless person. In sum, therefore, the fragmentation of contemporary economies is affecting not only individuals' work lives but even the processes relating to their ageing and death.

If these macabre results of social policy are to be avoided then other forms of financial support for care in older age need to be established, most appropriately on the lines of compulsory, but genuinely calculated, social insurance by which individuals can prepare for older age.[54] It is a bizarre effect of current and genuine social progress that more frequent survival to a later age should mean that older people may be forced to dispose prematurely of all they had hoped to pass on to another generation, endangering the entire idea of family lifetime itself.

COMMUNITY CARE AND THE DEBATE ON RESIDUALISM

According to *The Years Ahead* and to all subsequent policy pronouncements, social policy for older people in Ireland centres around the provision of 'community care', with the aspiration that some 90% of older people should be living in their own homes at all times.[55] Government policy is modulated by the different theoretical and practical interpretations given to it by the eight regional health boards, but some generalisations apply throughout the country – and indeed throughout Europe. Most older people look after themselves and their spouses or other relatives, according to the 1993 Eurobarometer. Care derives also from friends (6%) and neighbours, as well as from private paid help (11%). It is not clear how these proportions will change as higher proportions of people in Europe live singly. According to present trends, approximately a quarter of the population will shortly be living alone at any given time. On the European average, the Eurobarometer concludes, 13% of care is given by social services, and 3% by voluntary organisations. About one in ten of the general public give long-term care to someone in the family home as result of illness, disability or old age, and one in seven provide out-of-house care.

By far the largest part of all the caring that is done in Europe, therefore, is *not* done by government services. It is also important to stress that older people help younger ones, contributing directly or indirectly to the productive system, for example when grandmothers supply childcare for their working daughters. Moreover, in Ireland over 10% of older people are themselves engaged in voluntary work (the figure tops 25% in Denmark, Luxembourg and Holland). Most older people, therefore, are not in continuous receipt of public care and will not become so, but continue to play active parts in society.

In Ireland, three-quarters of those people who do require care are looked after by other members of the household. Three-quarters of these carers are female, and carers spend about forty-seven hours a week caring. The 1993 Eurobarometer reports that in Poland, as in Greece, Portugal and Spain, only 3–5% of care comes from private paid help. Only a small percentage of older people live in institutions – some 5% in Ireland, where the public services provide 9% of total care given (as against some 25% in the UK). Only a minority of those over 75 years of age suffer from any chronic illness or disability, and many even of these do not feel that the condition inhibits them from active participation in daily life. As far as the Eurobarometer's large-scale data can indicate, older people in Ireland are relatively sociable, three out of ten reporting that they use social amenities for mixed ages, and nine out of ten reading newspapers. In our fixation on the idea of older people as recipients of attention and resources, we forget that most of them are actively living their lives, just as other people are.

The majority of those who do need support are assisted under a variety of 'community care' programmes, on which much of the contemporary debate on 'residualism' is focused. Community care, which is intended to replace localised care in large institutions, has until recently been an enthusiastically accepted approach to most forms of contemporary care. Modes of aiding those seen as vulnerable in society tend to ebb and flow according to fashions related to the political, cultural and economic worlds of which they form part.[57] The contemporary presumption is in favour of active life in the community for older people. Nonetheless, scepticism has developed as to whether public agencies supply enough funding to make community care effective in any positive sense; whether it merely marks the *absence* of other arrangements as part of a cost-cutting exercise; whether enough residential care is made available to those who do need it, and whether it is not the case that excessive effort and responsibility is left to the (female) relations of vulnerable individuals. In effect, community care devolves very heavily on family involvement – particularly that of women. Community care therefore heavily affects the life courses of carers, particularly of female carers, who may cease needing to look after children in middle age only to find themselves obliged to care for their parents.

Residualism relates to a model of social welfare as providing a 'safety net' for emergencies but otherwise assuming that members of society will take care of themselves. Residual welfare models assume that needs are provided for in the normal course of events by private markets and the family, so that social policy is required to intervene temporarily only in emergencies. This may be contrasted with a model which sees social policy as an integrated part of society, taking a major part in distributing and allocating the means to a good life within it. It is true that the overtly charitable, discretionary nature of Irish support to older people has in theory declined, but the style, the contents and the distribution pattern of care for older people in Ireland give the impression that residualism has by no means disappeared.[58] Lundström and McKeown comment on the irregular and somewhat unpredictable distribution of home help for older people, and, as in Britain, most day care arrangements for older people are such that an individual would have to be in dire straits to take comfort from what is provided.[59]

Dr Michael Woods, TD, remarked, launching the Report on Home Help Services commissioned by the National Council for the Elderly, that 'It is the mark of a truly caring society that it ensures that its dependent elderly persons are well cared for'.[60] The tone of such a comment argues that anyone whose physical condition makes it difficult to do housework, say, may be categorised as a dependent elderly person. It implies too that the rationale for attending to the needs of older people is a charitable one. Charity is a matter of virtue rather than necessity; virtue can under some circumstances be found excessively expensive and some of the arrangements which have been made to accommodate older people to the pace of social change in Ireland might be considered costly. Many older farmers, especially in the West of Ireland, are enabled by state benefits to remain on their farms and older people enjoy the possibility of free travel.[61] Moreover, the tax system diverts much redistribution to non-income-earning households, particularly those which include older people, and subsidised health care also assists older people.[62] Breen and his colleagues go so far as to refer to a concentration of financial support and services on the elderly, a group traditionally seen as the 'deserving poor'.[63] The arrangements in question clearly indicate genuinely liberating measures; it is crucial not to allow them to be undermined by attitudes that construct older people as a group to be 'helped' – or not – as the rest of society sees fit, rather than as enjoying a free and dignified life as of right, because that is what living in Irish society is about.

The originators of community care first *intended* more than a conglomeration of benefits mitigating social change and enhancing family support. A composite picture of community care at its aspirational best can be compiled from two documents – the Western Health Board's *Services for the Aged*, published in 1985, and the *Review of Services for the Elderly and Four-Year Action Plan 1995–1998* published by the Eastern Health Board. The former evinces considerable insight into the phenomenon of care as it may actually be experienced, and the latter evinces a plethora of progressive detail coupled with refreshing honesty about areas in which aims have not, generally for reasons of funding, been accomplished. Both these boards have relatively high proportions of older people, though for opposite reasons: the Eastern area because it is urban and people have flocked to it, and the Western one because it is rural and younger people have left it. In the Eastern area, the proportion of people over 65 has increased faster than predicted, and the Western Health Board also has a high proportion of older people as compared to the national average (14.2%, as compared with 10.7%).

The main aim of *Services for the Aged* is preservation of independence, but it adds a phenomenological touch:

> Independence is directly affected by poverty and/or ill health and less obviously by a person's sense of security in themselves and their environment. This sense of security is influenced in turn not only by a person's adequacy of income and state of health, but by such matters as standard of housing, proximity of and support from neighbours, friends and relations, and by some degree of activity or at least involvement in the routine of the household. A fundamental objective of services for the aged must be to support and promote the positive features which reinforce a person's sense of independence and to seek to prevent or diminish the negative features. It is also crucial in planning or provision of services to remember that the nature and degree of response to the individual's needs must vary over time with his [sic] changing circumstances or capacity.[64]

Services for the Aged asserts that bad housing and loneliness are major problems in the West of Ireland, especially in areas suffering from rural depopulation. It rightly warns that while old people's parties and meals on wheels are laudable arrangements, they 'do little to produce that integration of old people into the normal patterns of community life which is their due'.[65] The document suggests, to go part of the way to meet this need, the construction of cluster housing with communal meeting places, canteen and laundry facilities, based on surveys of the wishes of older people. Some progress has been made in this region in, for instance, the provision of shared houses for older people to live in rather than homes. Other aims are still aspirational. The document asserts that older people should have the right to privacy and to decide their own affairs, with full information about options and their implications. They should have the final voice in decisions insofar as medical and hospital arrangements can make this possible. It avers that all medical and other services should take place in as home-like settings as possible, in size and location.[66]

The Eastern Health Board's aim is 'to maintain older people in dignity and independence at home in accordance with the wishes of older people as expressed in many research studies', as well as 'to restore to independence at home to those older people who become ill or dependent' and 'to encourage and support the care of older people in their own community by family, neighbours and voluntary bodies in every way possible'.[67] The Board hopes 'to provide high quality hospital or residential care for older people when they can no longer be maintained in dignity and independence at home' and 'to co-ordinate the existing services into a cohesive support package unrestricted by programme or service agency boundaries'. Here the 'sole objective' is to provide 'the best and most comprehensive range of care for the elderly'.[68] This, apart from its use of 'the elderly' rather than the preferred term 'older people', is characteristic of health board policy in Ireland, both in the conscientious but conventional quality of its aspirations and in its ambiguity between a residual and a citizenship approach to care. The reiterated terms dignity and independence show indications of the latter, but older people do not have a direct voice in this report and the terms dignity and independence are not furnished with any behavioural content. In the absence of such content the implication remains that older people can do whatever they like so long as no disaster occurs to bring them to the attention of the health board – and this, of course, is a residualist view. To rescue it from this implication, the policy would need to have been compiled with more input from older people and devised in a manner which accorded their arguments authority; it would need to contain enabling provisions, for example in support of further adult education or the use of older people's experience at work. This, apparently, is not yet part of the effective contemporary meaning of 'well-being' for older people in Ireland.[69]

The Eastern Health Board is also characteristic of the aspirations of health boards in Ireland in its emphasis on the use of interdisciplinary professional teamwork in community areas and in its wish to strengthen the role of the GP. GPs, therefore, are urged by the Eastern Health Board to take 'a holistic approach to the care of patients – including the elderly – taking full account of the psychological, social and environmental factors which influence the patient's health status'.[70] This praiseworthy aspiration is one whose fulfilment is impossible to imagine in the present state of medical education, which does almost nothing to prepare hard-pressed doctors for such gargantuan feats of human understanding. Nonetheless it is characteristic of European approaches to older people that health boards should plan to use interdisciplinary teams to provide outreach medical, nursing and paramedical services 'on a multi-disciplinary basis in the patient's own home'.[71] Note that no representative of older people is included on such teams, so that this is still care *for* older people rather than *by* or *with* them. Also, although the aim is to provide a community ward team for every 4,000 elderly, and to develop nine community units with some fifty beds each, there are not at present enough consultant psychiatrists and geriatricians for a full complement for each team.

Other community services in which public organisations are supported heavily by voluntary ones include the provision of home helps and meals on wheels. (In the Eastern Health Board area, the Board oversees home help for up to 4,200 people, and nearly a million meals on wheels per year to individuals' homes and to day centres, three-quarters of which are provided by grant-aided voluntary associations.) Both funding and means of assessing need vary markedly throughout the country, as indeed does the nature of co-operation between health boards and voluntary associations.[72] Often, the latter are partially funded by the Department of Health and also rely on their own fundraising. In some parts of the country, they are run by diocesan associations and other voluntary associations play a considerable (if often unsystematic) part in supporting older people.

Ill health constitutes one of the largest problems for older people, or at least one of the largest problems which contemporary forms of language allow them to discuss in interview situations.[73] Here it is essential that public policy should encourage preventive work and health promotion. A large, perhaps a predominant, proportion of conditions causing discomfort in older age are caused at much earlier life stages. This is an issue to which virtually no practical attention is paid in public health arrangements in Ireland today. Community care services provide services such as those in physiotherapy, chiropody, dentistry and ophthalmic/aural matters, but it is unclear to what extent these endorse health promotion measures. The Eastern Health Board approaches health promotion by focusing on smoking, alcohol, nutrition and diet, cholesterol and blood pressure, exercise and causes of accidents.[74] These tactics imply a diagnosis which is individual, not societal, and omits to consider that many causes of contemporary ill-health are socially constructed or environmental. For instance, concerns relating to physical fitness may arise not only from the obvious discomforts attaching to ill-health, but also at least in part because of the social exclusion of disabled people. Social and subjective meanings of ill-health may exercise independent effects on individuals' capacities to act as citizens in contemporary societies. Precisely those new social forms which confer freedom on healthy individuals, such as elective, geographically scattered acquaintances and interests, demand high degrees of physical mobility and fitness, and inhibit those who are not well.

In terms of the psychiatry of older age, there is a general insufficiency throughout the country.[75] Older age throws up psychiatric problems as does any other; in addition to the commonest problems of schizophrenia, depression, alcohol related problems and dementia, ordinary life and partnership related problems occur in older age as at any other period of life. This fact is widely ignored by the general public and often found surprising by older people themselves. Of those over 65, 5% suffer from dementia, increasing to 20% of those over 80; there are about 25,000 sufferers in Ireland.[76] Most of the care provided for these people is situated at primary care level which is to say that most sufferers remain at home and are cared for by relatives.[77] Lastly comes the question of dying and the care surrounding it: hospice places are in inadequate supply throughout the country, which has still to respond to the current prevalence of death in hospitals which are badly equipped to deal with it.

If the aspirations of the health boards are proving difficult to translate into reality, it is not only for financial reasons. The questions of 'caring' at home, who should feel obliged to do it and whether the public purse should pay for it, are related to the evaluation of interpersonal efforts in other (characteristically female) predicaments. The emphasis on 'caring' itself, while an understandable attempt to upgrade the status of efforts involved in giving practical and emotional support to another human being, may in the end endorse the puritanical notion that only work is worthwhile so that if any activity is worthwhile, it must count as work. By the same token, those cared for may be in danger of being reduced to objects of work upon whom technicist skills are exercised, rather than fellow subjects of human processes. Policy formulation processes do not lend themselves to the private and interpersonal language of human relations; policy debate on such questions imprints its own reifying mark. This leaves a silence at the centre where a developmental notion of the human person should provide legitimating criteria for decisions.

As Eamon O'Shea points out, older people in Ireland may be experiencing subtle social pressures to submit to a passive dependent, undemanding mode of thought and action.[78] Public policy may be exacerbating this, not only because financial pressures dictate the need to provide for the poorest first, which too easily implies a residualist attitude to the rest, but also because of the style of the provisions which are made. There is a startling contrast between provisions in Ireland (and in England) and those in countries such as Germany, where state facilities for older people are often inadequate in range of cover but do self-consciously attempt to communicate a positive message on ageing and the continuing development of the individual[79] (as reflected in theories of ageing by authors such as Erikson *et al.* 1986; Laslett, 1992 and Young and Schmuller, 1991). Lastly, it is in principle a crucial aspect of public policy that the public should know what the policy is. However, proactive information campaigns form an extremely minor aspect of health board preoccupations. If we were more conscious of the fact that health in old age is inseparable from health at other life stages, it might be easier to incorporate such campaigns, into public participation in community life in Ireland.

CONCLUSION: THE NEED FOR A NEW DEBATE ON AGEING

The *issues* dealt with in this chapter relate to processes affecting life courses in Irish society, but the *policies* concerned generally ignore life course issues and focus on 'older people' as a static group – a deserving group, no doubt, but not one relevant to the major concerns of the society. There are positive aspects of ageing in contemporary Ireland but nonetheless, the pigeonholing effect of contemporary policy-making is itself a major problem affecting older people. Moreover, policy on ageing here, as in Britain, is often in effect residual and passive – receiving care means having things *done* to you. This is despite the fact that the health boards have aspirations other than this and that individuals' expectations of older people they know appear generally well-meaning. Social policy on ageing, therefore, does not have the results which it is vaguely hoped that it will have. One precondition for mitigating this vagueness is the development of an aptly incisive language in which intentions can be expressed. Such a language must be developed through the day-to-day practice involved in campaigns, debates and decisions, where choices must be made and the allocation of resources of time and money must be argued about. The development of such a language is all the more pressing since it can be anticipated that much more public concern will develop in the future concerning euthanasia on the one hand and the ill-treatment of older people on the other. It is in a sense not unusual that weaker members of society should be vulnerable to injury or neglect, particularly if they possess property which other people would prefer to own. The form of argument, 'What does he/she need with all that?' is one which may appear appealing under some circumstances. Within a consumerist ethic, older people may be assumed to be less competent consumers than are people at earlier stages of their lives, or, if they do spend money, to be considered voracious or spendthrift. Acquaintances or relations may do their best to put an end to what they see as an inadmissible state of affairs.[80] This is an area where considerable further research is needed, for the extent of abuse of older people may be much greater than is currently realised.

In devising social policy in any of these areas it ought to be clear that notice should be taken of what older people actually want. This cannot be discovered – even by older people themselves – unless a form of public debate evolves in which new aspirations are formulated. At present, policy planners in Ireland find themselves in a position in which it is extremely difficult to assess what exactly is appropriate for answering the needs of older people or even for conceptualising these needs.[81] Of those older people surveyed across Europe for the 1993 Eurobarometer, over half said they were very or fairly satisfied with their lives, but one in five were not satisfied. We do not know what reasons this fifth had or how to interpret the verdicts of the rest, but overall the most important problems mentioned by older respondents in the Eurobarometer survey concerned money and loneliness. The latter term recurs in discourse relating to older people, but nonetheless it should be treated with caution as an acceptable blanket term which covers a heterogeneous collection of problems for which there may or may not exist an appropriate terminology. Whelan and Whelan, among others, emphasise that the type and degree of comfort derived from social contacts is a matter of the quality, not the quantity, of the relationships involved;[82] enhancing this quality may be no easy matter.[83]

Even though the processes of public policy constitute older people as a group, in the end they constitute them as a negative group – as a static collection of individuals who have stepped back from any creative form of development which might be interesting or exemplary for other members of society. Unless public policy is made the subject of dynamic social, moral and political argument, older people may find themselves drawn into a whirlpool of marginalisation – which will have negative consequences for everyone who grows older. That ageing should be socially constructed is inevitable, and this means that it is necessary to pay urgent attention to the forms this takes: constructing ageing means constructing living. 'Ageing' implicitly makes sense (or fails to make sense) of human life stages, prescribing what is tolerable in a certain society at a certain stage and what should be aimed at. Here, an excessive emphasis upon consumerism poses a special danger by obliterating differences between stages in favour of a blanket image of affluent youth, enthusiastic in purchasing terms. As many as possible are assimilated into this group, but all those who cannot see themselves as young(ish) and affluent are left with nothing to grow towards. Stages in ageing, therefore, are partially constituent of social structures. Public policy on ageing needs urgently to express an argument in which we show that we understand what ageing is, and what part it can play in constructing an inhabitable social structure. Policy, therefore, needs to be understood as actively argumentational, not lifelessly factual, and to be described as such in social and political texts. Furthermore, it should promote debate actively. One method of doing this is by using architectural language such as that described above.[84] Following cases of best practice from other settings, contentions can be communicated to the rest of society about the active capacities associated with ageing. But debate cannot be brought about simply by fiat, even if it can be encouraged in the mass media. Debate arises where there are courses of action to be decided, reasons to be defended, resources to be allocated. Local government in Ireland is in the course of being restructured with the aim of enhancing local participation. The more local communities have an active part in decisions affecting life courses, and the more older people's organisations enter these discussions, the more debate on ageing will become pressing and real.

CHAPTER 6

Community Empowerment *via* Partnership? The 'Local Community' in Rural Ireland's Area Based Development Regime

TONY VARLEY AND CHRIS CURTIN

INTRODUCTION

A striking feature of the 1990s was the readiness with which 'local communities' were invoked in official circles as holding part of the solution to many of Ireland's economic and social problems. Communities, we were told, possess a capacity to engage in enterprise and create employment, deliver a range of social services and contribute to the revitalising of local government and regional planning. Addressing the topic of integrated rural development, the National Development Plan 1989–93 declared that 'the priorities will be set by the communities themselves, who will be responsible for ensuring that local potential will be realised'.[1] Similarly the area based strategy to combat long-term unemployment, as outlined in the Programme for Economic and Social Progress, announced that it would have 'local communities as the primary movers'.[2] The participation of local communities featured equally centrally in the thinking behind the Department of Agriculture and Food's Pilot Programme for Integrated Rural Development (1988–90), the third European anti-poverty programme (Poverty 3) and in the generation of new European Economic Community/Union (EC/EU) area based rural development programmes – such as LEADER I and II and INTERREG – inspired by the restructuring of the Common Agricultural Policy, the bringing of the internal market project to completion and the combating of long-term tendencies towards rural decline. Most recently, Ireland's National Development Plan 1994–99 has spoken about 'empowering communities to sponsor innovative projects'.[3]

If this official rhetoric of the community as a central actor is to be taken seriously, we might expect to find 'local communities' as a leading force behind the appearance and operation of area based partnerships. We might additionally expect to see local communities being 'empowered' both by the experience of 'participation' and by the concrete benefits it confers. Before going further, however, we must ask: can 'communities' be considered to be agencies of collective action or collective actors in any strict sense? What, in other words, is implied by the statement that 'communities' are capable of action in their own right? What we have in mind in talking about community action is, in the first instance, the actions of those *groups* which explicitly claim to represent the locality or 'local community' and act on its behalf. By no means, of course, do 'community groups' of such an ilk exhaust the range of community action. What can be termed 'community based groups' must also be considered. The typical claim of 'community based groups', in contrast to 'community groups', is not to represent the interests or act in the name of localities or 'local communities'. Community based groups can be said to take some of their identity from being rooted in a particular locality, but their identity can mostly be thought of as constituted on some other basis. Class, gender, ethnicity and religion are just some of the many social markers around which community based groups may form and establish an identity.

Reflecting the multitude of organised interests in any locality, the list of Irish community based groups is likely to be both long and varied. It would certainly include local women's groups, local unemployed groups, local sporting clubs, even the local branches of political parties, to name but a few. All these cases can plausibly claim to have a 'local' in addition to some other 'community' dimension to their activities and identities. One suggestion about Irish community action in the 1980s was that community based groups had begun to outstrip, in number and vitality, community groups of the type so well exemplified by the community councils of Muintir na Tíre.[4]

We will call those who favour the idea of 'communities' (understood as including community and community based groups) playing a central role in local development communitarian populists (or simply communitarians). The first of three distinguishable communitarian claims is that local development can be organised around communities and therefore around popular participation. A second claim is that local development can be effective in meeting the aims set for it by community actors. On the basis of local development being at once participative and effective, communitarians are encouraged to expect that local development can contribute to the empowerment of community actors, in the sense that they can add to their capacity to control their own affairs.

Some contemporary observers suggest that conditions are becoming generally more favourable for community and voluntary actors to assert themselves as forces capable of shaping the course of social, political and economic transformation in modern society.[5] Opportunities are seen to be opening up in line with far-reaching social and economic change in the industrially advanced countries, rising official interest in flexible forms of state intervention (the area partnerships present a prime example) and in alternatives to direct public provision of a variety of welfare state-type services.[6]

Communitarians might be assumed to think that community and community based local groups are animated by a dynamic of their own. Indeed, in so far as the state can be numbered among the major centralising and large-scale forces in modern society, community action, especially those strains of it that are influenced by an anti-establishment analysis, might more likely be assumed to be directed at the state rather than originating within it or dependent upon it. The possibility that community actors may owe their survival, if not their very existence, to some external agency cannot at the same time be dismissed. Midgley reminds us that while there are those who favour 'community participation' and who present themselves as 'staunch advocates of local self-reliance, independence and autonomy and as stern critics of paternalism in all its guises', there are others who take quite a different view.[7] The belief of these others is that participative forms of local development typically owe their appearance to the initiatives of states or other external agencies, and that little or nothing can be sustained locally without on-going external assistance.[8]

There would appear to be a definite sense in which the rhetoric of the community as a dynamic force in its own right, as found in many of the official statements surrounding the Irish area based partnerships, veers towards an acceptance of that version of the communitarian populist vision of local development that accords an important role to the state. The intention, if the official rhetoric is to be believed at least, is to have 'local communities' become leading lights in the area partnerships, bringing them into existence, setting and implementing their agendas as well as being 'empowered' by the experience and by the material benefits that 'participation' makes possible.

How might a communitarian analysis imagine community actors to be empowered through participation in the area partnerships? Here we can suggest that not only should those community actors represented at board level stand formally 'equal' with other partners, but that their representatives should perceive the interests they speak for to be equal in practice. Any such perception implies *active* participation.[9] All community actors – whether represented at board level or not – if they are to find the area partnerships empowering should be able to use their participation as an effective means of advancing at least some of their major projects, and so hope to improve their own position while extending the community (however understood) dimension of local development in the process.

What we will call the elitist interpretation of community action seeks to pour cold water on the optimism that pervades communitarian expectations. The central contention of the elitist position, in relation to the area partnership phenomenon, would be that state or supranational elites (preeminently those associated with the EU), by virtue of the strategic position they occupy and the vastly superior resources at their disposal, will have no trouble at all in dominating all stages of the local area partnerships. With all the parameters set in advance, community actors are likely to end up being little better than puppets in the hands of state or supranational official elites. Another contention of the elitist position would be that popular participation in community action will be difficult to achieve and maintain, even at the best of times. This is so on account of the likelihood that community activists, reflecting local power structures and the pervasiveness of the so-called 'free riding' phenomenon,[10] will typically be few in number and be drawn from the ranks of the notables of local society.[11] A related pessimistic note sounded by our elitist analyst is that community or community based groups, even with locally powerful elements at the helm, will find it an uphill struggle to be effective in what they attempt to do and in sustaining their efforts in the medium to long term. Their weakness here reflects their dependence on voluntary effort, as well as the often hostile wider environment they are likely to face. The various difficulties attaching to external domination, local participation and effectiveness allow an elitist analysis to conclude that the prospects for popular empowerment can only be poor.

The communitarian and elitist positions outlined here present two very different interpretations of how community actors might fare in the context of the local area partnerships. Against the optimistic communitarian populist assumption, which would prefer to see community or community based groups at the centre of the action, the elitist position views local community actors as easily manipulated by powerful outside interests, who can be relied on to ruthlessly pursue their own agendas. On top of this, community actors are assumed to be under the control of local notables as well as generally weak.

ORIGINS OF THE PARTNERSHIPS

Are the Irish area partnerships to be seen as impositions from above or as the product of pressure exerted from below by organised community interests? Any answer to this question needs to distinguish between the origins of individual partnership programmes and the circumstances in which programmes come to be sited in specific places. What the evidence suggests is that the impetus for these programmes has come overwhelmingly from above, frequently in the form of joint initiatives with their member states.[12] Behind the Irish area partnerships can be found an official analysis – to be located more at the EU level than that of the Irish state – that agricultural overdevelopment and rural decline had reached crisis dimensions, and that the difficulties had become simply too immense for states, the EU or market forces to tackle on their own. Possibly the most comprehensive attempt to view rural problems in crisis terms is found in the analysis that preceded the appearance of LEADER I. By the late 1980s there was considerable apprehension within some EU circles at the scale of rural population decline (most acutely felt in remote, disadvantaged areas) and at the polluting, ecologically unsustainable character of heavily capitalised, intensive agriculture.[13] Similarly in Ireland, a dramatic shedding of agricultural labour, low agricultural incomes among the bulk of farmers and declining off-farm job opportunities had come to be officially recognised as problems that had attained, or were rapidly approaching, crisis proportions.[14] The limited effectiveness of existing policies to counter these tendencies, and the urgency of bringing forward new policy initiatives to deal with what was likely to be a worsening situation, made for Irish receptiveness to an EU LEADER I-type initiative.[15]

The primacy of an economic analysis of the rural problem shines through in the emphasis laid in LEADER I on agricultural diversification and on the need to stimulate small and medium-sized rural enterprise. This emphasis and the neglect of 'community development' are to be understood within the context of the wider effort to restructure the CAP and the desire to prepare European agriculture for the challenges of increased liberalisation of world trade under GATT. Taken together, these developments were viewed as threatening to undermine the income support regime that had sustained European agriculture over most of the post-war period and to aggravate existing difficulties both in the agricultural sector and in agriculture-dependent rural areas more generally.

If the EC Commission is to be given the prime credit for LEADER I's appearance, what principles were adopted in selecting those places that were to become LEADER I sites in Ireland? Perhaps the first thing to be noted is that there was no question of covering the entire country with

LEADER area partnerships. A fundamental dimension of the 'flexibility' of the approach was that it could pick and choose between areas to be included and excluded. Essentially the procedure adopted was that, in response to invitations and guidelines issued by the Department of Agriculture, Food and Forestry (DAFF – the designated 'intermediary body' between the Commission and the local sites), prospective local partnership groups were invited to compete with each other for inclusion in the programme. Some of these would-be area partnerships – Ballyhoura in East Limerick is a good example – were put together at the instigation of local community actors. Once DAFF had shortlisted and ranked a mix of applicants, the final decision regarding site selection lay with the EC Commission.

The Programme for Economic and Social Progress (PESP) area partnerships owe their existence, at one level, to Ireland's tradition of macro-political bargaining agreements that had inspired the appearance of PESP in 1990. More specifically, these PESP pilot partnerships were conceived as part of an official response to the crisis provoked by the alarming growth in long-term unemployment in the 1980s and the consequent emergence of intractable unemployment black-spots in rural and urban Ireland.[16] Reasoning that a comprehensive solution for long-term unemployment could never be found in the operation of market forces and standard labour market interventions alone, special measures (such as those to be pioneered by the area partnerships) came to be seen as having a potentially important part to play.[17] Significantly, the macro-political bargaining framework that gave rise to the PESP area partnerships did not acknowledge the 'community sector' among its recognised social partners. Nor, as things were to turn out, did 'local communities' have any say in choosing the sites for PESP area activity; these decisions were made centrally without consultation with local community interests.[18]

Of the three area partnership programmes under consideration, Poverty 3 was the one that most explicitly saw itself as contributing towards the heading-off of a legitimation crisis threatened by mass unemployment and rising levels of 'social exclusion'.[19] Poverty 3's appearance in the late 1980s can also be linked to the 'period of cautious optimism' which followed the completion of the internal market and the launch of the Social Charter of Fundamental Rights of Workers.[20] Whatever cautious optimism there may have been, however, was tempered by fears that the completion of the internal market would accentuate poverty levels in poor areas and 'peripheral' regions.

The underlying solution to problems of poverty and social exclusion may have been officially seen to reside in market-led economic growth, but again an important role came to be assigned to the creation of institutional arrangements capable of harnessing the energies of the public, private and voluntary sectors in dynamic area partnerships. The notion of an inclusive conception of partnership was also to fit well with the view taken by the creators of Poverty 3 that the different facets of 'social exclusion' could only be tackled by means of a wide and integrated set of policy measures.

As much as community actors may have had a prominent role to play in the implementation of the first and second European anti-poverty programmes in Ireland, they had no great say in the decision to create these programmes in the first place. In this, Poverty 3 was to prove to be no different. Applications for inclusion in Poverty 3 were invited by the Combat Poverty Agency (CPA). It was the CPA that then made recommendations and, once again, the final selection was left in the hands of EC Commission officials. In the case of the one successful rural Irish applicant, however, it was a local community group – Connemara West (based in Letterfrack) – that took the initiative in preparing the application, selecting the 'target groups' and recruiting the state partners.

We can say that the emergence of our three partnership programmes is to be seen as much more the outcome of a process of top-down decision-making than as a direct response to demands made locally or the mobilisation of local pressure. The official desire on the part of the EU authorities and the Irish state to be seen to be getting to grips with different, though inter-related, facets of what was taken to be a multi-stranded rural crisis was what was decisive in giving rise to the PESP and Poverty 3 area partnerships in particular. The area partnerships which have proliferated in recent years have, on the strength of an official analysis that has thought very much in crisis management terms, taken the form of new institutional arrangements designed to deal with major economic and social problems at *local* level.

IMPLEMENTING THE PARTNERSHIPS

If community actors have had little or no say in the appearance of the area schemes and but some small say in the issue of site selection, how central have they been to the area partnerships during their implementation phases? How well does the evidence of our three cases support the official rhetoric that the success of area initiatives will depend critically on the co-operation and active involvement of 'local communities'? Overall responsibility for administering the national LEADER I programme in Ireland rested with DAFF; it, in turn, was answerable to the EU's Directorate-General for Agriculture (DG VI). DAFF's supervisory role was exercised through formal contractual agreements with the sixteen selected local partnership groups,[21] the issuing of operating rules to cover matters such as funding criteria and grant aid eligibility, and the deployment of a team of inspectors whose task was to monitor and ensure conformity with the rules. Notwithstanding DAFF's attempt at imposing a uniform structure of control, significant differences were to characterise the LEADER I programme in Ireland. These are to be seen expressed in the size of catchment areas,[22] the budgets allocated and the composition of the boards of partnership groups.

The LEADER I partnerships may have been obliged to have a legally constituted board of directors, but many differences marked the composition of these directorates. Two of them stood out for their high proportion (76% and 90% respectively) of 'community' representatives.[23] On the other hand, community representation did not feature at all in three cases. The membership of one board was made up of local authority and state agency representatives to the total exclusion of private and community sector representation. Yet another directorate was remarkable for the absence of any representative of a state agency.[24] It seems that private enterprise failed to secure any board representation in four instances.

A great deal apparently depended in LEADER I on who was to emerge as the 'leading partner' at board level, a position occupied by 'voluntary community organisations' in six of the partnership areas.[25] When community organisations occupied the leading role, much emphasis fell on 'training and improving the capacity of the community to promote an integrated strategy for the benefit of all inhabitants of the area'.[26] By the same token, when the representatives of commercial interests became the leading partner, 'the main objectives related to encouraging new enterprises and helping existing businesses'.[27] Some evidence suggests that those representing community interests tended to be eclipsed by some of their colleagues in LEADER I; in particular, the statutory partners seem to have often held the upper hand.[28] Statutory partners, given the resources they could command and reflecting their preference for 'a "top-down" approach to planning', tended to resist developing a 'partnership process' and the power sharing this entailed, though much could depend on how well disposed individual officials proved to be.[29] 'In a number of cases', the LEADER I evaluators point out, 'the inflexibility of agency representatives was a cause of deep frustration for other partners'.[30]

There was also a sense in which the implementation of policy in LEADER I depended on building alliance among the area partnerships themselves. Established by representatives of the different LEADER I partnerships in May 1992 as a forum to discuss common problems and to co-ordinate negotiations with DAFF, the LEADER I representative body (known as the Irish LEADER Network or Comhar LEADER na hÉireann) set out to represent the interests of the individual partnerships before DAFF and the EU Commission, and to provide a conduit for the transfer of information and resources between groups. It was also intended to 'influence rural development policy at national and EU levels'.[31] The Network's success in negotiating cheap insurance cover provided individual partnerships with an incentive to join up and lend their support.[32]

One reason why DAFF welcomed the creation of an effective and strong representative body among the partnership groups sprang from its desire to offset the weakness and lack of experience of some of the non-state partners. DAFF's hope was that individual partnerships could learn much from each other and so allow each one to make greater headway than would otherwise be possible. At the same time, mindful of the need to safeguard its own authority, DAFF's view came to be that a balance had to be struck between using the Network as a buffer between itself and the partnership groups and dealing with the individual partnerships on a one-to-one basis. Apparently this was a reason why it chose not to make greater use of the Network in its relations with individual partnerships.

One rather important change to LEADER I's operating rules was to occur. Recipients of LEADER grant assistance were initially obliged to match official funding pound-for-pound;[33] the difficulties this caused community actors in garnering matching funding left them at a disadvantage. The authorities, following representations from the LEADER partnerships, eventually decided to allow contributions of voluntary labour to be used in lieu of matching funds.

When set against the LEADER I partnerships, the composition of the local PESP partnership boards displayed a greater measure of uniformity. Each of the PESP partnerships was required to form a company limited by guarantee. And each of the twelve local PESP partnership boards (four of which were rural) was typically composed of six social partner representatives (employers, trade unionists), six 'community' representatives and six state agency/department representatives.

With overall responsibility for direction and supervision of the individual PESP partnerships, a central review committee convened an operational team made up of representatives of employers, trade unionists, FÁS and the Department of Education. The appearance of the EU's global grant in 1992 made necessary a formal distancing of the PESP pilot area initiative from the Irish state. This was effected institutionally by the creation of the Area Development Management (ADM) company, five of whose fourteen board members purported to represent community interests in 1994.[34] Within both PESP and ADM, attention was paid to how the policy lessons flowing from the PESP partnerships were to be evaluated and disseminated. No formal attempt at alliance building comparable to LEADER I's Network developed among the PESP partnerships.[35]

In the official documentation, the PESP area initiative was defined as a 'community' response. What precisely this meant was unclear, though the capacity of local communities to act as real entities seems to have been assumed. Serious problems, many of which stemmed from 'intra-community rivalry and competition for scarce resources',[36] were experienced around the issues of how the community constituency was to be identified and how community representatives might be selected in a manner that would satisfy the requirements of democratic accountability.[37]

Community representatives, for their part, were to find that numerical equality was not sufficient to allow them to participate on anything like equal terms in the PESP area partnerships. Sarah Craig's account of why community representatives should view themselves as the weakest link in the partnership chain draws our attention to how the prior experience of 'community directors' had not prepared them for participation.[38] One source of this perceived weakness was the clash that was possible between the slower, consensual mode of decision-making favoured by some of the community representatives and the more executive and command styles of leadership and decision-making associated with state administration and private enterprise.[39] An equally basic difficulty, as Craig sees it, was that 'power structures at local level have not changed. Statutory agencies still maintain control over resources and there has been considerable resistance to any proposal that might alter this.'[40] Another source of dominating power is referred to in an in-depth study of one of the PESP partnerships when it is suggested that the technocratic discourse deployed by the professional staff could promote feelings of powerlessness among community activists.[41]

The foundation rules of Poverty 3 required that all 'model action' projects take the form of four-year partnerships between statutory and voluntary/community actors. While the Forum partnership of north-west Connemara had no national co-ordinating committee to answer to, nor any direct contact with a sponsoring department, it was answerable to the CPA, one of whose officials joined Forum's board of directors.[42] It had also to answer to Poverty 3's central executive at Lille, a body which imposed a tight set of reporting and financial procedures. Another official entity with which Forum had to deal was the Research and Development Unit (RDU), instituted to assist the Poverty 3 projects with evaluation procedures, ensure compliance with programme objectives, facilitate communication with regional and national policy-makers and disseminate information about the programme.

The Irish inter-project group of which Forum was a member came into being with Poverty 3 and fell away when it ended in June 1994. This network, reflecting the pilot and experimental nature of Poverty 3, concerned itself with wider policy implications as much as with issues of implementation. It was funded directly by the three Irish projects, the RDU and the CPA. The CPA and the RDU footed the bill for policy seminars and conferences organised to increase the programme's visibility and to influence public policy. The projects help to fund the production of a series of documents and reports.[43]

Once Forum got underway the adoption of a 'learning process' approach, which aimed at systematically taking account of the lessons of experience, meant that several changes were made to the composition of the Forum board and to its programme of work. These changes were to reflect the wishes of community actors as much as those of state partners. A related dynamic making for change in Forum was the struggle that developed between the adherents of two contrasting styles of pursuing community work. The first of these styles (particularly evident among some of the partnership's paid workers) emphasises the process of building up the capacity and awareness of local actors in line with democratic and emancipatory ideals. Such a process can prove to be a slow, drawn-out affair. What is taken as paramount in the second style of organising community action is the issue of demonstrating effectiveness in the short term. This second style finds its clearest expression in the emphasis which it attaches to the 'end product' of the development effort. Tension between 'process' and 'end product' styles ran through all of the local partnerships to some degree and was equally to mark the politics of pursuing community action in the Forum project.

THE BENEFITS TO COMMUNITY ACTORS OF PARTICIPATION

Three broad possibilities that range from the optimistic to the pessimistic can be contemplated in considering the benefits to community actors of participation in the area partnerships. The most optimistic scenario holds out the hope that participation can be potentially empowering for community actors. Participation is seen as presenting community actors with the opportunity to gain access to new resources and to deploy these in a manner that is to their own advantage. Community actors, by virtue of participation, can be expected to advance their own aims in significant ways and possibly to open up new arenas of activity for themselves. This optimistic possibility is very much in keeping with the communitarian populist ideal. In this version, community actors (at least those admitted to partnership status at board level), should stand formally equal with other partners, perceive themselves to be actually equal and develop a capacity to use the resources supplied by the partnerships to carry their own projects forward.

What may be described as an in-between possibility accepts that participation in the local partnerships may bring potential advantages to community actors (at board level and otherwise), but suggests that involvement may also impose heavy costs in the outlay of time and other scarce resources. These costs can be expected to weigh heaviest upon weak community actors that are wholly dependent on voluntary effort. Another likely consequence of participation is that the dynamics of the partnerships, especially the emphasis on showing tangible results quickly, are likely to pressure many community actors to think in terms of the 'product' rather than the 'process' of development.[44] A related point is that community actors cannot really look to the local partnerships, given their limited duration and terms of reference, for the type of life-cycle funding they may require if ever they are to realise their potential. Yet, dependent as they typically are on externally sourced assistance, they see themselves as having little choice but to become involved if they are not to be side-lined in a local development regime ever more dominated by area partnerships.

The most pessimistic of our three possibilities sees the cost to community actors of participation as excessively high. What is unmistakable, when the actual practice of the area partnerships is considered, is the sense in which state or state-like external actors possess the ability to set all the crucial parameters (funding, priorities, reporting procedures and programme length) of partnership activity, thus effectively constituting themselves as the controlling interest. The participation of community actors then brings with it the risks of co-optation, and the inability to exercise an advocacy role, oppose the state or use confrontational tactics against it. State or state-like actors, in short, are capable of operating a system in which they can shape community action in their own image.[45]

What support can be found for each of these three possibilities? Under what circumstances might community actors find participation in partnership-based area development to be potentially empowering, as the most optimistic possibility would have it? Certainly the architects of area interventions, with their language of empowerment and participation, hint at an agenda of emancipatory social, political and economic change *via* partnership. If the official rhetoric is to be believed, we might reasonably expect that participation would allow for 'the local community' to become a dynamic actor in the different area partnerships, and so pave the way for community empowerment. But have community actors found themselves to be formally equal with other partners? Have their representatives *seen* and *felt* the interests they represent to be equal? Have community actors been able to use the local partnerships to advance their own ends and help realise their own potential? Formal equality may be implied by the official rhetoric, and by some of the arrangements actually put in place, but it would be hard to conclude that community activists have usually seen or felt the interests they represent as partners to be equal to others (statutory ones especially) at board level. The view community activists take of the prospects for 'equality' between the various partnership strands is tied up with the question of who emerges as *central* to the workings of the area partnerships. Community interests have not as a rule possessed the resources or been sufficiently organised to become a *central* player in the area partnerships. Expressions of perceived or felt inequality on the part of representatives of community interests have been conspicuous in the PESP pilot area and LEADER I partnerships (though, as we have seen, community partners did become central to some of these). They have been significantly less apparent in Forum's case. Equal (in the numerical sense) community representation may have been explicitly provided for at board level in the PESP local partnerships, for instance, but this of itself did not constitute an organised community constituency, capable of participating on equal terms with other partners.

Community interests, on the other hand, have been able to use the partnerships to push some of their own work forward. We have seen how the 'learning process' approach adopted by Forum was to inspire substantial changes to the composition of the project's board and to its programme of work. The changes effected gave expression to the wishes of community actors as much as to those of state partners. Much came to depend in LEADER I on whether community organisations were able to become the 'leading partner' at board level.[46] When this occurred, a good deal of attention was paid to building the organisational capacity of community interests, primarily by means of training courses in areas as diverse as 'community development' and 'fish processing'.[47]

Perhaps the first thing to be said, in addressing the most pessimistic possibility, is that the recent official focus on communities as agents of local development presents us with a radical break with the past. Historically, the process of accumulation in Ireland was seen in official circles to be overwhelmingly a matter for the private and public sectors. In view of the highly centralised nature of public administration and the atrophy of local government in Ireland, tendencies that became more pronounced after political independence, the official climate for development that might possibly be informed by communitarian influences has been overwhelmingly adverse.[48] Equally, community actors were viewed as having only a negligible contribution to make to social service provision.[49] It has only been relatively recently, in the crisis ridden economic circumstances of the 1980s and typically in response to strong EU prompting, that an opening for some sort of alternative was created. Only then did the 'community', in the wave of local development programmes that have followed, come to be constituted as a significant actor in its own right, at least in the discourse of some policy-makers.

Opting for an identifiably elitist interpretation, some early commentators suggested that, for all the official rhetoric of communities empowering themselves *via* partnership to the point of holding their destinies in their own hands, these interventions were manifestly subject to tight and comprehensive central control. Such was to be seen in the origins, implementation and the benefits distributed by the area partnerships.[50] The ability of official elites to exert various forms of central control was taken to reflect a combination of their institutional power and the individual and collective weakness of community actors. The central implication of this pessimistic view of the area partnerships was that as long as the power imbalance between partners precluded participation for community actors on anything like equal terms, the best that those representing community interests could hope for was a subordinate form of participation.

Have things changed as the area partnership approach has matured? While their official sponsors may have desired to stimulate local participation, there simultaneously has been, as the experience of our three partnerships illustrates, a persistently strong desire to maintain tight (and, in LEADER's case, ever tighter) control over what was going on. Routinely, the control exerted is evident at all stages – preparatory, start-up and implementation – of the area partnership phenomenon. In particular, the later stages of LEADER I and of its successor, LEADER II have been marked by the way that central control has restricted the room to manoeuvre available to local non-statutory partners. The difficulties experienced with one of the LEADER I partnerships, where local autonomy was viewed officially to have got seriously out of hand, appear to have had much to do with inspiring a decidedly more control minded stance on the part of DAFF.[51] Needless to say, the tendency towards greater bureaucratic control in LEADER II has been in quite the opposite direction to that desired by the LEADER Network, which has found the application of tighter controls to be the cause of considerable despair. Toward the close of 1997, however, in response to much lobbying by the LEADER Network and deepening bureaucratic paralysis, DAFF agreed to make a number of substantial concessions to the local LEADER groups.[52]

Further support for the pessimistic possibility can be found in the overall situation in which the local partnerships have found themselves. The difficulties they have experienced in exerting themselves as a force to be reckoned with in national and supranational policy-making circles are amply illustrated in the failure to have a Poverty 4 programme succeed

Poverty 3 and in the uncertainty that currently surrounds the future of the LEADER and ADM partnerships. Problems of constituting and representing partnership interests have plagued some of the partnerships, as is evident in the obstacles encountered in negotiating formal standing for the LEADER Network.[53] In the case of the PESP partnerships, the initial situation was that the national co-ordinating team 'had a role in actually representing groups and partnerships *vis-à-vis* the statutory agencies and government departments'.[54] However, as the successor to the national co-ordinating team, ADM was 'never given that role' and as much as it may have 'a supporting role and may still lobby on behalf of the groups and partnerships', it lacks 'a mandate for representation'.[55] The contrast here with the position which the IFA and ICMSA have secured for themselves in representing farming interests in Irish agriculture's well established national policy community is striking.[56]

Are there any reasons why the situation might be less cut-and-dried than the pessimistic assessments sketched out here would imply? Our reading would suggest, in fact, that official thinking about community participation in the area partnerships, as well as the instrumental approach adopted to the area partnerships by many community actors, have tended to move in the direction of the in-between possibility relating to the benefits of participation for community actors. Two dimensions of this in-between possibility will now be considered. The first of these deals with how official actors have come to see the conditions in which community interests might realise their potential to benefit from the area partnerships. The second dimension focuses on the view taken by some community activists that organising a 'community sector' at national level will improve the position of community interests within the area partnerships as a whole.

Several general assumptions about 'community' participation can be detected in the early official thinking about the partnerships. Community involvement was deemed to be essential if the area programmes were to fulfil their potential. The interests of 'communities' tended to be treated as synonymous with those of 'the people' and the selection of legitimate representatives of community interests was expected to present no special difficulties. As things were to turn out, each of these assumptions was quickly to become problematic. In response to the difficulties, it has come to be acknowledged in official circles that admitting the 'community' has allowed a very diverse set of unevenly organised interests to be swept into the area partnerships.

Against such a background, the focus of official efforts, informed by a conviction that community actors would have to become more rationally organised entities in order to be more effective in the local development sphere, has come to fall heavily on building organisational capacities. In view of its weakness in disadvantaged areas and the inadequacy of resourcing (technical assistance, information and funding), the task of building organisational capacity was seen to present an especially challenging problem in the PESP area partnerships. In fact, on account of its weakness, the 'community sector' was viewed as sustaining 'participation in partnership activity over a long period' only with great difficulty.[57] So as to gear themselves for the requirement of participation, community actors were nonetheless urged to adopt a more rationalised approach. This would see them move towards greater professionalism and a full-time commitment. Greater dependence on paid staff was seen as complementing voluntarism as the central organising principle of community action.[58]

It was similarly realised within Forum that if community actors were to contribute more significantly to local development, their organisational capacities would have to be upgraded. To this end, a full-time community development worker was deployed to work with local community and community-based groups. Small amounts of financial aid (on average £250) were provided to seven community groups (with a total of 265 members) to help develop leadership skills, undertake project development and evaluation, acquire media presentation familiarity and establish contacts with kindred groups in other districts. Assistance was also provided to four community groups to improve their buildings and meeting rooms. Three groups were aided in their efforts to prepare local development plans.

A more general feature of Forum's approach to capacity-building was the point it made of highlighting the collective side to the genesis and the combating of social exclusion. The approach it settled on was to single out certain categories – such as women, the elderly, small farmers and fishers – as being at particular risk of poverty. The idea was to seek either to constitute these categories as collective actors or to add to the capacities of those already functioning as organised entities. Such aims were more easily realised in some cases than in others. Forum assisted in the formation of seven women's groups and, in conjunction with FÁS and the Western Health Board, helped design and implement an educational and training programme for women. The approach Forum took in relation to the elderly involved committing funds to the establishment of three resource centres, organising a programme of social events, improving the provision of public transport and co-ordinating housing repairs. A conscious effort was made, in the project's attempts to develop local aquaculture and tourism, to assist those who had tended to be passed over by conventional policy measures.

Forum may have experienced little or no success in changing national policy, but it was able to exert some influence over the manner local agencies and departments did their work. Most of the statutory partners involved in Forum have learned much about the changing needs of north-west Connemara people and several have come to review the manner they actually deliver their services. The Western Health Board, to take an example, has explored new ways of combining with voluntary associations to provide services for the elderly. New forms of support for small-scale fishermen and shellfish farmers were launched by Bord Iascaigh Mhara.

If official actors have come to see the organisation of community action as weak and crying out to be placed on a more rational basis, how have community activists viewed the position of the interests they purport to represent in the area partnerships? Reserving a place on area partnership boards for 'community "partners" may be seen by many community activists as an important breakthrough, but this cannot conceal how relatively weak and unequal they often take the interests they represent to be. The partnerships are widely acknowledged, on the other hand, as offering a new and promising set of opportunities to get things done.[59] It is this pragmatic interest in moving things forward that appeals most concretely to many community activists. The challenge, as these see it, is to exploit the material and institutional resources the area partnerships bring with them to the advantage of the community interests they profess to represent.

The success with which community actors can manipulate the area partnerships to their own advantage can be said to depend on a large number of contingencies. Pre-existing strength, based on a more-or-less established tradition of community organisation and achievement, as the case of Connemara West in Letterfrack well illustrates, can obviously be important in accounting for the siting of partnerships and the dynamics of their operations. The ability of both local community actors and local partnerships groups to establish supralocal alliances for themselves may, both in the short and longer terms, make a substantive difference to the position in which they find themselves, especially a relation to the 'power' struggles being waged with other partners or with interests outside the partnerships.

A number of possibilities for coalition and alliance building within the area partnership context have begun to materialise. A potentially important learning experience for community activists was provided by the chance to join alliances, such as the one the LEADER I Network formed. The coalition of partnership groups put together by the LEADER Network conferred practical as well as morale-boosting benefits,[60] though a good deal of frustration and in-fighting has been registered as well.[61]

Is there a sense in which the general situation of community interests within the area partnerships is linked to their ability to constitute themselves as a more powerful presence at the supralocal level? The obstacles to this happening should not be under-estimated. Reflecting the weakness and fragmentation of community action and the false starts and discontinuities that have characterised many attempts at supralocal organisation, the ability of community interests to unite with a view to forming a 'sector' in Ireland has typically been problematic. Of course, some particular strands of community action have achieved more success than others.[62] There are some indications, however, that steps have been taken in the 1990s to counter the weakness of community actors as a nationally organised interest in Ireland. In particular, the project of 'the community sector as social partner' has been adopted by some nationally organised bodies (especially the Community Workers Co-operative).[63] Very critically, some official bodies have come around to viewing community actors as national-level partnership material.[64] The result has been that a place has recently been reserved for the so-called 'community and voluntary sector' in a number of national-level sites where policies are considered and changes proposed.[65] Perhaps the best evidence of the evolving pattern is found in the community and voluntary sectors' membership of the National Economic and Social Forum (NESF), and in the Community Platform's involvement in the *Partnership 2000* negotiations.[66] The hope of community activists is that these developments will strengthen the hand of community partners in the area partnerships in a way that will make local conditions more conducive to community empowerment.

However, it has not all been plain sailing. In particular, the democratic mandate of the emergent community sector has come under renewed threat from local government politicians who have always regarded themselves to be the only legitimately constituted representatives of local communities.[67] They resent what they see to be the privileging of community actors and their own exclusion from the area partnerships.[68] The claim of these local councillors that, as duly elected public representatives, they have a superior right to that of community actors to represent localities, seems to have been accepted in the 1996 Howlin proposal to assign overall responsibility for the Irish area partnerships to the Department of the Environment.

Apart from the movement to find room for local authority representatives, the area partnership phenomenon, and the resources and opportunities for career advancement that have accompanied it, have inspired a good deal of jockeying for position between state departments and agencies. That these power struggles have proceeded without any reference to community actors yields a telling insight into where power resides at one crucial level. As long as agriculture dominated the rural development agenda the Department of Agriculture's central position was guaranteed. But as soon as the boundaries were pushed outwards, other departments, each with its own sphere of area activity, have struggled to come into the frame.

The gist of Minister Howlin's proposals of late 1996 to concentrate overall responsibility in the Department of the Environment indicates not only that a greater measure of central control was on the cards but that the Department had won out in the inter-departmental struggle for control.[69] Howlin's White Paper, *Better Local Government: A Programme for Change*, states that 'The Government has decided that the local government and local development systems will be integrated on completion of the current round of structural funds programmes'.[70] Practical steps to realise such an aim are set forth in the recent *Task Force on Integration of Local Government and Local Development Systems* report, one of whose recommendations is that 'local development groups set up under EU programmes, be they Partnerships, LEADER groups, or other such groups, shall post-1999 have county/city councillors on their boards'.[71] The Task Force does advise, however, that the 'community and voluntary sector' be given representation alongside the 'traditional social partners' on the new County/City Development Boards, which it recommends be instituted without delay.[72] With something akin to the Howlin reforms likely to go through, community actors may conceivably find themselves in a position in which they can advance their own interests, not least by exploiting the official rhetoric of community control which looks set to continue to infuse the area partnerships into the future.

Three possibilities have been outlined and assessed in this section in considering the benefits to community interests of participation in the area partnerships. The complexity and diversity of the area partnerships are underscored by the ease with which evidence can be found to support the optimistic, pessimistic and in-between possibilities regarding the benefits to community interests of participation. It is hard to find general circumstances in which the power imbalance in the area schemes, which pessimists would regard as leaving community partners severely disadvantaged, might be countered. On the other hand, the pragmatic view that state officials increasingly take that the 'community's' ability to contribute to local development can be improved by means of organisational capacity building is one that many community activists would not disagree with. Of itself, this official pragmatism presents a chance for community interests to expand their 'room to manoeuvre' in moving their projects on. A supralocal dimension to community action may be of equal importance, at least indirectly, if community actors are to get more out of the area partnerships in the longer term.

PARTNERSHIP: THE WAY TO COMMUNITY EMPOWERMENT?

Two distinctly different interpretations of how community actors might fare in the context of the local area partnerships are found in the communitarian and elitist positions that were outlined at the beginning of this chapter. The communitarian populist would prefer to see community actors at the centre of the action while, from a vantage point of cynical realism, elitist would see community actors as the pawns of powerful outside interests and, very likely, under the control of local elites. How do these contrasting positions stand up in light of our discussions so far? It would be impossible to argue that community actors are central to the initial appearance of the Irish area partnerships. Their creators, instead, are to be found far away from rural localities in the power centres of Brussels and Dublin. Yet behind the official thinking that has shaped the new area initiatives rest the convictions that neither the state nor the EU are to be regarded as omnipotent, and that the time has now come for local actors (including organised community interests) to assert themselves as more central players in the process of local development. This line of thinking can be said to be consistent with the much-vaunted EU doctrine of subsidiarity as well as with the new right's preference for diminishing the state's role and reasserting the primacy of market forces in late capitalist societies.

Conceptions of crisis have supplied a huge stimulus to the official thinking embodied in the area partnership approach. The official view that the crisis conditions afflicting rural areas are structural in nature resonates with that theme in modern social science which sees contemporary society as periodically beset by deep-seated disruptions that have the potential to reach crisis proportions. How the state and supranational bodies like the EU are affected by and deal with the decisive decision-making moments these crises present has attracted much attention. In an analysis that is pertinent to the present case, Pickvance and Preteceille take the official response to crisis conditions as involving two basic movements – a shrinkage of state responsibilities and interventions (as evidenced in privatisation programmes and the proliferation of subcontracting arrangements) and, secondly, the simultaneous constitution of an array of new actors as players in more flexible forms of local intervention.[73] Both these tendencies are evident in Ireland, with the area partnerships supplying a significant example of the second movement.

Lying behind the three area partnerships we have been discussing was the official idea that the talents of a range of collective actors could be pooled in a formalised division of labour capable of stimulating a cycle of accelerated local development or even, as in two of our three cases, of combating processes of 'social exclusion'. All of this was to be brought about by creating new institutions that could provide representation to 'local communities' as well as to other organised interests, capable of constituting themselves as 'partners' in the new area development regime. The flexibility of this form of development intervention stemmed not only from its relatively short lifespan and its refusal to be tied indefinitely to particular locations, but also from the emphasis placed on the preparation of customised local plans and the anticipated devolution of decision-making power to local partnership groups. The vagueness of the notion of 'community' has also made for flexibility by allowing the state to find a place for certain organised community elements within the area partnership process while passing over others.

Have the area partnerships allowed community actors to empower themselves by participating as equals at board level and by using the available resources as a means to the achievement of some of their own ends, along the lines imagined by an optimistic communitarian analysis? There can be no doubt that some local partnerships did acquire a certain discretion over matters such as board composition, territory covered and the prioritising of different types of projects.[74] What is also clear is that some community actors have been able to participate in the areas partnerships in a way that has delivered benefits to them and allowed them make headway with some of their aims.[75] At the same time it is hardly surprising, given the disparity of resources commanded by the different partnership strands, that many community activists would dismiss the idea of equality between the different interests represented on area partnership boards as verging on the utopian. At least in the short term, the best that can be hoped for from the area-based approach is that community interests can succeed in using them instrumentally to advance their own prospects. Whether the area partnerships eventually evolve into something akin to power-sharing arrangements will depend more on pragmatic, instrumental considerations than on how well the various formal power differences that militate against 'equality' between partners can be offset.

To what extent can the claims of the elitist position be supported? It is indisputable that the area partnerships we have been discussing have opened up opportunities for the state and EU authorities to shape community action in ways that allow it to serve the achievement of official ends. But is there confirmation of the elitist assumption that the power imbalance between partners in the board room precludes participation on anything like equal terms for the representatives of community interests? A number of points can be made here. The gap that has opened up between the official portrayal of the area partnerships as an exercise in the devolution of power and the large body of evidence indicating central control in the way these initiatives actually work might seem to point to an inevitable tendency for official rhetoric and reality to drift far apart. Yet, as immensely constraining as the formal structures and procedures of the area partnerships may be for community actors, are they capable of determining the entire process in all its detail and of leaving community actors powerless? We have placed considerable stress in our discussion here on the possibility that community actors can find their participation enabling in the sense that sufficient room to manoeuvre can be created to allow them to exploit the opportunities the area partnerships bring with them, as well as improve their position *vis-à-vis* other partners. Not only do the politics of the area partnerships revolve around the possession of resources, they centre as well on the manner in which the different actors can use their bargaining power to best advantage. Quite crucial, therefore, is the manner in which the different sets of interests compete to exercise power, play the cards they acquire or are dealt and handle the pressures that impinge upon decision-making. That the boundaries between policy formation and implementation are potentially vague and shifting, especially in new and experimental policy departures such as the area partnerships, arguably plays into the hands of community actors in all of this.

These observations accord with that theme in the literature on 'actor-oriented' policy negotiation which highlights the difficulties encountered in trying to read off the process of implementation from the letter of official policy.[76] The exponents of the negotiation approach insist that policy as formulated high up must always be interpreted by those charged with its implementation lower down. Depending on how much discretion there is in decision-making, the scope for the actual making or remaking of policy at the implementation stage may be considerable. Community actors stand to do well at the level of implementation to the extent that experimentation and innovation are encouraged, that other partners are prepared to be supportive and make concessions to community interests and that community activists themselves become adept at playing the politics of partnership.

Another consideration to be borne in mind is that the direction in which the area partnerships has been moving can be interpreted as broadly favourable to community actors. As with LEADER I, 'community development' tended initially to be of secondary importance to the PESP local partnerships, whose stock-in-trade was the organisation of innovative educational and training projects that aimed to provide and upgrade labour market skills. What focus there was on community development was aimed at drawing attention to the need for a broad socio-economic approach to tackling the problems of long-term unemployment, the redirection of some 'centrally located services to a community setting' and the highlighting of the 'need for a review of representative community structures'.[77] Only with the advent of ADM in 1992 did the community development dimension of the PESP partnerships began to loom appreciably larger. Funds, under the provisions of the EU global grant, could then be allocated to 'capacity building among local organisations'.[78] Similarly, in contrast to the tendency of LEADER I which, as O'Hara and Commins point out, was to move the '. . . emphasis from community and social development to enterprise and business development', the subsequent decision by the Operational Programme for Local Urban and Rural Development (OPLURD) to target social exclusion 'has provided a counter-balance to the promotion of individual enterprise in rural development. It has led many rural development groups to adopt a broader development agenda, combining economic and social actions'.[79]

Some evidence of the power of local elites comes from an in-depth study of one of the twelve PESP cases. O'Reilly's specific contention, in fact, is that the general dominance of commercial interests in local society has tended to be carried over into the area partnerships.[80] Further support for a class analysis reading of the area partnerships as an institutional framework in which those partners representing the interests of economically dominant classes can take precedence over others comes from the Office of the Comptroller and Auditor General's uncovering of the power of local commercial elites in some of the LEADER I partnerships. That 'some of the projects grant aided were promoted by Board members or by persons with whom they were closely connected', the Comptroller and Auditor General notes, did '. . . give rise to a possible conflict of interest'[81] It was in response to such criticisms that the then Minister of State with responsibility for rural development, Jimmy Deenihan, promised that the LEADER II area partnerships (1994–9) would be made subject to a set of tighter central controls.[82]

Another way of approaching the issue of the domination of local elites is to ask how the participation of disadvantaged interests has been encouraged by the area partnership approach. It appears that representatives of the long-term unemployed were absent by and large from most of the original PESP directorates.[83] A recent study of women's involvement in the area partnerships observes how 'overall, women said they felt peripheral to partnership structures rather than central to establishing priorities and making decisions'.[84] The low turnover of representatives would also tend to support elitist expectations. Haase *et al.* observe that while there is 'invariably a healthy demand for seats on Boards and Committees . . . the lack of movement of personnel . . . and the fact that new people do not seem to be emerging' have to be matters for concern.[85]

CONCLUSIONS

By way of summing up, it can be suggested that the ability of community actors to bend the local partnerships to their own purposes (at least to some degree) provides some support for the communitarian populist position. Participation may add to the capacity of community actors to control their own affairs. Community activists would also point out, however, that what has been achieved is but a beginning and that there is still an awful long way to go before the ideal of community empowerment can become a tangible reality. The distribution of power within the partnerships, as we have seen, has frequently fallen far short of formal as well as perceived equality for community partners. An elitist reading would find further encouragement in the ability of external and local elites to determine many of the basic dynamics of the area partnerships. Creating 'room to manoeuvre' and seizing the chance, as far as organised community interests are concerned, inevitably take on a certain complexion when the commitment the state (and the EU) are prepared to provide is but intermittent and refuses to go beyond special, fixed-term area development schemes. The short lifespans of the area partnerships, as well as their sometimes excessively bureaucratic styles, are not conducive to building an enduring framework of trust in which community actors might be inclined to commit themselves more deeply to the process. Instrumentalism is encouraged on all sides by the basic dynamics of the area-based partnership regime.

Since the area partnerships were born of crisis conditions, are they likely to disappear once the current crises fade or pass? One answer to this question might be that despite Ireland's recent economic advances, the condition many rural areas in Ireland have settled into is now arguably one of permanent crisis, even if some local elements do well as the process of agricultural restructuring runs its course.

LEADER I has been followed by LEADER II and, to judge from the expansion that has occurred (by 1997, there were eighteen ADM-financed rural partnership companies and thirty-three rural community groups functioning under OPLURD), the whole approach associated with the PESP area development initiative has progressed from the experimental stage to become a recognisable feature of Ireland's Local Development Programme (1994–9). The general approach (in whatever guise) may be here to stay,[86] but much uncertainty surrounds the future of specific programmes.[87] Poverty 3 has come and gone without any EU successor programme taking its place. With both the expanded set of PESP area initiatives and LEADER II also now finished, and with no guarantees that extensions will be granted to existing partnerships, the always thorny issue of continuity looks like being raised as never before.

Notes

Introduction

1 Lee, J. J. (1992) *Ireland 1912–85: Politics and Society*, Cambridge: Cambridge University Press.
2 Sabel, C. (1995) *Ireland: Local Partnerships and Social Innovation*. Paris: OECD.

Chapter 1

1 Lee, J. J. (1992) *Ireland 1912–85: Politics and Society*, Cambridge: Cambridge University Press. See also O'Grada, C. (1994) *Ireland 1780–1939: An New Economic History*, Oxford: Oxford University Press.
2 See Breen *et al.* (1990) *Understanding Contemporary Ireland: State, Class and Development in the Republic of Ireland*, Dublin: Gill and Macmillan; Crotty, R. (1986) *Ireland in Crisis: A Study in Capitalist Colonialist Underdevelopment*, Dingle: Bandon Books; Girvin, B. (1989) *Between Two Worlds: Politics and Economy in Independent Ireland*, Dublin: Gill and Macmillan; O'Mally, E. (1989) *Industry and Economic Development: The Challenge for the Latecomer*, Dublin: Gill and Macmillan.
3 See Gray, A. (ed.) (1997) *International Perspectives on the Irish Economy*, Dublin: Indecon Economic Consultants.
4 O'Grada, C. (1997) *op. cit.*, p. 234.
5 Bradley *et al.* (1997) 'Interpreting the Recent Irish Growth Experience', in Duffy, D., Fitzgerald, J., Kearney, I. and Shorthall, F. (eds) *Medium-Term Review: 1997–2003*, Dublin: Economic and Social Research Institute.
6 Krugman, P. (1991) *Geography and Trade*, Cambridge, Mass: MIT Press. Also (1995) *Development, Geography and Economic Theory*, Cambridge: Cambridge University Press.
7 Boylan, T. A. (1988) 'Economic Development in a Small Open Economy: Aspects of the Irish Experience', *Manchester Papers on Development*, Vol. 4, pp. 244–71.
8 National Economic and Social Council (1996) *Strategy into the 21st Century*, Report No. 99. Dublin: National Economic and Social Council.
9 *Ibid.*
10 Leddin, A. J. and B. M. Walsh (1995) *The Macro-Economy of Ireland*, 3rd edition. Dublin: Gill and Macmillan.
11 O'Hagan, J. W. (ed.) (1995) *The Economy of Ireland: Policy and Performance of a Small European Economy*, Dublin : Gill and Macmillan.
12 O'Grada, C. (1997) *A Rocky Road: The Irish Economy Since the 1920s*, Manchester: Manchester University Press.
13 Leddin, A. J. and B. M. Walsh (1995) *The Macro-Economy of Ireland*, 3rd edition. Dublin: Gill and Macmillan.

14 Barry, F. (ed.) (1999) *Understanding Ireland's Economic Growth*, London and New York: Macmillan, p. 1.
15 European Economy, 1996 *The Economic and Financial Situation in Ireland: Ireland in the Transition to EMU*, Report and Studies, no. 1, Brussels: European Commission, p. 1.
16 Leddin, A. J. and B. M. Walsh (1997) 'Economic Stabilisation, Recovery, and Growth: Ireland 1979–96', *Irish Banking Review*, Summer, pp. 2–17.
17 O'Hagan, J. W. (ed.) (1995) *The Economy of Ireland: Policy and Performance of a Small European Economy*, Dublin: Gill and Macmillan.
18 Giavazzi, F. and M. Pagano (1990) 'Can Fiscal Contractions be Expansionary? Tales of Two Small European Countries', in O. Blanchard and S. Fischer (eds), *The National Bureau of Economic Research, Macroeconomics Annual 1990*, Cambridge, Mass: MIT Press; McAleese, D. (1990) 'Ireland's Economic Recovery', *Irish Banking Review*, Summer, pp. 18–32; Barry, F. and M. B. Devereux (1995) 'The Expansionary Fiscal Contracton Hypothesis: A Neo-Keynesian Analysis', *Oxford Economic Papers*, Vol. 47, pp. 249–64.
19 Bradley, J., Whelan, K. and J. Wright (1993) *Stabilisation and Growth in the EC Periphery: A Study of the Irish Economy*, Aldershot: Avebury.
20 Leddin, A. J. and B. M. Walsh (1997) 'Economic Stabilisation, Recovery, and Growth: Ireland 1979–96', *Irish Banking Review*, Summer, pp. 2–17.
21 Walsh, B. M. (1996) 'Stabilisation and Adjustment in a Small Open Economy: Ireland, 1979–95', *Oxford Review of Economic Policy*, Vol. 12 (3), pp. 74–86.
22 Leddin, A. J. and B. M. Walsh (1997) 'Economic Stabilisation, Recovery, and Growth: Ireland 1979–96', *Irish Banking Review*, Summer, pp. 2–17.
23 Honohan, P. (1999) 'Fiscal Adjustment and Disinflation in Ireland: Settling the Macro Basis of Economic Recovery and Expansion', in F. Barry (ed) *Understanding Ireland's Economic Growth*, London and New York: Macmillan.
24 Kenny, G. and D. McGettigan (1996) 'Non-Traded, Traded and Aggregate Inflation in Ireland', *Technical Paper 3/RT/96, Central Bank of Ireland*, p. 89.
25 Middlemas, K. (1995) *Orchestrating Europe: The Informal Politics of the European Union 1973–1995*, London: Fontana Press.
26 Tansey, P. (1998) *Ireland at Work: Economic Growth and the Labour Market 1987-1997*, Dublin: Oak Tree Press.
27 O'Hagan, J. W. (ed.) (1995) *The Economy of Ireland: Policy and Performance of a Small European Economy*, Dublin: Gill and Macmillan; Boylan, T. A. (1988) 'Economic Development in a Small Open Economy: Aspects of the Irish Experience', *Manchester Papers on Development*, Vol. 4.
28 Forfas (1996) *Shaping Our Future*, Dublin: Forfas.
29 White Paper on Education (1995) *Shaping Our Education Future*, Dublin: Stationery Office.
30 Leddin, A. J. and B. M. Walsh (1997) 'Economic Stabilisation, Recovery, and Growth: Ireland 1979–96', *Irish Banking Review*, Summer.

31 Jones, C. I. (1998) *Introduction to Economic Growth*, New York: W. W. Norton.

32 Bradley, J., Fitzgerald, J., Honohan, P. and I. Kearney (1997) 'Interpreting the Recent Irish Growth Experience', in Duffy, D., Fitzgerald, J., Kearney, I. and Fergal Shorthall (eds) *Medium-Term Review; 1997–2003*, Dublin: Economic and Social Research Institute.

33 Mankiw, G. N., Romer, D. and D. N. Weil (1992) 'A Contribution to the Empirics of Economic Growth', *Quarterly Journal of Economics*, 107 (2), pp. 407–37.

34 Bradley, J., Fitzgerald, J., Honohan, P. and I. Kearney (1997) 'Interpreting the Recent Irish Growth Experience', in Duffy, D., Fitzgerald, J., Kearney, I. and Fergal Shorthall (eds) *Medium-Term Review; 1997–2003*, Dublin: Economic and Social Research Institute.

35 This phrase was first used by Crowley and McLaughlin (1997) *Under the Belly of the Tiger: Class, Race, Identity and Culture in the Global Ireland*, Dublin: Irish Reporter Publications.

36 See Taylor, G. (1996) 'Labour Market Rigidities, Institutional Impediments and Managerial Constraints: Some Reflections on the Recent Experience of Macro-Political Bargaining in Ireland', *The Economic and Social Review*, Vol. 27 (3), pp. 253–77.

37 Roche, W. K. (1997) 'Pay Determination, the State and the Politics of Industrial Relations', in T. V. Murphy and W. Roche (eds) *Irish Industrial Relations in Practice*, Dublin: Oak Tree Press.

38 O'Hearn, D. (1997) 'The Celtic Tiger: The Role of the Multinationals', in E. Crowley and J. Mcloughlin (eds) *Under the Belly of the Tiger: Class, Race, Identity and Culture in the Global Ireland*, Dublin: Irish Reporter Publications.

39 O'Hearn, D. (1998) *Inside the Celtic Tiger: The Irish Economy and the Asian Model*, London: Pluto Press; Sweeney, P. (1998) *The Celtic Tiger: Ireland's Economic Miracle Explained,* Dublin: Oak Tree Press.

40 O'Hearn, D. (1998) Inside the Celtic Tiger: *The Irish Economy and the Asian Model*, London: Pluto Press, p. 157.

41 Murphy, A. (1998) *The Celtic Tiger – The Great Misnomer: Economic Growth and the Multi-Nationals in Ireland in the 1990s*, Dublin: MMI. p. 3.

42 Callan, T. B. and B. Nolan (1998) 'Poverty and Policy', in S. Healy and B. Reynolds (eds) *Social Policy in Ireland: Principles, Practice and Problems*, Dublin: Oak Tree Press; Callan, T., Nolan B., Whelan B. J., Whelan, C. T. and J. Williams (1996) *Poverty in the 1990s: Evidence from the Living in Ireland Survey*, Dublin: Oak Tree Press.

43 Curtin, C., Haase, T. and H. Tovey (eds) (1996) *Poverty in Rural Ireland: A Political Economy Perspective*, Dublin: Oak Tree Press and Combat Poverty Agency; Pringle, D. G., Walsh, J. and M. Hennessy (eds) (1999) *Poor People, Poor Places: A Geography of Poverty and Deprivation in Ireland*, Dublin: Oak Tree Press.

Chapter 2

1 Bertie Ahern, *Irish Times* 5.11.1998.
2 Streeck, W. (1992) *Social Institutions and Economic Performance: Studies of Industrial Relations in Advanced Capitalist Economies*. London: Sage; Goldthorpe, J. (ed.) (1984) *Order and Conflict in Contemporary Capitalism*. Oxford: Clarendon Press; Lash, S. and J. Urry (1987) *The End of Organised Capitalism*. Cambridge: Polity Press; Gobeyn, M. J. (1993) 'Explaining the Decline of Macro-Political Bargaining Structures in Advanced Capitalist Societies', *Governance: An International Journal of Policy and Administration*. Vol. 6, pp. 3–22.
3 The term flexible specialisation has emerged as an umbrella concept encompassing a wide range of processes within contemporary capitalism. For those such as Piore and Sabel ((1984) *The Second Industrial Divide: Possibilities for Prosperity*. New York: Basic Books), the mass production techniques of the long post-war boom have been replaced by a new paradigm in which flexibility in production becomes axiomatic. the concept has become extremely contentious. In general terms, however, the components of this new paradigm include changes in both product and labour markets, new forms of flexibility in the workforce (both numerical and functional), product diversification and the emergence of smaller production units operating for niche markets. For alternative views on what are the main features of this new, emerging era see Hirst and Zeitlin (1991) 'Flexible Specialisation Versus Post-Fordism: Theory Evidence and Policy Implications', *Economy and Society*. Vol. 20, pp. 1–56; (1990) 'Regulation Theories in Retrospect and Prospect', Economy and Society 19 pp. 152–216. For a critical discussion of this concept see A. Pollert (1988) 'The Flexible Firm: Fixation or Fact?' *Work Employment and Society*, Vol 2., pp. 281–316; R. Hyman (1988) 'Flexible Specialisation: Miracle or Myth?' in R. Hyman and W. Streeck, *New Technology and Industrial Relations*. Oxford: Blackwell; Clarke (1988); 'What in the F*****'s Name is Post-Fordism?' in N. Gilbert, R. Burrows and A. Pollert (eds) *Fordism and Flexibility: Divisions and Change*. Basingstoke: Macmillan; Warde (1994); 'Consumers, Consumption and Post-Fordism', in R. Burrows and B. Loader (eds) *Towards a Post-Fordist Welfare State*. London: Routledge.
4 Taylor, G. (1996) 'Labour Market Rigidities, Institutional Impediments and Managerial Constraints: Some Reflections on the Recent Experience of Macro-Political Bargaining in Ireland', *Economic and Social Review*, Vol. 27, no. 3, pp. 253–77.
5 *Ibid.*
6 Goldthorpe, J. (ed.) (1984) *Order and Conflict in Contemporary Capitalism*. Oxford: Clarendon Press.
7 *Ibid.*, p. 328.
8 *Ibid.*, p. 329.
9 *Idem*. Streeck ((1992) *op. cit.*, p. 215)) contends that the spread of de-

regulation occurred because it represented an assault upon the 'accumulated rigidities' of the post-war mixed economy. The position of Lash and Urry ((1987) *op. cit.* p. 280) is more complex. They argue that the collapse of corporatist bargaining is part of a wider process of disorganisation which capitalism is experiencing. Thus they suggest that 'corporatism begins tendentially to wither – largely because of the disorganised capitalist decline in size, resources and homogeneity of the working class. With internationalisation capital ceases to be a national class creating divisions between export oriented firms and the rest of organised labour.

10 Streeck, W. (1992) *op. cit.*, p. 211.

11 *Ibid.*, p. 212.

12 *Ibid.*, p. 213.

13 For Gobeyn, it is possible to identify a further four domestic and international economic factors which demand a more 'capitalist oriented' explanation of the decline of macro-political bargaining structures: the entrenchment of high levels of structural unemployment in those sectors of the economy which had high levels of trade union density; the increased mobility of capital; reductions in tariffs and international barriers and, finally, the expansion of capitalist investment opportunities. For Gobeyn, corporatism is being 'rendered obsolete' by interrelated trends which have weakened the bargaining powers of trade unions and, therefore, question the efficacy of 'extensive nationally based concertative linkages'. For more detail see Gobeyn, M. J. (1993) *op. cit.* For a detailed critique of Gobeyn's position see Taylor, G. (1996) *op. cit.*

14 Lash and Urry (1987) *op. cit.*, p. 233.

15 *Ibid.*, pp. 233–4.

16 *Ibid.*, p. 5.

17 *Ibid.*, p. 234.

18 It would be misleading to suggest that this was an original intention of Goldthorpe's schema, since, at various junctures, he wishes to distance himself from establishing any form of preference. Thus, Goldthorpe states that: 'In sum, what may be maintained is that over recent decades western capitalist societies have moved in divergent directions in their responses to economic problems and further that, in consequence, they now face different sets of political choices in which real ideological alternatives are in fact inherent. *Which alternatives will be pursued, to what extent, and with what degree of success are questions that cannot be answered in advance* (my emphasis) (Goldthorpe, J. (1984), *op. cit.* p. 42.

19 Taylor (1996) *op. cit.*

20 *Ibid.*

21 It may not be very meaningful to assert that either decentralised and centralised forms of bargaining are more effective. As Calmfors notes, where there exists highly centralised bargaining and highly decentralised bargaining optimal outcomes may be produced. However, as he points out, 'it is unrealistic to expect one universally optimal set of bargaining institutions to exist in all countries'. (Calmfors, L. (1993) 'Centralisation

of Wage Bargaining and Macroeconomic Performance: A Survey', *OECD Working Papers*, no 131.)

22 Brown, W. A., and Walsh, J. (1991) 'Pay Determination in Britain in the 1980s: The Anatomy of Decentralisation', *Oxford Review of Economic Policy*. Vol. 7, pp. 45–59.

23 Purcell, J. (1991) 'The Rediscovery of the Management Prerogative: The Management of Labour Relations in the 1980s', *Oxford Review of Economic Policy*. Vol. 7, pp. 33–43.

24 Walsh, J. (1993) 'Internalisation v Decentralisation: An analysis of Recent Developments in Pay Bargaining', *British Journal of Industrial Relations*. Vol. 31, no. 3, p. 416.

25 Marsh, D. (1992) *The New Politics of British Trade Unionism: Union Power and the Thatcher Legacy*. London: Macmillan.

26 O'Donnell, R. (1998) 'Social Partnership in Ireland: Principles and Interactions', in O'Donnell, R. and J. Larragy (eds) *Negotiated Economic and Social Governance and European Integration*. Luxembourg: European Commission.

27 Dore, R. (1988) 'Rigidities in the Labour Market', *Government and Opposition*. Vol. 23, no. 4, pp. 393–412.

28 See Marsh (1992) *op. cit.*

29 See Dore (1988) *op. cit.* Rowthorn argues that such wage-efficiency considerations have an important bearing upon the issue of centralisation and decentralisation of bargaining. Moreover, the issue is perhaps a little more complex than either Dore or Streeck acknowledge. For example, Calmfors notes that there are at least two types of firm that would prefer decentralised forms of negotiation to decentralised forms of negotiation: strong wage-effort-profit firms, which require relative wages and those with a weak such link that want low wage relativities. See Rowthorn, R. E. (1992) 'Centralisation, Employment and Wage Dispersion', *Economic Journal*, Vol. 102; Calmfors (1993) *op. cit.*

30 Streeck, W. (1988) 'Comment on Ronald Dore, Rigidities in the Labour Market', *Government and Opposition*, pp. 413–23; Streeck (1992) *op. cit.*

31 Rubery, J. and F. Wilkinson (eds) (1994) *Employer Strategy and the Labour Market*. Oxford: Oxford University Press, p. 13.

32 Rhodes, M. (1998) 'Globalisation, Labour Markets and Welfare States: A Future of Competitive Corporatism?' In Rhodes, M. and Y. Meny, *The Future of European Welfare: A New Social Contract?* London: Macmillan.

33 *Ibid.*

34 Hayek, F. (1960) *The Constitution of Liberty*. London: Routledge.

35 An interesting comparative analysis of some of the complex themes associated with this type of argument has been undertaken by Pfaller and Gough. They suggest that their findings do not prove that welfare statism is linked to diminishing economic performance. See Pfaller, A. and I. Gough (1991) *Can the Welfare State Compete? A Comparative Study of Five Advanced Capitalist Countries*. London: Macmillan.

36 Dore (1988) *op. cit.*

37 Streeck (1988) *op. cit.*, p. 417.

38 *Ibid.*, p. 419.

39 In Streeck's opinion, Diversified Quality Production (DQP) 'requires a rich supply of individually non-appropriable production factors' and, furthermore, that 'industrial restructuring towards high levels of product diversity and quality is impeded by a neo-classical institutional environment that gives rational possessive individualism precedence over collective, co-operative and collusive action'. Streeck (1992) *op. cit.*, p. 22.

40 Taylor (1996) *op. cit.*

41 Streeck (1988) *op. cit.*, p. 419.

42 See *Irish Times* 5.11.1998. This is not to suggest that there are not tensions emerging in discussions for a successor programme to Partnership 2000. The persistence of poverty and the failure to address the equitable distribution of the Celtic Tiger's wealth has been compounded by revelations of systematic tax avoidance during the late 1980s and early 1990s. The public sector unions are becoming increasingly concerned at the direction that the later agreements have taken.

43 O'Donnell (1998) *op. cit.*

44 *Irish Times* 5.11.1998.

45 Hardiman, N. (1988) *Pay Politics and Economic Performance in Ireland 1970-87*. Oxford: Clarendon Press.

46 O'Riordan, M. (1996) 'Towards A European Social Pact: The Irish Experience'. Paper presented to European Trade Union Institute Conference, Brussels, 1996.

47 *Ibid.*

48 For a review of PESP see the report of the Central Committee (1992) *Progress Achieved Under PESP* Pn 0447.

49 Under the terms of PESP, increases in pay at national level were divided into three years. Year one (4%), year two (3%) and year three (3.75%). In addition, Clause Three allowed local negotiations up to a ceiling of 3% basic pay. In contrast, the breakdown under PCW was year one (2%), year two (2.5%), year three - first six months (2.5%) and second six months (1%). Separate agreements were made in both the public sector and the construction industry.

50 *Industrial Relations News* (1992), Vol. 37, p. 11.

51 The SIPTU report was based on 187 cases covering 749 companies. See *Industrial Relations News* (1992), Vol. 37, p. 12

52 *Industrial Relations News* (1992), Vol. 37.

53 Department of Employment (1993) *Survey of Local Bargaining*. Dublin.

54 Labour Relations Commission Annual Report 1992.

55 *Industrial Relations News* (1992), Vol. 36, p. 19.

56 Labour Relations Commission Annual Report 1993. The Commission stated that items covered in trade-offs were varied but included flexibility, multi-skilling, redeployment, interchangeability, continuous working, the introduction of new technology and industrial peace clauses. 75% of cases referred were resolved. 66 cases were sent to the labour court which was

almost three times the previous year's amount.

57 It is important to add a note of caution here. While recent figures suggest that part-time work is common, it is only so for a relatively small proportion of organisations who responded to the Price Waterhouse Cranfield Project. However, as an emerging feature, it is common across organisational ownership (Irish, UK, US). See Morley, M., Gunningle, P. and N. Hearty (1994) 'The Flexibilisation of Work Practices in Ireland: Gradual Incrementalism or Radical Path Breaking Developments', Administration. Vol. 42, no. 1, pp. 92–111.

58 Morley *et al.* (1994) *op. cit.*

59 O'Riordan (1996) *op. cit.*

60 *Ibid.*, p.6.

61 *Ibid.*

62 Labour Relations Commission Annual Report 1994.

63 O'Riordan (1996) p. 7.

64 However, NESF noted that the schemes introduced by the government fell short of their expectations, both in terms of conditions and payments.

65 O'Riordan (1996) *op. cit.*

66 Partnership Agreement (1997), p. 68.

67 *Ibid.*, p. 80.

68 Labour Relations Commission Annual Report 1997, p. 18.

69 Evidence from a recent survey analysis in the UK suggests that British firms are largely 'improvisers and empiricists' and even where evidence of strategic behaviour could be found, it applied only to a small group of firms. See Rubery and Wilson (1994) *op. cit.*, p. 10.

70 Rubery and Wilson, for example, suggest that 'employers have a wide range of objectives that are not necessarily compatible. They argue that the 'need to manufacture and maintain consent may be an important constraint of the exercise of power by managers'. See Rubery and Wilson (1994) *op. cit.*

Chapter 3

1 Ferrera, M. (1997) 'New Problems, Old Solutions? Recasting Social Protection for the Future of Europe', pp. 119–28, in *European Social Policy Forum: A Summary*. Luxembourg: European Commission.

2 *Idem.*

3 Social protection expenditure is any expenditure involved in meeting costs incurred by individuals or households as a result of the materialisation of the existence of certain risks, contingencies or needs, insofar as this expenditure gives rise to the intervention of a 'third party', without there being any simultaneous equivalent counterpart by the beneficiary. See Eurostat (1997a) 'Social Protection in the European Union', *Statistics in Focus: Population and Social Conditions* (3), p. 73.

4 European Commission (1995) *Europe: Social Protection*. Luxembourg: Directorate General for Employment, Industrial Relations and Social

Affairs, p. 59.

5 PPS refers to purchasing power standard which is a measure reflecting the real purchasing power of a currency within the country concerned, providing a better indication than the exchange rate of the volume and structure of goods and services and the relative level of GDP. European Commission (1995) *Europe: Social Protection*. Luxembourg: Directorate General for Employment, Industrial Relations and Social Affairs, p. 75.

6 European Commission (1995) *Europe: Social Protection*. Luxembourg: Directorate General for Employment, Industrial Relations and Social Affairs, pp. 68–81.

7 Alber, J. (1988) 'Continuation and Change in the Idea of Welfare State', *Policy and Society*, Vol. 16, no. 4, pp. 451–68.

8 Ploug, N. and Kvist, J. (1996) *Social Security in Europe: Development or Dismantlement?* The Hague: Kluwer Law International.

9 Esping-Anderson, G. (1990) *The Three Worlds of Welfare Capitalism*. Cambridge: Politics Press; Leibfried, S. (1992) 'Towards a European Welfare State? On Integrating Poverty Regimes into the European Community', in Farge, Z. and J. E. Kolberg (eds) *Social Policy in a Changing Europe*. Boulder, Colorado: Westview Press; Ploug and Kvist (1996) *op. cit.*; Ferrera, M. (1996) 'The Southern Model of Welfare in Social Europe', *Journal of European Social Policy*, Vol. 6, no. 1, pp. 17–37.

10 Esping-Anderson (1990) *op. cit.*

11 Jarre, D. (1991) 'Subsidiarity in Social Services Provision in Germany', *Social Policy and Administration*, Vol. 25, no. 3, pp. 211–17.

12 Van Kesbergen, K. (1995) *Social Capitalism. A Study of Christian Democracy and the Welfare State*. London: Routledge.

13 Esping-Anderson (1990) *op. cit.*

14 Gough, I. *et al.* (1997) 'Social Assistance in OECD Countries', *Journal of European Social Policy*, 7 (1), pp. 17–43.

15 Mishra, R. (1993) 'Typologies of the Welfare State Comparative Analyses: The "Liberal" Welfare State'. *Paper presented at the Conference: Comparative Research on Welfare States in Transition*, Oxford, September 9–12.

16 Kosonen, P. (1994) *European Integration: A Welfare State Perspective*. Helsinki: University of Helsinki, Sociology of Law Series.

17 Kemeny, J. (1995) 'Theories of Power in the Three Worlds of Welfare Capitalism', *Journal of European Social Policy*, Vol. 5, no. 2, pp. 87–96.

18 See Taylor Gooby, P. (1991) 'Welfare State Regimes and Welfare Citizenship', *Journal of European Social Policy*, Vol. 1, no. 2, pp. 93–105; O'Connor, J. S. (1993) 'Gender, Class and Citizenship in the Comparative Analysis of Welfare States: Theoretical and Methodological Issues', *British Journal of Sociology*, Vol. 44, no. 3, pp. 501–19.

19 Bonoli, G. (1997) 'Classifying Welfare States: A Two Dimensional Approach', *Journal of Social Policy*, Vol. 26, no. 4, pp. 351–72.

20 Liebfried (1992) *op. cit.*

21 Ferrera (1996) *op. cit.*

22 Katrougalos, G. S. (1996) 'The South European Welfare Model: The

Greek State. In Search of an Identity', *Journal of European Social Policy* Vol. 6, no. 1, pp. 39–59.

23 Bonoli (1997) *op. cit.*, pp. 356–9.

24 Cousins, M. (1997) 'Ireland's Place in the Worlds of Welfare Capitalism', *Journal of European Social Policy*, Vol. 7, no. 3, pp. 223–35.

25 Alber, J. (1995) 'A Framework for the Comparative Study of Social Services', *Journal of European Social Policy*, Vol. 5, no. 2, pp. 131–49.

26 Jones, C. (1985) *Patterns of Social Policy: An Introduction to Comparative Analysis*. London, Tavistock.

27 Alber (1995) *op. cit.*

28 Anttonen, A. and J. Sipila. (1996) 'European Social Care Services: Is it Possible to Identify Models?' *Journal of European Social Policy*, Vol. 6, no. 2, pp. 87–100.

29 Liebfried, S. (1993) 'Towards a European Welfare State?' in Jones, C. (ed), *New Perspectives on the Welfare State in Europe*. London: Routledge.

30 O'Connell, P. J. and D. B. Rottman (1992) 'The Irish Welfare State in Comparative Perspective'. In J. H. Goldthorpe and C. T. Whelan (eds) *The Development of Industrial Society in Ireland*. Oxford: Oxford University Press.

31 *Ibid.*

32 Report of the Pensions Board (1998) *Securing Retirement Income: National Pensions Policy Initiative*. Dublin: The Pensions Board.

33 Whelan, C. T. and Whelan, B. (1988) *The Transition to Retirement*. Dublin: The Economic and Social Research Institute.

34 *Ibid.*

35 Nolan, B. (1991) *The Utilisation and Financing of Health Services in Ireland*. Dublin: The Economic and Social Research Institute.

36 Rottman, D. and Reidy, M. (1988) *Redistribution Through State Social Expenditure in the Republic of Ireland: 1973–1980*. Dublin: National Economic and Social Council.

37 Tussing, A. D. (1985) *Irish Medical Care Resources: An Economic Analysis*. Dublin: The Economic and Social Research Institute.

38 Nolan (1991) *op. cit.*

39 Commission on Health Funding (1989) *Report on Health Funding*, Dublin.

40 O'Connell and Rottman (1992) *op. cit.*

41 Callan, T., B. Nolan, C. T. Whelan with S. Creighton (1989) *Poverty, Income, and Welfare in Ireland, General Research Series*. Dublin: The Economic and Social Research Institute.

42 *Ibid.*

43 Callan, T., Nolan, B., Whelan, B. J., Whelan, C. T. and J. Williams (1996a) *Poverty in the 1990s: Evidence from the Living in Ireland Survey*. Dublin: Oak Tree Press.

44 Nolan, B. (1999) 'Monitoring Poverty Trends', *Poverty Today*, July–August, 4–5.

45 Callan et al. (1996a) *op. cit.*

46 Nolan (1999) *op. cit.*

47 Ploug and Kvist (1996) *op. cit.*
48 See Hills, J. (1993) *The Future of Welfare: A Guide to the Debate*. York: Joseph Rowntree Foundation.
49 Esping-Anderson (1996a) 'After the Golden Age? Welfare State Dilemmas in a Global Economy', in G. Esping-Andersen (eds), *Welfare States in Transition: National Adaptations in Global Economies*. London: Sage Publications.
50 Lindbeck, A. (1995) 'Hazardous Welfare State Dynamics', *American Economic Review*, Vol. 85, no. 2, pp. 9–15.
51 *Ibid.*
52 Layard, R., Nickell, S. and R. Jackman (1991) *Unemployment: Macroeconomic Performance and the Labour Market*. Oxford: Oxford University Press.
53 Esping-Anderson (1996a) *op. cit.*
54 Atkinson, A. B. (1993) 'Conclusion', in A. B. Atkinson and G. V. Mogensen (eds) *Welfare and Work Incentives – A North European Perspective*. Oxford: Clarendon Press.
55 McLaughlin, E. (1994) 'Employment, Unemployment and Social Security', in A. Glyn and D. Miliband (eds) *Paying for Inequality*. London: Rivers Oram Press.
56 Geary, P. T. (1989) 'The Measurement and Alleviation of Poverty: A Review of Some Issues', *The Economic and Social Review*, Vol. 20, No. 4.
57 Blank, R. (1994) 'Introduction', in R. Blank (ed.) *Social Protection vs Economic Flexibility: is there a trade-off?* Chicago University Press.
58 Sali-Martin, X. (1997) 'Transfers, Social Safety Nets, and Economic Growth', *IMF Staff Papers*, 44 (1), pp. 82.
59 Barr, N. (1993) *The Economics of the Welfare State*. 2nd edition. London: Weidenfeld and Nicolson.
60 Atkinson (1993) *op. cit.*
61 Mangan, I. (1993) 'The Influence of EC Membership on Irish Social Policy and Social Services', in S. O Cinneide (ed.) *Social Europe: EC Social Policy and Ireland*. Dublin: Institute of European Affairs.
62 Springer, B. (1992) *The Social Dimension of 1992: Europe Faces a New EC*. New York: Praeger.
63 European Commission (1993) *Growth, Competitiveness, Employment: The Challenges and Ways Forward into the 21st Century*. Luxembourg: Office for Official Publications of the European Communities.
64 Kuper, B. O. (1994) 'The Green and White Papers of the European Union: The Apparent Goal of Reduced Social Benefits', *Journal of European Social Policy*, Vol. 5, no. 2, pp. 129–37.
65 Adnett, N. (1995) 'Social Dumping and European Economic Integration', *Journal of European Social Policy*, Vol. 5, no. 1, pp. 1–12.
66 Leibfried, S. and Pierson, P. (1995) 'Semi-Sovereign Welfare States: Social Policy in a Multitiered Europe,' in Leibfried, S. and P. Pierson (eds) *European Social Policy: Between Fragmentation and Integration*. Washington DC: The Brookings Institution.

67 Marshall, T. H. (1975) *Social Policy*. London, Hutchinson.

68 Majone, G. (1993) 'The European Community Between Social Policy and Social Regulation', *Journal of Common Market Studies*, Vol. 31, no. 2, pp. 153–70.

69 Leibfried, S. and Pierson, P. (1995) *op. cit.*

70 Caporaso, J. A. (1996) 'The European Union and Forms of State: Westphalian, Regulatory or Post-Modern', *Journal of Common Market Studies*, Vol. 34, no. 1, pp. 29–52.

71 Report of the Expert Working Group on the Integration of the Tax and Social Welfare Systems (1996). *Integrating Tax and Social Welfare*. Dublin: Stationery Office.

72 Blackwell, J., O'Shea, E., Moane, G. and P. Murray (1992) *Care Provision and Cost Measurement: Dependent Elderly People at Home and in Geriatric Hospitals*. Dublin: The Economic and Social Research Institute.

73 European Commission (1993) *op. cit.*

74 National Economic and Social Forum (1995) *Jobs Potential of the Services Sector, Report No. 7*. Dublin: National Economic and Social Forum.

75 Keane, M., Kennedy, V., Gannon B. and C. O. Muiri (1996) *Pilot Projects for the Benefit of the Long-Term Unemployed*. Western Regional Authority, Ireland. Report on Stages 1 & 2, Brussels: European Commission.

76 Parker, H. (1989) *Instead of the Dole: An Enquiry into the Integration of the Tax and Benefit Systems*. London: Routledge; Callan, T., O'Donoghue, C. and C. O'Neill (1994) *An Analysis of Basic Income Schemes for Ireland*. Dublin: The Economic and Social Research Institute; Ward, S. (1994) 'A Basic Income System for Ireland'. In B. Reynolds and S. Healy (eds) *Towards an Adequate Income for All*. Dublin: Justice Commission, Conference of Religious in Ireland; Healy, S. and Reynolds, B. (1995) 'An Adequate Income Guarantee For All', in Healy, S. and B. Reynolds (eds) *An Adequate Income For All: Desireability, Viability Impact*. Dublin, Conference of Religious of Ireland.

77 Atkinson, A. B. (1992) 'Social Policy, Economic Organisation and the Search for a Third Way', in Ferge, Z. and J. E. Kolberg (eds) *Social Policy in a Changing Europe*. Frankfurt am Main, Campus Verlag.

78 Callan *et al.* (1994) *op. cit.*

79 Department of Enterprise and Employment (1996) *Growing and Sharing our Employment: Strategy Paper on the Labour Market*. Dublin, Stationery Office; Report of the Expert Working Group on the Integration of the Tax and Social Welfare Systems (1996). *Integrating Tax and Social Welfare*. Dublin: Stationery Office.

80 Meade, J. E. (1989) *Agathotopia: The Economics of Partnership*. Aberdeen: Aberdeen University Press.

81 Sen, A. (1992) *Inequality Re-examined*. Oxford: Clarendon Press; Sen, A. (1993) 'Capability and Well-Being', in M. Nussbaum and A. Sen (eds) *The Quality of Life*. Oxford: Clarendon Press.

82 Sen, A. (1992) *op. cit.*

83 Marshall, T. H. (1950) *Citizenship and Social Class*. Cambridge:

Cambridge University Press.

84 Esping-Anderson (1996b) 'Positive-Sum Solutions in a World of Trade-Offs?', in G. Esping-Andersen (ed.) *Welfare States in Transition: National Adaptations in Global Economies*. London: Sage Publications.

85 Le Grand, J. (1991) *Equity and Choice*. London: HarperCollins; Cohen, G. A. (1993) 'Equality of What? On Welfare, Goods and Capabilities', in M. Nussbaum and A. Sen (eds) *The Quality of Life*. Oxford: Clarendon Press.

86 Le Grand, J. (1997) 'Knights, Knaves or Pawns? Human Behaviour and Social Policy', *Journal of Social Policy*, Vol. 26, no. 2, pp. 149–69.

Chapter 4

1 Culliton, J. (1992) 'A Time for Change: Industrial Policy for the 1990s'. *Industrial Policy Review Group*. Dublin: Stationery Office.

2 Taylor, G. (1998) 'Conserving the Emerald Tiger: The Politics of Environmental Regulation in Ireland', in *Environmental Politics*, Vol. 7, no. 4, pp. 53–74.

3 See Scannell, Y. (1990) 'Legislation and Toxic Waste Disposal in Ireland', in *Environmental Protection and the Impact of European Community Law*. Papers from the Joint Conference with the Incorporated Law Society of Ireland. Irish Centre for European Law, Trinity College, Dublin. Also, a succession of legislative documents has left local authorities responsible for air and water pollution controls, sanitation and waste management. These include the Local Government (Planning and Development) Acts of 1963 and 1976, the Local Government (Water Pollution) Act, 1977 and the Local Government (Planning and Development) Regulations of 1977. The Air Pollution Act, 1987, was a consolidation of the various EC Directives and it retained local government responsibility for enforcement of air pollution controls. Most other EC Directives relating to the environment were incorporated into the Irish environmental regime by making government regulations under the EEC Act, 1972 (Coyle, C. (1994) 'Administrative Capacity and the Implementation of EU Environmental Policy in Ireland', in Baker, S., Milton, K. and S. Yearley (eds) *Protecting the Periphery: Environmental Policy in the Peripheral Regions of the European Union*. London: Frank Cass, p. 67).

4 The Fisheries Acts 1959–62 typified many of the flaws in the regulatory regime. Organised largely on a voluntary basis it did not provide protection against ground water pollution from agricultural activity because it offered a defence to the polluter on the grounds that s/he had taken all reasonable care to prevent entry. See Scannell, Y. (1993) 'Agriculture and Environmental Law' in Feehan, J. (ed.) *Environment and Development in Ireland*. Dublin: The Environmental Institute.

5 Taylor (1998) *op. cit.*

6 Leech, B. C. (1989) *The Administrative and Technical Arrangements for Environmental Management in Ireland*, Vols 1 and 2, unpublished PhD dis-

sertation, Trinity College, Dublin. Keohane's research highlights the example of one local authority environmental officer who drew up planning permission for Penn Chemicals in 1975. The company, which was expanding the range of products to be produced at the plant, got an extension to the original planning permission. However, no additional air pollution control conditions were added to the original planning permission. As Keohane notes, this meant that either the environmental officer involved was not aware that methyl mercaptan was going to be a by-product of the new process or he was not aware of its deleterious properties. Either way a serious lack of expertise was demonstrated. See Keohane, K. (1987) *Dependent Industrialisation, Crisis Transfer and Crisis Displacement: The Transnational Pharmaceutical Industry and the Irish Republic*, unpublished MA Thesis, UCC.

7 See Taylor (1998) *op. cit.* Also see Scannell (1990) *op. cit.* Confidence in the regulatory functions assumed by local authorities was further undermined by the fact that they were exempt from many of the pollution controls they were supposed to be enforcing on others. Most notably, they did not have to obtain permits for waste management procedures and there was nothing in Irish law to prevent sanitary authorities from discharging list 1 dangerous substances into ground water or to prevent sanitary services authorising indirect discharge to ground water.

8 Allen, R. and T. Jones (1990) *Guests of the Nation; People of Ireland versus the Multi-nationals*, London: Earthscan Publications; Keohane, K. (1989) 'Toxic Trade-Off: The Price Ireland Pays for Industrial Development', *The Ecologist*, Vol. 19, no. 4, pp. 144–6.

9 The difficulties inherent in the regulatory role performed by public bodies which act as both gamekeeper and poacher was replicated at a national level when the Department of the Environment's portfolio extended beyond environmental regulation to include responsibilities for housing, roads, sanitary services and local authority functions.

10 Leonard, H. J. (1988) *Pollution and the Struggle for the World Product; Multi-national Corporations, Environment and International Comparative Advantage*. Cambridge: Cambridge University Press, p. 187.

11 Adshead, M. (1996) 'Beyond Clientelism: Agricultural Networks in Ireland and the EU', *West European Politics*, Vol. 19, no. 3, pp. 583–608, p. 593.

12 Taylor (1998) *op. cit.*

13 Lee, J. J. (1992) *Ireland 1912–1985: Politics and Society*. Cambridge: Cambridge University Press, p. 473.

14 Leonard (1998) *op. cit.*

15 Allen and Jones (1990) p. 257.

16 Keohane (1987) *op. cit.*

17 Allen and Jones (1990) p. 257 (emphasis added).

18 Barry, U. and Jackson, P. (1989) 'Women's Employment and Multinationals in Ireland; The Creation of a New Female Labour Force', in D. Eleson and R. Pearson (eds) *Women's Employment and Multi-nationals in*

Europe, Macmillan, London.

19 Taylor (1998) *op. cit.*

20 Leonard (1998) *op. cit.*, p. 127.

21 Leonard (1998) *op. cit.*

22 The IIRS advised government and local authorities on acceptable norms for industrial practice in relation to effluents and hazardous waste. It was a key actor in presenting a scientific defence of ISA projects and was an important part in the policy community's attempts to construct a new discourse around environmental regulation. For more detail see Taylor 1988 (*op. cit.*). For more detail on policy networks see Marsh, D. and R. A. W. Rhodes (1992) *Policy Networks in British Government.* Oxford University Press.

23 *Irish Times* 16.9.1989.

24 *Irish Times* 11.9.1989. Further controversy surrounded the decision of Bord Pleanála to grant planning permission for the Radio Tara long range radio transmission mast, despite the fact that the inspector who conducted the oral hearing into the matter strongly recommended against this in his report. The Labour councillor for the area in which the mast would be located claimed that the decision to allow planning permission was granted under extreme political pressure, and pointed out that government support for the scheme was underlined by its inclusion in the *Programme for National Recovery*.

25 In 1987, Merrell Dow announced plans to set up a plant in Killeagh in the Womanagh Valley in County Cork. The residents in the area objected to the location, primarily on the basis that a pharmaceutical plant should be located in an industrial estate as opposed to the rural setting of Killeagh. However, the company got planning permission despite all the local opposition. The local authority decision was appealed and following an oral hearing, An Bord Pleanála upheld the decision, although with a number of conditions. A case was taken to the High Court on the jurisdiction of Bord Pleanála to make a decision on the matter in the light of alleged deficiencies in the information submitted in the planning application. The High Court ruled that An Bord Pleanála did indeed have the power to make the decision in this case and the court refused to overturn the decision of the planning authorities. In the end, after nearly three years of controversy and amid calls for the Minister for the Environment to intervene, the company announced its decision to pull out of Ireland altogether. They cited a merger with another company and a consequent need to reevaluate their production needs as the reason. Many feel that local opposition to the project was a more credible reason. Suffice it to say, the case was highly publicised and served to focus the attention of the public on the arguments of those who saw Ireland's environment threatened by the forces of development.

26 *Irish Times*, 5.9.1989.

27 A political consensus had emerged on the need for an overhaul of legislation. The Workers' Party, for instance, had made calls for such an

agency in May of 1989 in their environmental policy document 'The Environment is Where We Live' (*Irish Times*, 5 May, 1989). Similarly, the Labour Party produced a policy document on World Environment Day entitled 'Proposals for a Socialist Environment' which called for, among other things, the creation of a National Environmental Agency (*Irish Times*, 6 June, 1989). It was a theme also taken up in Fine Gael's policy document on the environment, 'A Clean Environment'.

28 Dáil Debates 1991, Vol. 411, 1256–7.

29 Environmental Data Services (ENDS) (1994) p. 184.

30 Pat Nolan of Hamilton Osborne Kings *Irish Times*, 24.6.1998.

31 Environmental Protection Agency (1994) *Environmental Protection Agency. Integrated Pollution Control Licensing: A Guide to Implementation and Enforcement in Ireland*. Wexford.

32 *Ibid.*

33 There has been considerable debate in public policy circles about the role of state intervention and the appropriate tools for policy intervention in the environmental arena. For more detail see Janicke, M. (1990) *State Failure*. Cambridge: Polity Press; Weale, A. (1992) *The New Politics of Pollution*. Manchester: Manchester University Press; Eckersly, R. (ed.) (1996) *Markets, the State and the Environment*. London: Macmillan.

34 *Irish Times*, 28.5.1998.

35 ENDS (1994) *op. cit.*

36 Taylor, G. (1998a) 'Me Thinks thou Do'st Protest Too Much: Oral Hearings, Public Registers and Environmental Democracy in Ireland' *Irish Planning and Environmental Law Journal*. Vol. 5, no. 4, pp. 143–55.

37 To date, the EPA has sought seven successful prosecutions from 376 IPC licensees in recent years. The fines ranged from £450 against Liffey Meats to £1,050 against Castlemahon. The total fines, including costs awarded to the agency, ranged from £2,718–£7,945 (EPA, 1997, p. 28). Two prosecutions have also been made, one against health boards for the illegal operation of incinerators and the other against Proctor and Gamble for the pollution of the water supply at Nenagh, Co. Clare.

38 EPA (1994) *op. cit.*

39 Taylor (1998a) *op. cit.*

40 ENDS (1994) *op. cit.*

41 EPA (1997) *op. cit.*

42 *Ibid.*, p. 19.

43 Gilmore, Dáil Debates, Vol. 411, pp. 1301, 1992.

44 Harney, Dáil Debates, Vol. 418, p. 959.

45 Howlin, Dáil Debates, Vol. 418, p. 957.

46 Taylor (1998) *op. cit.*

47 Harney, Dáil Debates, Vol. 418, p. 959, 1992.

48 Taylor (1998) *op. cit.*

49 EPA Act 1992, p. 64. It is important to recognise that an oral hearing is only one of several mechanisms the agency has at its disposal to control licences. It is, for example, empowered to review licences if there has been

a 'material change that could have not been reasonably foreseen when the licence was granted or where evidence was not available, or new standards relating to the contents or nature of the emission are concerned or the effects of the emission on the environment or the means for the better control of the emissions are prescribed'.

50 Taylor (1998a) *op. cit.*
51 EPA (1994) *op. cit.*, p. 11.
52 Taylor (1998a) *op. cit.*; EPA (1994) *op. cit.*, emphasis added.
53 Taylor (1998a) *op. cit.*
54 EPA (1994) *op. cit.*, p. 5.
55 Browne, Dáil Debates, 1994, p. 573.
56 Howlin, Dáil Debates, 1995, p. 337.
57 Gilmore, Dáil Debates 1991, Vol. 411, p. 1297.
58 *Ibid.*, pp. 1293–4.
59 Garland, Dáil Debates 1991, Vol. 411, p. 2431–2.
60 Regan, S. (1994) 'Advice and Training in Agriculture to Meet the Change in the Direction of Farming', in M. Moloney (ed.) *Agriculture and the Environment: Proceedings of a Conference on the Integration of EC Environmental Objectives with Agricultural Policy held in the RDS from March 9–11, 1994.* Royal Dublin Society, Dublin.
61 *Ibid.*, p. 75.
62 *Ibid.*, p. 25.
63 *Irish Times*, 28.12.1996.
64 Regan (1994) *op. cit.*
65 *Farmers' Journal*, 5.10.1996.
66 *Farmers' Journal*, 12.10.1996.
67 Deenihan, Dáil Debates, 26.1.1995 p. 539.
68 This includes cumulative afforestation i.e. within 500 metres by, or on behalf of, a single developer over a three year period where the afforestation would result in a total area planted exceeding seventy hectares.
69 Howlin, Dáil Debates 1996, Vol. 465, p. 458.
70 Deenihan, Dáil Debates 1995, Vol. 454, p. 1334.
71 Howlin, Dáil Debates 1995, Vol. 453, pp. 2000–2.

Chapter 5

1 The author wishes to thank the Health Research Board, Ireland, and the Centre for Health Promotion Studies, NUI, Galway, for supporting research on which this article is in part based.
2 Dáil Éireann Democratic Programme 1919.
3 T. H. Green, for example (1883), had definite ideas about how character develops and what circumstances and settings are optimum for it, and he certainly saw moral and political development as dynamic. Discussions of this nature have grown less popular during the course of this century. It may be that the sheer scale of contemporary public policy initiatives, and their need to rely on relatively static statistical data, itself carries a

momentum which disguises the dynamic nature of the development of life courses. See Green, T. H. (1883) in Bradley, A. C. (ed.) *Prolegomena to Ethics*. Oxford: Clarendon Press.

4 This generalisation may apply less completely to countries such as the USA owing to the American culture of public discussion of moral and subjective issues. On the other hand, the generation conflict sometimes alleged to be occurring in the USA is not yet general in Ireland.

5 Edmondson, Ricca (1994) 'The Impact of Context and the Transformation of Plans: The Case of Older People', paper to European Consortium for Political Research Joint Sessions, Madrid.

6 Arensberg, Conrad and Kimball, Solon (1940) *Family and Community in Ireland*. Cambridge, Mass: Harvard University Press, p. 158.

7 *Ibid*., pp. 167–8.

8 Like other witnesses to Irish rural society this century, Arensberg and Kimball preface their account of older people by drawing attention to the extreme domination of the father in rural life:

> Here there is an absolute coincidence of 'social' and economic' factors within single relationships. In the case of a small farmer and his son, there is only one relationship; to separate their social from their economic activities is meaningless (p. 62) . . . In the Irish family, the sons and the daughters are equally subordinate; there is no formal distinction made between them . . . Rural Ireland knows neither primogeniture nor junior right. Except as age differences separate them informally, the brothers occupy the same status both within and outside the family group. Thus neighbours and other outsiders refer to them all alike as 'the boys' of the farmer's family (p. 63) . . . In choosing the son to remain upon the farm, the father has full power of decision (p.65) . . . Similarly with several old bachelors. A nephew moves in and works the farm, but the old fellow keeps strict control even to regulating the nephew's expenditures for amusement (p. 69).

These relationships of what the authors term extreme superordination and extreme subordination include the supervision by the elderly of the sexual and reproductive lives of their children. It is the father who is chiefly instrumental in matchmaking (see p. 109). He decides when to give over his farm to the heir he has chosen to inherit, and the other children must remain celibate or leave the farm, often for emigration. The father then selects a suitable wife for the son to remain: 'the initiative in the matter lies with the owner of the farm, usually the father of the boy'. One of the author's respondents, a lady now in her eighties, remembers with considerable scorn the time when the men making a match would pace the land, 'valuing every bit of scrub and bush for what it was worth'; she recalls their deliberations as 'ridiculous' but the fact remains that they had it in their power who married whom. Another lady in her eighties told me, 'I didn't want to get married but my father wouldn't let me stop at home'. However, there is no evidence that she regretted the course her life subsequently took. See Arensberg and Kimball (1940) *op. cit.*

9 Hareven, Tamara (1982) 'The Life Course and Aging in Historical Perspective', in T. Hareven, and K. Adams (eds) *Ageing and Life Course Transitions: An Interdisciplinary Perspective*. London: Tavistock, pp.1–26.

10 Brown, T. (1985) *Ireland: A Social and Cultural History* (2nd edn). London: Fontana.

11 Murphy, T. (1986) *Bailegangáire*. Dublin. Gallery Press.

12 Heath, A. (1981) *Social Mobility*. Glasgow, Collins; Clancy, P., Drudy, S., Lynch, K. and O'Dowd, L. (1995) *Irish Society: Sociological Perspectives*. Dublin: Institute For Public Administration.

13 Finch, J. (1989) *Family Obligations and Social Change*. Cambridge: Polity Press.

14 Breen, R., Hanan, D., Rottman, D. and Whelan, Christopher (1990) *Understanding Contemporary Ireland*. Houndmills: Macmillan.

15 O'Shea, E., Donnison, D., Larragy, J. *et al.* (1991) *The Role and Future Development of Nursing Homes in Ireland*. Dublin: National Council for the Elderly.

16 *Ibid.*

17 In the state of Arizona, for example, proportions of elderly people are so considerable that it is claimed that they are in a position to determine the outcome of elections.

18 See Lundström, F. and McKeown, K. (1994) *Home Help Services for Elderly People in Ireland*. Dublin: National Council for the Elderly. Research by Jennifer Oren shows that it is not possible to use ordinary channels to obtain reliable information about how many older people in Ireland are helped, how and to what extent, by whom. Though some Health Boards, such as the Eastern Health Board, provide relatively detailed overall accounts of their activities, others give only vague indications of the extent of their work and specific research projects (such as Lundström and McKeown's) are need to discover what actually happens.

19 Guillemard, Anne-Marie (1986) 'Social Policy and Ageing in France', in Phillipson, C. and Walker, A. (eds) *Ageing and Social Policy: A Critical Assesment*. London: Gower, pp. 263–79.

20 Agencies such as the National Council on Ageing and Older People and many others attempt to fill some gaps and do excellent work, but it is questionable to what extent they can be expected to compensate for this type of democratic deficit.

21 Victor, C. (1991) *Health and Health Care in Later Life*. Buckingham: Open University Press.

22 Deborah Stone insists rightly that 'policy-making is a constant discursive struggle over the criteria of social classification, the boundaries of problem categories, the intersubjective interpretation of common experiences, the conceptual framing of problems, and the definitions of ideas that guide the ways people create the shared meanings which motivate them to act. These discursive struggles involve far more than manipulative rhetoric. The institutionally disciplined rhetorics of policy and planning influence

problem selection as well as problem analysis, organisational identity as well as administrative strategy and public access as well as public understanding. Stone, D. (1988) *Policy Paradox and Political Reason*. Glenview, Ill.: Scott Forestman, pp. 1–2.

23 Policy constitutes attitudes and behaviour differentially as it refers to those who make policy, those who are directly affected by it and the general public. These related phenomena should be a subject of empirical study themselves.

24 Edmondson, R. (1984) *Rhetoric in Sociology*. London: Macmillan.

25 Berger, J. (1967) *The Sacred Canopy*. Garden City, N.Y.: Doubleday.

26 Phillipson, C. (1993) 'The Sociology of Retirement', in J. Bond *et al.* (eds) *Ageing in Society*. London: Sage, pp.180–99.

27 Fischer, F. and Forester, J. (eds) (1993) *The Argumentative Turn in Policy Analysis and Planning*. London: UCL Press, p. 2.

28 Walker, A. (1993) 'Poverty and Inequality in Old Age', in J. Bond *et al.* (eds) *Ageing in Society*. London: Sage, pp. 280–303.

29 Neugarten B. and Neugarten D. (1986) 'Changing Meanings of Age', pp. 33–52 in Alan Pifer and Lydia Bronte (eds) *Our Aging Society: Paradox and Promise*. New York, Norton.

30 *Ibid.*

31 Mayer, K. U. and Müller, W. (1986) 'The State and the Structure of the Life-Course' in Sorensen, A. B., Weilnert, E. and Sherrod, L. (eds) *Human Development and the Life-Course, Multidisciplinary Perspectives*. Hillsdale, NJ: Erlbaum Publishers.

32 Phillipson, C. and Walker, A. (eds) (1986) *Ageing and Social Policy: A Critical Assesment*. London: Gower.

33 Walker (1986) *op. cit.*

34 The director of a social services centre in Berlin said of one elderly lady who was crippled but had continued to knit and sew, 'It was handcrafts that saved her life' (interview, July 1997). The woman in question had used these resources to remain connected to socially respected activity in her setting.

35 Phillipson (1993) *op. cit.*

36 Breen *et al.* (1990) *op. cit.*

37 Fahey, T. and Murray, P. (1994) *Health and Autonomy Among the Over-65s in Ireland*. Dublin: National Council for the Elderly.

38 O'Shea, E. (1993) *The Impact of Social and Economic Policies on Older People in Ireland*. Dublin: National Council for the Elderly.

39 *Sunday Times*, 21.1.1996.

40 Guillemard (1986) *op. cit.*

41 Whelan, C. T. and Whelan, B. J. (1988) *The Transition to Retirement*. Dublin: Economic and Social Research Institute.

42 For instance, the *Irish Times* (8.7.1995, p. 14) reported that the AIB was offering severance packages to everyone over 50 in a strategy intended to save money for the organisation. This is not to say that early retirement is never a welcome option – mortality figures indicated that it may help to

save lives in some cases. The question is how to combine the possibility of early retirement with a recognition that older people are as capable of positive contributions as anyone else, and is some cases, more so.

43 The government minister who at one point referred to them as 'antechambers to death' was forced to recant.

44 Harries, K. (1997) *The Ethical Function of Architecture*. Cambridge, Mass: MIT Press.

45 One indicator of public expectations about older people is given by the leisure activities for older people supported by public organisations in the Republic. These tend to characteristically take the form of bingo sessions, rather than allowing bingo to form part of a palette of options.

46 O'Shea *et al.* (1991) *op. cit.*

47 Interview by author 1995.

48 Western Health Board (WHB) (1985) *Services for the Aged*. Galway: WHB, pp. 12–13.

49 *Ibid.*, p. 13.

50 *Ibid.*, p. 16.

51 *Ibid.*, pp. 16–17.

52 Dr A., interview April 1995.

53 O'Shea (1993) *op. cit.*

54 O'Shea *et al.* (1991) *op. cit.*

55 Department of Health (1988) *The Years Ahead: A Report of the Working Party on Services for the Elderly*. Dublin: GPSO.

56 Anderson, R. (1992) 'Promoting Health in the Elderly', pp. 45–56, in C. Kelleher (ed.) *The Future for Health Promotion*. Galway: Centre for Health Promotion Studies.

57 A number of writers have drawn attention to the fact that it seemed unassailably reasonable to the Victorians to relate their caring to economies of scale; in contrast, in the past thirty years or so, this notion of reasonableness has been virtually demolished. The transient power of assumptions about reasonableness is exhibited again in works such as that by Cumming and Henry. The authors describe their study as having started in a circle of 'friends, colleagues and a handful of very old people', among whom ideas were started about what 'healthy, economically secure old people' are 'like'; these ideas were applied to the wider group of the survey, in a shuttle process of cross-fertilisation with the original idea – namely that old age involves progressive 'disengagement' from the mainstream of society. In their work, the authors unintentionally reify a specific social world, assuming that its particular attitudes are universal. See Cumming, E. and Henry, W. (1961) *Growing Old: The Process of Disengagement*. New York: Basic Books.

58 Contrast Kaim-Caudle's words: 'The term Social Policy may be taken to imply conduct based on deliberation, action brought about as the result of decision influenced by ideology. This is an over-simplification in most countries; social policy in practice is largely the result of historical accident, the operation of pressure groups, and the determination and

ability of outstanding personalities . . . Insurance Companies and Medical Associations have in all countries attempted to influence social security legislation. In few have they been as successful as the Republic. The influence of the church on government social policy in the state is certainly very pronounced in all stages of education. Little is known about its influence in the other spheres with the exception of one famous incident – the Mother and Child Bill – in the early 1950s. The level and scope of the services in the Republic is limited by the unfavourable age structure, the comparatively low GNP per head and the peculiar (by European standards) employment structure . . . This framework hardly encourages the building of a Welfare Society.' In relation to clerical contributions, Kaim-Caudle refers to the stimulating influence of the Bishop of Clonfert, Dr Dignan, in suggesting reform to social insurance and health services (p. 40) away from the 'degrading' poor-law model in operation in the 1940s (p. 27). He might also have mentioned the influence of Archbishop McQuaid on the development of social work in the same period. Policy on ageing is not referred to extensively in Kaim-Caudle's text except for occasional references to the age at which the Old Age Pension could be received – at 70 (see pp. 62–7). 'Old age pensions amount to approximately one third of the minimum wage of an agricultural worker and to about a sixth of male industrial earnings' (p. 67). See Kaim-Caudle, P. (1967) *Social Policy in the Irish Republic*. London, Routledge and Kegan Paul.

59 Lundström and McKeown (1994) *op. cit.*

60 *Ibid.*, p. 6.

61 Breen *et al.* (1990) *op. cit.*, p. 78.

62 *Ibid.*, pp. 88, 96.

63 *Ibid.*, p. 97.

64 WHB (1995) *op. cit.*, p. 6.

65 *Ibid.*, p. 11.

66 *Ibid.*, pp. 11–12.

67 Eastern Health Board (EHB) (1995) *Review of Services for the Elderly and Four-Year Action Plan 1995–1998*. Dublin, p. 1.

68 *Idem.*

69 The European Foundation for the Improvement of Living and Working Conditions has issued two working papers (numbers WP/91/EN and WP/95/33/EN) which begin to address the issue of older people in employment; but employment issues in Europe are currently so confused that it would be unwise to expect policies beneficial to older people to emerge without considerable pressure.

70 EHB (1995) *op. cit.*, p. 25.

71 *Ibid.*, p. 38.

72 Lundström and McKeown (1994) *op. cit.*

73 Fahey and Murray (1994) *op. cit.*

74 EHB (1995) *op. cit.*, p. 21.

75 See for example EHB (1995) *op. cit.*, p. 69.

76 EHB (1995) *op. cit.*, p. 45.
77 There isn't yet much recurrent, systematic evidence of ill-treatment of older people in various forms of care, familial or otherwise, but this is partly because the topic remains profoundly under-researched. In one interview by the author, an ex-nurse said that she had left her profession because of its persistent (though unintentional) humiliation and neglect of older people whose dignity might on occasion be affronted to the extent of influencing matters of life and death for them. Until more public debate takes place about appropriate standards of care and support, it will remain impossible to respond adequately to such claims.
78 O'Shea, E. (1992) *Coming of Age in Europe*. Brussels: Directorate-General 5, European Commission.
79 This is reflected in the theories of ageing by author such as Erikson, E. H., Erikson, J. M., Kivnick, H. Q. (1986) *Vital Involvement in Old Age: the Experience of Old Age in Our Time*. New York: Norton; Laslett, P. (1992) A Fresh Map of Life: the Emergence of the Third Age. London: Weidenfeld and Nicolson; Young, M. and Schuller, T. (1991) *Life After Work: The Arrival of the Ageless Society*. London: HarperCollins.
80 One bank manager in another European country whom I asked to estimate how often older clients of his were forced or encouraged to disgorge funds by relatives suggested 10% as a possible figure. It is not clear how the veracity of this witness is itself affected by the fact that he himself then attempted to buy property from an elderly lady at considerably less than market value.
81 Note 19 p. 180
82 Whelan and Whelan (1988) *op. cit.*
83 note 20
84 Harries (1997) *op. cit.*

Chapter 6

1 Government of Ireland (1989) *National Development Plan, 1989–1993*. Dublin: Stationery Office, p. 65.
2 *Ibid.*, p. 75.
3 *Ibid.*, p. 69.
4 Crickley, A. and M. Devlin (1990) 'Community Work in the Eighties – An Overview'. In *Community Work in Ireland: Trends in the 80's, Options for the 90s*. Dublin: Combat Poverty Agency, p. 54.
5 Hirst, P. (1994) *Associative Democracy: New Forms of Economic and Social Governance*. Oxford: Polity Press.
6 O'Donovan, O. and T. Varley (1995) *Paid Employment in the Voluntary Sector: A Review of the Literature*. Galway: Centre for Public Policy Studies Working Paper, SSRC, University College Galway.
7 Midgley, J. (1986) *Community Participation, Social Development, and the State*. London: Methuen, p. 35.
8 *Ibid.*, p. 38.

9 This communitarian populist ideal of participation resembles in certain respects the 'ideal speech situation' of Habermas in which equal access to relevant information and equal opportunity to participate in debates is open to all participants. See Habermas, J. (1984) *The Theory of Communicative Action, Reason and the Rationalisation of Society*. Oxford: Polity Press and (1987) *The Theory of Communicative Action, II. A Critique of Functionalist Reason*. Oxford: Polity Press.

10 Olson, who argues that individuals as a rule will be unwilling to bear the costs of collective actions if they can avoid it and if they can hope to gain without participating, provides what has become the classical account of the free riding phenomenon. See Olson, M. (1968) *The Logic of Collective Action: Public Goods and the Theory of Groups*. New York: Schocken Books.

11 An argument along these lines would be consistent with Eipper's account (1986) of Bantry which portrays a town as effectively in the tight grip of a 'ruling trinity' of businessmen, politicians and Catholic priests. The coalition thus put together is presented as capable of dominating the representation of the locality, though not the entire arena of local community action. Eipper, C. (1986) *The Ruling Trinity. A Community Study of Church, State and Business in Ireland*. Aldershot: Gower.

12 The impact membership of the EU has had across a wide range of Irish policy areas has much impressed the commentators. O'Halpin's general review notes how 'in recent years an increasing number of the decisions that matter have come to be taken at European Community level'. The 'major impetus for rural development in the Republic in the 1980s is traced by Commins to the difficulties being experienced at EU level with the CAP and the decision to adopt the SEM project. See O'Halpin, E. (1992) 'Policy Making'. In Coakley, J. and M. Gallagher (eds) *Politics in the Republic of Ireland*. Galway: PSAI Press; Commins, P. (1993) 'Rural Development in the Republic of Ireland'. In Murray, M. and J. Greer, (eds) *Rural Development in Ireland*. Aldershot: Avebury.

13 European Commission (1988) *The Future of Rural Society*. Brussels: European Commission.

14 Kearney, B., Boyle, G. E. and J. A. Walsh (1994) *EU LEADER I Initiative in Ireland; Evaluation and Recommendations*. Dublin: Department of Agriculture, Food and Forestry, pp. 9–10.

15 LEADER I, which was to operate during the 1991–94 period and was to be followed by LEADER II (1995–99), became the first of a series of special EU inspired rural development programmes. It had been preceded in Ireland by the Department of Agriculture and Food's Pilot Programme for Integrated Rural Development (1988–90). See O'Malley, E. (1992) *The Pilot Programme for Integrated Rural Development 1988–90*. Dublin: The Economic and Social Research Institute.

16 Almost 20% of the Republic's estimated labour force was out of work by 1992–93. See McCarthy, C. (1993) 'A Review of the Crisis'. In C. Keane (ed.) *The Jobs Crisis*. Cork: Mercier Press.

17 See Nolan, B., Whelan, C. T. and J. Williams (1998) *Where are Poor Households? The Spatial Distribution of Poverty and Deprivation in Ireland.* Dublin: Oak Tree Press in association with Combat Poverty Agency, for a critique of the reasoning behind area based interventions in Ireland.

18 Initially in 1991, £500,000 was made available to cover staffing costs; the projects became eligible to draw down global grant funding in 1992.

19 The tradition of social analysis out of which notions of 'social exclusion' have come are usefully discussed in Room, G. (1995) 'Poverty in Europe: Competing Paradigms of Analysis', *Policy and Politics*, 23 (2): 103–13 and in Shucksmith, M. and P. Chapman (1998) 'Rural Development and Social Exclusion', *Sociologia Ruralis*, 38 (2): 225–242.

20 Poverty 3, Central Unit, 'Community Programme to Foster Economic and Social Integration of the Least Privileged Groups up to the year 2000', Conference on Combatting Social Exclusion, Fostering Integration, Brussels, 2–3 April 1992.

21 Officially there were sixteen groups but a process of segmentation quickly resulted in one group effectively operating as two separate entities.

22 The LEADER I territories in Ireland were essentially new spatial units, though sometimes they did coincide with existing local authority boundaries. One partnership area, for example, extended across two whole counties (Cavan and Monaghan). Two others covered single counties. (See Kearney *et al.* (1994) *op. cit.*, pp. 4–5.) On average, £2.04 million was allocated per group but the money actually distributed ranged from £60,000 (in the case of Erris) to £3,200,000 (in Dulhallow/West Cork) at the time of evaluation.

23 Kearney *et al.* (1994) *op. cit.*, p. 103.

24 *Idem.*

25 Kearney *et al.* (1994) *op. cit.*, p. 109.

26 *Idem.*

27 *Idem.*

28 The specific suggestion of the LEADER I evaluators is that 'the community representatives are sometimes not sufficiently skilled to enable them to participate effectively in a formal Board, especially when confronted by more skilful representatives of the statutory sector on whom they depend for many resources'. See Kearney *et al.* (1994) *op. cit.*, p. 110.

29 Kearney *et al.* (1994) *op. cit.*, p. 110.

30 *Idem.* Also see Frazer, H. (1996) 'The Role of Community Development in Local Development'. In P. Conroy *et al. Partnership in Action: The Role of Community Development and Partnership in Ireland.* Galway: The Community Workers' Co-operative, pp. 41–2.

31 *Info-LEADER*, No. 27, September 1994, pp. 1–2.

32 LEADER II, *The Future of Rural Ireland*, July 1993, p. 16.

33 This requirement to supply matching funds, in the view of some interviewed activists, worked in such a way as to ensure that LEADER's impact on combating social exclusion could only be negative. Walsh, J., Craig, S. and D. McCafferty (1998) *Local Partnership for Social Inclusion?*

Dublin: Oak Tree Press in association with Combat Poverty Agency.

34 At this point, too, the National Co-ordinating Committee went out of existence to be replaced by the ADM executive. It was to the Department of the Taoiseach and to a new Inter-departmental Committee on Local Development that ADM became answerable. Craig, S. with K. McKeown (1994) *Progress Through Partnership: Final Evaluation Report on the PESP Pilot Initiative on Long-term Unemployment*. Dublin: Combat Poverty Agency, pp. 95–9.

35 The same is no longer true of the present-day generation of ADM sponsored partnerships. See European Social Fund Evaluation Unit (1999) *ESF and the Local Urban and Rural Development Operational Programme*. Dublin: European Social Fund Evaluation Unit, pp. 149–51.

36 Craig (1994) *op. cit.*, p. 32.

37 *Ibid.*, pp. 20, 31–2; Combat Poverty Agency (1995) *Community Participation: A Handbook for Individuals and Groups in Local Development Partnerships*. Dublin: Combat Poverty Agency, pp. 4, 9–24.

38 Craig (1994) *op. cit.*, p. 90.

39 *Idem*. Sabel, C. (1996) *Ireland: Local Partnerships and Social Innovation*. Paris: OECD, pp. 82–4.

40 Craig (1994) *op. cit.*, p. 63; Webster, C. M. (1991) 'How Far Can You Go? The Role of the Statutory Sector in Developing Community Partnership'. Unpublished MA thesis, University College Galway, p. 58.

41 O'Reilly, P. (1994) 'Whose Plan Is It Anyway? Struggles Over the Attribution of Meaning in the Planning Process'. Unpublished MA thesis, Department of Political Science and Sociology, University College Galway, p. 189.

42 With a budget amounting to £1,733,869, the Forum project was able to support a complement of seven full-time and eleven part-time paid staff when operating at full tilt.

43 Mernagh, M. and P. Commins (1997) *In From the Margins: Social Inclusion in the Europe of the New Millennium: Some Lessons from Poverty 3*. Dublin: Research and Development Unit, SICCDA.

44 Lumb, R. (1990) 'Rural Community Development: Process versus Product'. In Henry Buller and Susan Wright (eds) *Rural Development: Problems and Practices*. Aldershot: Avebury.

45 Rolston contends that such a state of affairs has already been substantially realised in Northern Ireland.

46 Kearney *et al.* (1994) *op. cit.*, p. 109.

47 *Ibid.*, pp. 115–16.

48 Barrington, T. (1975) *From Big Government to Local Government*. Dublin: Institute of Public Administration.

49 As the case of church controlled education makes clear, the same cannot be said of all sections of the Irish voluntary sector. See Breen *et al.* (1990) *op. cit.*

50 Varley, T. (1991) 'Power to the People? Community Groups and Rural Revival in Ireland'. In Reynolds, B. and S. Healy (eds) *Rural Development*

Policy: What Future for Rural Ireland? Dublin: Conference of Major Religious Superiors; Webster (1991) *op. cit.*

51 See *Sunday Independent*, 14.2.1993.

52 See *Irish Times*, 7.11.1997; *Sunday Tribune*, 15.6.1997; *Operating Rules for LEADER II* (Department of Agriculture and Food, Circular No. 24/97, 20.11.1997).

53 See *Sunday Tribune*, 15.6.1997.

54 Haase, T., McKeown, K. and S. Rourke (1996) *Local Development Strategies for Disadvantaged Areas: Evaluation of the Global Grant, 1992–1995*. Dublin: Area Development Management Limited, p. 92.

55 *Idem.*

56 Adshead, M. (1996) 'Beyond Clientelism: Agricultural Networks in Ireland and the EU', *West European Politics*, Vol. 19, no. 3, pp. 583–608.

57 Craig (1994) *op. cit.*, p. 31.

58 For a discussion of some of the dynamics of paid work in Irish community action, see O'Donovan and Varley (1995) *op. cit.*

59 Walsh *et al.* point out, in relation to LEADER in Kerry, that the 'ability of a locally based group to determine the allocation of significant project funding . . . created a very high degree of interest among the community at large and expectations on the part of the community of their directors'. See Walsh *et al.* (1995) *op. cit.*

60 Kearney *et al.* (1994) p. 115.

61 Frustration seems to have arisen very considerably with the tightening of bureaucratic control under LEADER II (see *Sunday Tribune*, 15.6.1997).

62 The new wave of women's groups presents what is arguably the best contemporary example among community based groups. Not only have these increased dramatically in number, but they have also begun a process of constituting themselves as regionally and nationally organised interests (see O'Donovan and Ward (1999) O'Donovan, O. and E. Ward (1999) 'Networks of Women's Groups in the Republic of Ireland' in Galligan, Y., Ward, E. and R. Wilford (eds) *Contesting Politics: Women in Ireland, North and South*. Boulder, Colorado: Westview Press in association with PSAI Press). As this strand of community action has flourished, the much older national federation of organised rural women, the Irish Countrywomen's Association, whose appeal nowadays appears to be confined to older women in the main, has entered a period of contraction and decline.

63 At the 1994 conference of the Community Workers' Co-operative in Kilkenny, it was agreed that 'if the Government was committed to partnership, then the [community] sector must be accorded social partner status and included in bodies from which the sector had been so far excluded'. Watt, P. (1997) 'The Community Platform'. In Fahy, K. (ed.) *Strategies to Encourage Participation*. Galway: Community Workers Co-operative, p. 67.

64 Much the same tendency is to be found in Northern Ireland (see Kearney, J. (1997) 'Achieving Equality for the Voluntary and Community Sector in Policy Making'. In K. Fahy (ed.) *Equality Policies and Social Change*.

Galway: Community Workers Co-operative and Northern Ireland Council for Voluntary Action; Rolston, B. (1997) 'Overview of Community Development in Northern Ireland', *Inishowen Development Journal*, Summer: pp. 15–19). O'Donnell and Thomas suggest that the broadening of the existing social partnership framework in the south to make room for the community and voluntary sector '. . . was certainly encouraged by the growth in stature and standing of some third-pillar groups as a result of their performance both within NESF and in local-level partnership initiatives. They had, moreover, garnered considerable support for national level inclusion amongst the key players, including the leadership of ICTU, the senior civil servants in the Departments of the Taoiseach and Tánaiste and also critically from across the political spectrum, as all of the party leaders had articulated the need to develop a broader-based national consensus'. See O'Donnell, R. and D. Thomas (1998) 'Partnership and Policy-Making', in Healy, S. and B. Reynolds, (eds) *Social Policy in Ireland: Principles, Practice and Problems*. Dublin: Oak Tree Press, p.127. See also McCarthy, D. (1998) 'The Genesis and Evolution of the Irish State's Commitment to Social Partnership at Local Level'. In P. Kirby and D. Jacobson (eds) *In the Shadow of the Tiger: New Approaches to Combating Social Exclusion*. Dublin: Dublin City University Press. Also see NESF (1997) *A Framework for Partnership – Enriching Strategic Consensus through Participation, Forum Report No. 16*. Dublin: National Economic and Social Forum, pp. 112–14.

65 These include the Structural Fund Operational Programme monitoring committees, the National Economic and Social Forum, the Advisory Committee for the Local Employment Service, the Partnership 2000 agreement, the Task Force on the Travelling Community, the Commission on the Status of People with Disabilities, the Irish National Committee for the European Year Against Racism and the National Anti-Poverty Strategy.

66 In the run-up to Partnership 2000, a broad alliance of mainly community based groups, all united around the aim of 'furthering the interests of those experiencing poverty and exclusion', was assembled as the Community Platform. Community Platform (1997) *Achieving Social Partnership: The Strategy and Proposals of the Community Platform at the Partnership 2000 Negotiations*. Dublin: The Community Platform, pp. 7–34).

67 O'Cearbhaill, D. and T. Varley (1998) 'Community Group/State Relationships: The Case of West of Ireland Community Councils'. In R. Byron (ed.) *Public Policy and the Periphery: Problems and Prospects in Marginal Regions*. Belfast: Association for the Study of Marginal Regions.

68 See also Sabel (1996) *op. cit*., pp. 85–6; *Task Force on Integration of Local Government and Local Development Systems* (1998) Dublin: Department of the Environment and Local Government, p. 10. This is not to say that the advent of the area partnerships has not been turned into another resource in the hands of clientelist minded politicians. A number of instances can

be pointed to where the selection of partnership sites was given a clientelist spin by senior politicians, claiming to have used their power to influence siting decisions.

69 Government of Ireland (1996) *Better Local Government: A Programme for Change*. Dublin: The Stationery Office, pp. 26–32.

70 Department of the Environment (1996) *Better Local Government: A Programme for Change*. Dublin: The Stationery Office, p. 27.

71 Task Force (1998) *op. cit.*, p. 14.

72 i., p. 15.

73 Pickvance, C. and E. Preteceille (1991) 'Introduction: The Significance of Local Power in Theory and Practice'. In Pickvance, C. and E. Preteceille (eds) *State Restructuring and Local Power*. London: Pinter.

74 In discussing 'the dialectic of local development' in one of the Scottish LEADER I areas (the Western Isles, Skye and Lochalsh), where 'the discourses of the Gael and crofting were prominent on the policy agenda by the time that LEADER I was announced', Ray goes so far as to suggest that in certain respects the initiative 'was co-opted by the local context' (original emphasis). See Ray, C. (1996) *The Dialectic of Local Development: The Case of the EU LEADER I Rural Development Programme*. Newcastle: Centre for Rural Economy, Department of Agricultural Economics and Food Marketing, University of Newcastle upon Tyne, p. 28.

75 The recent verdict Walsh *et al.* arrive at, in their account of the South Kerry Development Partnership, is that 'while the exercise of decision-making has not been without its difficulties for local community representatives, the general feeling is that it is infinitely preferable to the remote decision-making which has shaped the fortunes of the area in the past. Both the confidence and sense of responsibility of the communities have been boosted and this has led to a greatly increased level of activity. A number of new community groups has been set up, and established groups that were inactive have been revitalised as a result of the general stimulus that the Partnership has provided. As a result, the capacity of the area to engage in development activity has been enhanced'. See Walsh *et al.* (1998) *op. cit*, p. 219. O'Neill relates, in a similar fashion, how the prospect of LEADER funding inspired the creation of five of the thirty-one local community organisations he studied in south-west Mayo. See O'Neill, G. (1997) 'A Study of the Involvement of Local Community Organisations in the LEADER Rural Development Programme in South-west Mayo, 1991–1994'. Unpublished MRD thesis, Department of Economics, University College, Galway, p. 33.

76 Long, N. (1992) 'From Paradigm Lost to Paradigm Regained? The Case for the Actor-oriented Sociology of Development'. In Long, N. and A. Long (eds) *Battlefields of Knowledge: The Interlocking of Theory and Practice and Social Research and Development*. London: Routledge, pp. 20, 24; Arce, A. and N. Long (1992) 'The Dynamics of Knowledge: Interfaces between Bureaucrats and Peasants'. In N. Long and A. Long (eds) *Battle-*

fields of Knowledge: The Interlocking of Theory and Practice and Social Research and Development. London: Routledge; Lipsky, M. (1980) *Street-Level Bureaucracy: Dilemmas of the Individual in Public Service*. New York: Russell Sage Foundation.

77 Craig (1994) *op. cit.*, p. 78.

78 *Ibid.*, p. 95. It seems that 30% of ESF spending on the Irish area partnerships in 1997, as funnelled through ADM, went on 'community development actions'. ESF (1999) *op. cit.*, p. xvi.

79 O'Hara, P. and P. Commins (1998) 'Rural Development: Towards the New Century'. In Healy, S. and B. Reynolds (eds) *Social Policy in Ireland: Principles, Practice and Problems*. Dublin: Oak Tree Press, p. 274.

80 O'Reilly (1994) *op. cit.* p. 137. Nine of the twelve partnership board chairpersons appear to have had business backgrounds. See Craig (1994) *op. cit.*, p. 22.

81 A number of breaches of the guidelines regarding the funding of certain types of excluded projects (golf courses and conventional retail services are examples) have been documented. Office of the Comptroller and Auditor General (1995) *The LEADER Programme*. Dublin: Stationery Office, p. 17.

82 See *Irish Times*, 27.9.1994.

83 Craig (1994) *op. cit.*, p. 120. Frazer (1996) *op. cit.*, pp. 48–9.

84 Faughnan, P., McEvoy, M. and P. Tobin (eds) (1997) *Gender Equality in the Partnerships: Women's Experience*. Dublin: CAN (Community Action Network), p. 8.

85 Haase *et al.* (1996) *op. cit.*, p. 87.

86 A recent evaluation of the ESF funded partnerships in Ireland provides a qualified endorsement. See ESF (1999) *op. cit.*

87 Sabel (1996) *op. cit.*, p. 11.

Bibliography

Adnett, N. (1995) 'Social Dumping and European Economic Integration', *Journal of European Social Policy*, Vol. 5, no. 1, pp. 1–12.

Adshead, M. (1996) 'Beyond Clientelism: Agricultural Networks in Ireland and the EU', *West European Politics,* Vol. 19, no. 3, pp. 583–608.

Alber, J. (1988) 'Continuation and Change in the Idea of Welfare State', *Policy and Society*, Vol. 16, no. 4, pp. 451–68.

——(1995) 'A Framework for the Comparative Study of Social Services', *Journal of European Social Policy*, Vol. 5, no. 2, pp. 131–149.

Allen, R., and T. Jones (1990) *Guests of the Nation; People of Ireland versus the Multi-nationals*, London: Earthscan Publications.

Anderson, R. (1992) 'Promoting Health in the Elderly', pp. 45–56, in C. Kelleher (ed.) *The Future for Health Promotion.* Galway: Centre for Health Promotion Studies.

Anttonen, A. and J. Sipila (1996) 'European Social Care Services: Is it Possible to Identify Models?' *Journal of European Social Policy*, Vol. 6, no. 2, pp. 87–100.

Area Development Management Limited (1994) *Annual Report 1993.* Dublin: ADM.

Arce, A. and N. Long (1992) 'The Dynamics of Knowledge: Interfaces between Bureaucrats and Peasants', in N. Long and A. Long (eds) *Battlefields of Knowledge: The Interlocking of Theory and Practice and Social Research and Development*. London: Routledge.

Arensberg, Conrad and Kimball, Solon (1940) *Family and Community in Ireland.* Cambridge, Mass: Harvard University Press.

Atkinson, A. B. (1992) 'Social Policy, Economic Organisation and the Search for a Third Way', in Ferge, Z. and J. E. Kolberg (eds) *Social Policy in a Changing Europe*. Frankfurt am Main, Campus Verlag.

Atkinson, A. B. (1993) 'Conclusion', in A. B. Atkinson and G. V. Mogensen (eds) *Welfare and Work Incentives – A North European Perspective*. Oxford: Clarendon Press.

Baker, S. (1988) 'Dependent Industrialisation and Political Protest: Raybestos Manhatten in Ireland'. *Government and Opposition*, Vol. 22, no. 3, pp. 352–358.

Barr, N. (1993) *The Economics of the Welfare State* (2nd edn). London: Weidenfeld and Nicolson.

Barrington, T. (1975) *From Big Government to Local Government*. Dublin: Institute of Public Administration.

Barry, F. (1991) 'Irish Recovery 1987–90: Economic Miracle?' *Irish Banking Review*, Winter.

——(ed.) (1999) *Understanding Ireland's Economic Growth*, London and New York: Macmillan.

——and M. B. Devereux (1995) 'The Expansionary Fiscal Contraction Hypothesis: A Neo-Keynesian Analysis', *Oxford Economic Papers*, Vol. 47.

——and Bradley, J. and E. O'Malley (1999) 'Indigenous and Foreign Industry: Characteristics and Performance', in F. Barry (ed.) *Understanding Ireland's Economic Growth*, London and New York: Macmillan.

Barry, U. and Jackson, P. (1989) 'Women's Employment and Multinationals in Ireland; The Creation of a New Female Labour Force', in D. Eleson and R. Pearson (eds) *Women's Employment and Multi-nationals in Europe*, Macmillan, London.

Benson, F. L. and Associates, Matheson Ormsby and Prentice and Ove Arup (1992) 'The Impact of Planning, Licensing and Environmental Issues on Industrial Development; A Report to the Industrial Policy Review Group'. Stationery Office, Dublin.

Berger, J. (1967) *The Sacred Canopy*. Garden City, NY: Doubleday.

Bertola, G. and A. Drazen (1993) 'Trigger Points and Budget Cuts: Explaining the Effects of Fiscal Austerity', *American Economic Review*, Vol. 83, pp. 11–26.

Black, B. (1994) 'Labour Market Incentive Structures and Employee Performance', in *British Journal of Industrial Relations.* Vol. 32–1, pp. 99–111.

Black, W. A. (1993) 'The Contraction of Collective Bargaining in Britain'. *British Journal of industrial Relations*. 31–2, pp. 189–200.

Blackwell, J., O'Shea, E., Moane, G. and P. Murray (1992) *Care Provision and Cost Measurement: Dependent Elderly People at Home and in Geriatric Hospitals*. Dublin: The Economic and Social Research Institute.

Bond, J., Coleman, P., Peace, S. (eds) (1993) *Ageing in Society: an Introduction to Social Gerontology*. London: Sage.

Bonoli, G. (1997) 'Classifying Welfare States: A Two Dimensional Approach', *Journal of Social Policy*, Vol. 26, no. 4, pp. 351–72

Boylan, T. A. (1988) 'Economic Development in a Small Open Economy: Aspects of the Irish Experience', *Manchester Papers on Development*, Vol. 4.

Bradley, J., Whelan, K. and J. Wright (1993) *Stabilisation and Growth in the EC Periphery: A Study of the Irish Economy*, Aldershot: Avebury.

Bradley *et al.* (1997) 'Interpreting the Recent Irish Growth Experience', in Duffy, D., Fitzgerald, J., Kearney, I. and Shorthall, F. (eds) *Medium-Term Review: 1997–2003*. Dublin: Economic and Social Research Institute.

Breen *et al.* (1990) *Understanding Contemporary Ireland: State, Class and Development in the Republic of Ireland*. Dublin: Gill and Macmillan.

Brown, T. (1985) *Ireland: A Social and Cultural History* (2nd edn). London: Fontana.

Brown, W. A. and Walsh, J. (1991) 'Pay Determination in Britain in the 1980s: The Anatomy of Decentralisation', *Oxford Review of Economic Policy*. Vol. 7, pp. 45–59.

Callan, T., Nolan, B., Whelan, B. J., Whelan, C. T. and J. Williams (1996) *Poverty in the 1990s: Evidence from the Living in Ireland Survey*. Dublin: Oak Tree Press.

——and B. Nolan (1998) 'Poverty and Policy', in S. Healy and B. Reynolds (eds) *Social Policy in Ireland: Principles, Practice and Problems*. Dublin: Oak Tree Press.

——and B. Nolan, C. T. Whelan with S. Creighton (1989) *Poverty, Income, and Welfare in Ireland, General Research Series*. Dublin: The Economic and Social Research Institute.

——and O'Donoghue, C. and C. O'Neill (1994) *An Analysis of Basic Income Schemes for Ireland*. Dublin: The Economic and Social Research Institute.

——and Nolan, B., Whelan, B. J., Whelan, C. T and J. Williams (1996a) *Poverty in the 1990s: Evidence from the Living in Ireland Survey*. Dublin: Oak Tree Press.

——and Nolan, B. and C. T. Whelan (1996b) *A Review of the Commission on Social Welfare's Minimum Adequate Income*. Dublin: The Economic and Social Research Institute.

Calmfors, L. (1993) 'Centralisation of Wage Bargaining and Macroeconomic Performance: A Survey', *OECD Working Papers, no 131*.

——and J. Driffel (1988) 'Bargaining Structure, Corporatism and Macroeconomic Performance', *Economic Policy, No. 6*. pp. 14–61.

Caporaso, J. A. (1996) 'The European Union and Forms of State: Westphalian, Regulatory or Post-Modern', *Journal of Common Market Studies*, Vol. 34, no. 1, pp. 29–52.

Central Statistics Office (1996) *Revised Economic Indicators since 1960*. Dublin: Central Statistics Office.

Christoff, P. (1996) 'Ecological Modernisation, Ecological Modernities'. *Environmental Politics*. Vol. 35, no. 3, pp. 476–501

Clarke, S. (1988) 'What in the F****'s Name is Post-Fordism?' in N. Gilbert, R. Burrows and A. Pollert (eds) *Fordism and Flexibility: Divisions and Change*. Basingstoke: Macmillan.

Cohen, G. A. (1993) 'Equality of What? On Welfare, Goods and Capabilities', in M. Nussbaum and A. Sen (eds) *The Quality of Life*. Oxford: Clarendon Press.

Collins, T. (1991) 'Conflict Resolution as an Environmental Management Strategy', in Feehen, J. (ed.) *Environment and Development in Ireland*. Dublin: The Environmental Institute.

Combat Poverty Agency (1995) *Community Participation: A Handbook for Indi-*

viduals and Groups in Local Development Partnerships. Dublin: Combat Poverty Agency.

Commins, P. (1993) 'Rural Development in the Republic of Ireland', in Murray, M. and J. Greer (eds) *Rural Development in Ireland.* Aldershot: Avebury.

Commission on Health Funding (1989) *Report on Health Funding*, Dublin.

Commission on Social Welfare (1986) *Report of the Commission on Social Welfare.* Dublin: Stationery Office.

Community Platform (1997) *Achieving Social Partnership: The Strategy and Proposals of the Community Platform at the Partnership 2000 Negotiations.* Dublin: The Community Platform.

Cousins, M. (1997) 'Ireland's Place in the Worlds of Welfare Capitalism', *Journal of European Social Policy*, Vol. 7, no. 3, pp. 223–235

Coyle, C. (1994) 'Administrative Capacity and the Implementation of EU Environmental Policy in Ireland', in Baker, S., Milton, K. and S. Yearley (eds) *Protecting the Periphery: Environmental Policy in the Peripheral Regions of the European Union.* London: Frank Cass.

Craig, S. with K. McKeown (1994) *Progress Through Partnership: Final Evaluation Report on the PESP Pilot Initiative on Long-term Unemployment.* Dublin: Combat Poverty Agency.

Crickley, A. and M. Devlin (1990) 'Community Work in the Eighties – An Overview', in *Community Work in Ireland: Trends in the 80's, Options for the 90s.* Dublin: Combat Poverty Agency.

Crotty, R. (1986) *Ireland in Crisis: A Study in Capitalist Colonialist Underdevelopment.* Dingle: Bandon Books.

Crowley, E. and J. MacLaughlin (eds) 1997 *Under the Belly of the Tiger: Class, Race, Identify and Culture in the Global Ireland.* Dublin: Irish Reporter Publications.

Culliton, J. (1992) 'A Time for Change: Industrial Policy for the 1990s', *Industrial Policy Review Group.* Dublin: Stationery Office.

Cumming, E. and Henry, W. (1961) *Growing Old: The Process of Disengagement.* New York: Basic Books.

Curtin, C., Haase, T. and H. Tovey (eds) (1996) *Poverty in Rural Ireland; A Political Economy Perspective*, Dublin: Oak Tree Press and Combat Poverty Agency.

Department of Enterprise and Employment (1996) *Growing and Sharing our Employment: Strategy Paper on the Labour Market.* Dublin, Stationery Office.

Department of the Environment (1996) *Better Local Government: A Programme for Change.* Dublin: The Stationery Office.

Department of Health (1988) *The Years Ahead: A Report of the Working Party on Services for the Elderly.* Dublin: GPSO.

Dodd, V. A. and W. S. T. Champ (1993) 'Environmental Problems Associated with Intensive Animal Production Units, with reference to the catchment area of

Lough Sheelin', in Blackwell, J. and F. Convery (eds) *Promise and Performance: Irish Environmental Policies Analysed.* University College Dublin: The Resource and Environmental Policy Centre.

Dore, R. (1988) 'Rigidities in the Labour Market', *Government and Opposition.* Vol. 23, no. 4. pp. 393–412.

Duffy, D., Fitzgerald, J., Kearney, I. and Shorthall, F. (eds) *Medium-Term Review: 1997–2003*, Dublin: Economic and Social Research Institute.

Durkan, J. (1992) 'Social Consensus and Incomes Policy', *Economic and Social Review.* Vol. 23, no. 3, pp. 347–364.

Eastern Health Board (EHB) (1995) *Review of Services for the Elderly and Four-Year Action Plan 1995–1998.* Dublin.

Eckersly, R. (ed.) (1996) *Markets, the State and the Environment.* London: Macmillan.

Edmondson, R. (1984) *Rhetoric in Sociology.* London, Macmillan.

——(1994) 'The Impact of Context and the Transformation of Plans: The Case of Older People', paper to European Consortium for Political Research Joint Sessions, Madrid.

——(1995) 'Critical Ethnography and Policy on Ageing'. UCG: Centre for Public Policy Working Papers, SSRC.

——(1997) 'Older People and Life-Course Construction in Ireland', in Pearl Tracey and Anne Cleary (eds) *Readings in the Sociology of Health and Illness in Ireland.* Dublin: UCD Press.

——and Nullmeier, F. (1997) 'Knowledge and Rhetoric as Contexts for Political Action, in R. Edmondson (ed) *The Political Context of Collective Action: Argumentation, Power and Democracy.* London: Routledge.

Eipper, C. (1986) *The Ruling Trinity. A Community Study of Church, State and Business in Ireland.* Aldershot: Gower.

Environment Council (1980) *A Policy for the Environment.* Dublin: Stationery Office.

Erikson, E. H., Erikson, J. M., Kivnick, H. Q. (1986) *Vital Involvement in Old Age: the Experience of Old Age in Our Time.* New York: Norton.

Esping-Anderson, G. (1990) *The Three Worlds of Welfare Capitalism.* Cambridge: Polity Press.

——(1996a) 'After the Golden Age? Welfare State Dilemmas in a Global Economy'. In G. Esping-Andersen (eds), *Welfare States in Transition: National Adaptations in Global Economies.* London: Sage Publications.

——(1996b) 'Positive-Sum Solutions in a World of Trade–Offs?' In G. Esping-Andersen (ed.) *Welfare States in Transition: National Adaptations in Global Economies.* London: Sage Publications.

Eurobarometer (1993) *Age and Attitudes: Main Results of a Eurobarometer Survey.* Brussels: Directorate-General 5, European Commission.

European Commission (1988) *The Future of Rural Society.* Brussels: European

Commission.
——(1993) *Growth, Competitiveness, Employment: The Challenges and Ways Forward into the 21st Century*. Luxembourg: Office for Official Publications of the European Communities.
——(1994) *European Social Policy: A Way Forward for the Union*. Luxembourg: Directorate General for Employment, Industrial Relations and Social Affairs.
——(1995) *Europe: Social Protection*. Luxembourg: Directorate General for Employment, Industrial Relations and Social Affairs.
——(1998) *Social Protection in Europe 1997*. Luxembourg: Directorate General for Employment, Industrial Relations and Social Affairs.
European Economy (1996) *The Economic and Financial Situation in Ireland: Ireland in the Transition to EMU*, Report and Studies, No. 1, Brussels: European Commission.
European Social Fund Evaluation Unit (1999) *ESF and the Local Urban and Rural Development Operational Programme*. Dublin: European Social Fund Evaluation Unit.
Eurostat (1996) *Social Portrait of Europe*. Luxembourg: Office for Official Publications of the European Communities.
——(1997a) 'Social Protection in the European Union', *Statistics in Focus: Population and Social Conditions* (3).
——(1997b) 'Gross Domestic Product and its Components: First Values for 1996', *Statistics in Focus, Economy and Finance* (1).
Fahey, T. and Murray, P. (1994) *Health and Autonomy Among the Over-65s in Ireland*. Dublin: National Council for the Elderly.
Faughnan, P., McEvoy, M. and P. Tobin (eds) (1997) *Gender Equality in the Partnerships: Women's Experience*. Dublin: CAN (Community Action Network).
Fenlon, R. M. (1993) 'The Water Pollution Control Act: An Evaluation', in Blackwell, J. and F. Convery (eds) *Promise and Performance: Irish Environmental Policies Analysed*. UCD: The Resource and Environmental Policy Centre.
Ferrera, M. (1996) 'The Southern Model of Welfare in Social Europe', *Journal of European Social Policy*, Vol. 6, no. 1, pp. 17–37.
——(1997) 'New Problems, Old Solutions? Recasting Social Protection for the Future of Europe', pp. 119–128, in *European Social Policy Forum: A Summary*. Luxembourg: European Commission.
Finch, J. (1989) *Family Obligations and Social Change*. Cambridge: Polity Press.
Fischer, F. and Forester, J. (eds) (1993) *The Argumentative Turn in Policy Analysis and Planning*. London: UCL Press.
Forfas (1996) *Shaping Our Future*, Dublin: Forfas.
Frazer, H. (1996) 'The Role of Community Development in Local Development', in P. Conroy *et al. Partnership in Action: The Role of Community Development and Partnership in Ireland*. Galway: The Community Workers' Co-operative.
Geary, P. T. (1989) 'The Measurement and Alleviation of Poverty: A Review of

Some Issues', *The Economic and Social Review*, Vol. 20, No. 4.

Giavazzi, F. and M. Pagano (1990) 'Can Fiscal Contractions be Expansionary? Tales of Two Small European Countries', in O. Blanchard and S. Fischer (eds), *The National Bureau of Economic Research, Macroeconomics Annual 1990*, Cambridge, Mass: MIT Press.

Girvin, B. (1989) *Between Two Worlds: Politics and Economy in Independent Ireland*, Dublin: Gill and Macmillan.

Gobeyn, M. J. (1993) 'Explaining the Decline of Macro-Political Bargaining Structures in Advanced Capitalist Societies', *Governance: An International Journal of Policy and Administration*, Vol. 6, pp. 3–22

Goldthorpe, J. (ed.) (1984) *Order and Conflict in Contemporary Capitalism*. Oxford: Clarendon Press.

Gough, I. *et al.* (1997) 'Social Assistance in OECD Countries', *Journal of European Social Policy*, 7 (1), pp. 17–43.

Government of Ireland (1989) *National Development Plan, 1989–1993*. Dublin: Stationery Office.

——(1991) *Programme for Economic and Social Progress*. Dublin: Stationery Office.

——(1993) *Ireland: National Development Plan 1994–1999*. Dublin: Stationery Office.

——(1994) *National Development Plan, 1994–9*. Dublin: Stationery Office.

——(1996) *Better Local Government: A Programme for Change*. Dublin: The Stationery Office.

Grabosky, P. (1996) 'Governing at a Distance: Self-Regulating Green Markets', in Eckersly, R. (ed.) *Markets, the State and the Environment*. London: Macmillan.

Gray, A. (ed.) (1997) *International Perspectives on the Irish Economy*, Dublin: Indecon Economic Consultants.

Green, T. H. (1883) in Bradley, A. C. (ed.) *Prolegomena to Ethics*. Oxford: Clarendon Press.

Greenpeace (1993) *Stop Legal Pollution: The M.V. Solo Irish Tour 1993*. Dublin: Greenpeace Ireland.

Grove-White, R. (1993) 'Environmentalism; A New Moral Discourse for a Technological Society?' in Milton, K. (ed.) *Environmentalism: The View From Anthropology*. London: Routledge.

Guillemard, Anne-Marie (1986) 'Social Policy and Ageing in France', in Phillipson, C. and Walker, A. (eds) *Ageing and Social Policy: A Critical Assesment*. London: Gower, pp. 263–279.

Guiomard, C. (1995) *The Irish Disease and How to Cure It*. Dublin: Oak Tree Press.

Haase, T., McKeown, K. and S. Rourke (1996) *Local Development Strategies for Disadvantaged Areas: Evaluation of the Global Grant, 1992–1995*. Dublin: Area Development Management Limited.

Habermas, J. (1984) *The Theory of Communicative Action, Reason and the Rationalisation of Society*. Oxford: Polity Press.

——(1987) *The Theory of Communicative Action, II. A Critique of Functionalist Reason*. Oxford: Polity Press.

——(1989) *The New Conservatism*. Oxford: Polity Press.

Hardiman, N. (1988) *Pay Politics and Economic Performance in Ireland 1970-87*. Oxford: Clarendon Press.

Hareven, Tamara (1982) 'The Life Course and Aging in Historical Persepctive', in T. Hareven, and K. Adams (eds) *Ageing and Life Course Transitions: An Interdisciplinary Perspective*. London: Tavistock, pp.1–26.

Harney, Mary. (1991) 'The Irish Environmental Protection Agency', in Feehen, J. (ed.) *Environment and Development in Ireland*. Dublin: The Environmental Institute.

Harries, K. (1997) *The Ethical Function of Architecture*. Cambridge, Mass., MIT Press.

Hayek, F. (1960) *The Constitution of Liberty*. London: Routledge.

Healy, S. and Reynolds, B. (1995) 'An Adequate Income Guarantee For All', in Healy, S. and B. Reynolds (eds) *An Adequate Income For All: Desireability, Viability Impact*. Dublin, Conference of Religious of Ireland.

Heath, A. (1981) *Social Mobility*. Glasgow, Collins.

Hills, J. (1993) *The Future of Welfare: A Guide to the Debate*. York: Joseph Rowntree Foundation.

——and Ditch, J. and H. Glennerster (1994) *Beveridge and Social Security*. Clarendon Press. Oxford.

Hirst, P. (1994) *Associative Democracy: New Forms of Economic and Social Governance*. Oxford: Polity Press.

——and J. Zeitlin (1991) 'Flexible Specialisation Versus Post-Fordism: Theory Evidence and Policy Implications', *Economy and Society*. Vol. 20, pp. 1–56.

Honohan, P. (1999) 'Fiscal Adjustment and Disinflation in Ireland: Settling the Macro Basis of Economic Recovery and Expansion', in F. Barry (ed.) *Understanding Ireland's Economic Growth*, London and New York: Macmillan.

Hyman, R. (1987) 'Strategy or Structure: Capital, Labour and Control', *Work Employment and Society*, Vol. 1, no. 1, pp. 25–56.

——(1988) 'Flexible Specialisation: Miracle or Myth?', in R. Hyman and W. Streeck, *New Technology and Industrial Relations*. Oxford: Blackwell.

Industrial Development Authority (1989) *IDA Industrial Plan 1978–1982*. Dublin: IDA.

Info-LEADER (Monthly news bulletin of the LEADER Programme of the European Commission). Brussels: European Commission.

Inter-Departmental Environment Committee (1977) *Report to the Minister for the Environment on Pollution Control*. Dublin: Stationery Office.

Institute for Industrial Research and Standards (1977) *The Role of the IIRS in the Environmental Field*. Dublin: IIRS.

Janicke, M. (1990) *State Failure*. Cambridge: Polity Press.

Jarre, D. (1991) 'Subsidiarity in Social Services Provision in Germany', *Social Policy and Administration*, Vol. 25, no. 3, pp. 211–17.

Jessop, B., (1990) 'Regulation Theories in Retrospect and Prospect', *Economy and Society* 19, pp. 152–216.

Jones, C. (1985) *Patterns of Social Policy: An Introduction to Comparative Analysis.* London, Tavistock.

Jones, C. I. (1998) *Introduction to Economic Growth*, New York: W. W. Norton.

Kaim-Caudle, P. (1967) *Social Policy in the Irish Republic*. London, Routledge & Kegan Paul.

Katrougalos, G. S. (1996) 'The South European Welfare Model: The Greek State. In Search of an Identity', *Journal of European Social Policy*, Vol. 6, no. 1, pp. 39–59.

Keane, M., Kennedy, V., Gannon B. and C. O. Muiri (1996) *Pilot Projects for the Benefit of the Long-Term Unemployed*. Western Regional Authority, Ireland. Report on Stages 1 & 2, Brussels: European Commission.

Kearney, B., Boyle, G. E. and J. A. Walsh (1994) *EU LEADER I Initiative in Ireland; Evaluation and Recommendations*. Dublin: Department of Agriculture, Food and Forestry.

Kearney, J. (1997) 'Achieving Equality for the Voluntary and Community Sector in Policy Making', in K. Fahy (ed) *Equality Policies and Social Change*. Galway: Community Workers Co-operative and Northern Ireland Council for Voluntary Action.

Kelleher, C. (1993) *Measures to Promote Health and Autonomy for Older People: A Position Paper*. Dublin: National Council for the Elderly.

Kemeny, J. (1995) 'Theories of Power in the Three Worlds of Welfare Capitalism', *Journal of European Social Policy*, Vol. 5, no. 2, pp. 87–96.

Kennedy, K. (1993) *The Unemployment Crisis in Ireland*. Cork: Cork University Press.

——and Giblin, T. and D. McHugh (1988) *The Economic Development of Ireland in the Twentieth Century*. London: Routledge.

Kennelly, B. and E. O'Shea (1997) 'Efficiency, Values and Social Welfare Policy', *Administration*, 45 (2), pp. 3–20.

Kenny, G. and D. McGettigan (1996) 'Non Traded, Traded and Aggregate Inflation in Ireland', *Technical Paper 3/RT/96*, Central Bank of Ireland.

Keohane, K. (1987) *Dependent Industrialisation, Crisis Transfer and Crisis Displacement: The Transnational Pharmaceutical Industry and the Irish Republic*. Unpublished MA thesis, UCC.

——(1989) 'Toxic Trade-Off: The Price Ireland Pays for Industrial Development', *The Ecologist*, Vol. 19, no. 4, pp. 144–6.

Kosonen, P. (1994) *European Integration: A Welfare State Perspective*. Helsinki: University of Helsinki, Sociology of Law Series.

Krugman, P. (1991) *Geography and Trade*, Cambridge, Mass: MIT Press.

——(1995) *Development, Geography and Economic Theory*, Cambridge: Cambridge University Press.

Kuper, B. O. (1994) 'The Green and White Papers of the European Union: The Apparent Goal of Reduced Social Benefits', *Journal of European Social Policy*, Vol. 5, no. 2, pp. 129–137.

Lash, S. and J. Urry (1987) *The End of Organised Capitalism*. Cambridge: Polity Press.

Laslett, P. (1992) *A Fresh Map of Life: the Emergence of the Third Age*. London: Weidenfeld and Nicolson.

Layard, R., Nickell, S. and R. Jackman (1991) *Unemployment: Macroeconomic Performance and the Labour Market*. Oxford: Oxford University Press.

LEADER II (1993) *The Future of Rural Ireland*. Cavan: Irish LEADER Network.

Leddin, A. J. and B. M. Walsh (1995) *The Macro-Economy of Ireland* (3rd edn). Dublin: Gill and Macmillan.

——(1997) 'Economic Stabilisation, Recovery, and Growth: Ireland 1979–96', *Irish Banking Review*, Summer.

Lee, J. J. (1989) *Ireland 1912–85: Politics and Society*, Cambridge: Cambridge University Press.

——(1990) *Ireland 1912–1985*. Cambridge: Cambridge University Press.

Leech, B. C. (1989) *The Administrative and Technical Arrangements for Environmental Management in Ireland*, Vols 1 and 2. Unpublished PhD dissertation, Trinity College, Dublin.

Le Grand, J. (1991) *Equity and Choice*. London: HarperCollins.

——(1997) 'Knights, Knaves or Pawns? Human Behaviour and Social Policy', *Journal of Social Policy*, Vol. 26, no. 2, pp. 149–169.

Leibfried, S. (1992) 'Towards a European Welfare State? On Integrating Poverty Regimes into the European Community', in Farge, Z. and J. E. Kolberg (eds) *Social Policy in a Changing Europe*. Boulder, Colorado: Westview Press.

——(1993) 'Towards a European Welfare State?', in Jones, C. (ed), *New Perspectives on the Welfare State in Europe*. London: Routledge.

——(1994) 'The Social Dimension of the European Union: En Route to Positively Joint Sovereignty?', *Journal of European Social Policy*, Vol. 4, no. 4, pp. 239–62.

——and Pierson, P. (1995) 'Semi-Sovereign Welfare States: Social Policy in a Multitiered Europe', in Leibfried, S. and P. Pierson (eds) *European Social Policy: Between Fragmentation and Integration*. Washington DC: The Brookings Institution.

Leonard, H. J. (1988) *Pollution and the Struggle for the World Product; Multinational Corporations, Environment and International Comparative Advantage*. Cambridge: Cambridge University Press.

Lindbeck, A. (1995) 'Hazardous Welfare State Dynamics', *American Economic Review*, Vol. 85, no. 2, pp. 9–15.

Lipsky, M. (1980) *Street-Level Bureaucracy: Dilemmas of the Individual in Public*

Service. New York: Russell Sage Foundation.

Long, N. (1992) 'From Paradigm Lost to Paradigm Regained? The Case for the Actor-oriented Sociology of Development', in Long, N. and A. Long (eds) *Battlefields of Knowledge: The Interlocking of Theory and Practice and Social Research and Development*. London: Routledge.

Lumb, R. (1990) 'Rural Community Development: Process versus Product', in Henry Buller and Susan Wright (eds) *Rural Development: Problems and Practices*. Aldershot: Avebury.

Lundström, F. and McKeown, K. (1994) *Home Help Services for Elderly People in Ireland*. Dublin: National Council for the Elderly.

Lynch, K. and McLaughlin, E. (1995) 'Caring Labour and Love Labour', pp. 250–92 in P. Clancy *et al.* (eds) *Irish Society: Sociological Perspectives*. Dublin: IPA.

Madden, P. (1992) 'Towards Health Promotion of the Elderly'. Unpublished paper.

Majone, G. (1993) 'The European Community Between Social Policy and Social Regulation', *Journal of Common Market Studies*, Vol. 31, no. 2, pp. 153–70.

Mangan, I. (1993) 'The Influence of EC Membership on Irish Social Policy and Social Services', in S. O Cinneide (ed.) *Social Europe: EC Social Policy and Ireland*. Dublin: Institute of European Affairs.

Mankiw, G. N., Romer, D. and D. N. Weil (1992) 'A Contribution to the Empirics of Economic Growth', *Quarterly Journal of Economics*, 107 (2).

Marsh, D. (1992) *The New Politics of British Trade Unionism: Union Power and the Thatcher Legacy*. London: Macmillan.

——and R. A. W. Rhodes (1992) *Policy Networks in British Government*. Oxford University Press

Marshall, T. H. (1950) *Citizenship and Social Class*. Cambridge: Cambridge University Press.

——(1975) *Social Policy*. London, Hutchinson.

Mayer, K. U. and Müller, W. (1986) 'The State and the Structure of the Life-Course', in Sorensen, A. B., Weilnert, E. and Sherrod, L. (eds) *Human Development and the Life-Course, Multidisciplinary Perspectives*. Hillsdale, NJ: Erlbaum Publishers.

McAleese, D. (1990) 'Ireland's Economic Recovery', *Irish Banking Review*, Summer.

McCarthy, C. (1993) 'A Review of the Crisis', in C. Keane (ed) *The Jobs Crisis*. Cork: Mercier Press.

McCarthy, D. (1998) 'The Genesis and Evolution of the Irish State's Commitment to Social Partnership at Local Level', in P. Kirby and D. Jacobson (eds) *In the Shadow of the Tiger: New Approaches to Combating Social Exclusion*. Dublin: Dublin City University Press.

McCarthy, E. and S. Yearley (1995) 'The Irish Environmental Protection Agency:

The Early Years', *Environmental Politics*, Vol. 4, no. 4, pp. 258–64.

McGrath, B. (1996) 'Environmentalism and Property Rights: The Mullaghmore Interpretative Centre Dispute', *Irish Journal of Sociology*, Vol. 6, pp. 25–48.

McLaughlin, E. (1994) 'Employment, Unemployment and Social Security', in A. Glyn and D. Miliband (eds) *Paying for Inequality*. London: Rivers Oram Press.

Meade, J. E. (1989) *Agathotopia: The Economics of Partnership*. Aberdeen: Aberdeen University Press.

Mernagh, M. and P. Commins (1997) *In From the Margins: Social Inclusion in the Europe of the New Millenium: Some Lessons from Poverty 3*. Dublin: Research and Development Unit, SICCDA.

Middlemas, K. (1995) *Orchestrating Europe: The Informal Politics of the European Union 1973–1995*. London: Fontana Press.

Midgley, J. (1986) *Community Participation, Social Development, and the State*. London: Methuen.

Milton, K. (ed.) (1993) *Environmentalism: The View From Anthropology*. London: Routledge.

Mishra, R. (1993) 'Typologies of the Welfare State Comparative Analyses: The "Liberal" Welfare State'. *Paper presented at the Conference: Comparative Research on Welfare States in Transition*, Oxford, September 9–12.

Morley, M., Gunningle, P. and N. Hearty (1994) 'The Flexibilisation of Work Practices in Ireland: Gradual Incrementalism or Radical Path Breaking Developments', *Administration*. Vol. 42, no. 1, pp. 92–111.

Mullally, G. (1993) *Challenging the Illusion of Powerlessness; Social Movements, the Transnational Pharmaceutical Industry and the State in the Republic of Ireland*. Unpublished MA Thesis, University College Cork.

Murphy, A. (1994) *The Irish Economy: Celtic Tiger or Tortoise?* Dublin: MMI.

——(1996) 'The Two Faced Economy', in *Proceedings of Conference on Measuring Economic Growth organised by Central Statistics Office and Irish Economic Association*. Dublin: Central Statistics Office.

——(1998) *The Celtic Tiger – The Great Misnomer: Economic Growth and the Multi-Nationals in Ireland in the 1990s*. Dublin: MMI.

Murphy, T. (1986) *Bailegangáire*. Dublin. Gallery Press.

National Economic and Social Council (1996) *Strategy into the 21st Century*, Report No. 99. Dublin: National Economic and Social Council.

National Economic and Social Forum (1995) *Jobs Potential of the Services Sector, Report No. 7*. Dublin: National Economic and Social Forum.

——(1997) *A Framework for Partnership - Enriching Strategic Consensus through Participation, Forum Report No. 16*. Dublin: National Economic and Social Forum.

Neugarten B. and Neugarten D. (1986) 'Changing Meanings of Age'; pp. 33–52, in Alan Pifer and Lydia Bronte (eds) *Our Aging Society: Paradox and Promise*. New York, Norton.

Nolan, B. (1991) *The Utilisation and Financing of Health Services in Ireland*. Dublin: The Economic and Social Research Institute.

——(1999) 'Monitoring Poverty Trends', *Poverty Today*, July–August, 4–5.

——and Whelan, C. T. and J. Williams (1998) *Where are Poor Households? The Spatial Distribution of Poverty and Deprivation in Ireland*. Dublin: Oak Tree Press in association with Combat Poverty Agency.

Ó Cearbhaill, D. and T. Varley (1998) 'Community Group/State Relationships: The Case of West of Ireland Community Councils', in R. Byron (ed.) *Public Policy and the Periphery: Problems and Prospects in Marginal Regions*, Belfast: Association for the Study of Marginal Regions.

O'Connell, P. J. and D. B. Rottman (1992) 'The Irish Welfare State in Comparative Perspective', in J. H. Goldthorpe and C. T. Whelan (eds) *The Development of Industrial Society in Ireland*. Oxford: Oxford University Press.

O'Connor, J. and Thompstone, K. (1986) *Nursing Homes in the Republic of Ireland: A Study of the Private and Voluntary Sector*. Dublin: National Council for the Aged.

——and Ruddle, H., O'Gallagher, M., Murphy, E. (1988) *The Caring Process: A Study of Carers in the Home*. Dublin: National Council for the Aged.

——and J., Ruddle, H. and O'Gallagher, M. (1989) *Sheltered Housing in Ireland: its Role and Contributions in the Care of the Elderly*. Dublin: National Council for the Aged.

O'Connor, J. S. (1993) 'Gender, Class and Citizenship in the Comparative Analysis of Welfare States: Theoretical and Methodological Issues', *British Journal of Sociology*, Vol. 44, no. 3, pp. 501–19.

O'Connor, P. (1994) 'Very Close Parent-Child Relationships: the Perspective of the Elderly Person', *Journal of Cross-Cultural Gerontology* 9, pp. 53–76.

O'Donnell, R. (1998) 'Social Partnership in Ireland: Principles and Interactions', in O'Donnell, R. and J. Larragy (eds) *Negotiated Economic and Social Governance and European Integration*. Luxembourg: European Commission.

——and C. O'Reardon (1996) 'Ireland's Experiment in Social Partnership, 1987–96'. Paper presented to workshop Dublin, 1996.

——and D. Thomas (1998) 'Partnership and Policy-Making', in Healy, S. and B. Reynolds (eds) *Social Policy in Ireland: Principles, Practice and Problems*. Dublin: Oak Tree Press.

O'Donovan, O. and T. Varley (1995) *Paid Employment in the Voluntary Sector: A Review of the Literature*. Galway: Centre for Public Policy Studies Working Paper, SSRC, University College Galway.

——and E. Ward (1999) 'Networks of Women's Groups in the Republic of Ireland', in Galligan, Y., Ward, E. and R. Wilford (eds) *Contesting Politics: Women in Ireland, North and South*. Boulder, Colorado: Westview Press in association with PSAI Press.

Office of the Comptroller and Auditor General (1995) *The LEADER Programme*.

Dublin: Stationery Office.

O'Grada, C. (1994) *Ireland 1780–1939: An New Economic History*, Oxford: Oxford University Press.

——(1997) *A Rocky Road: The Irish Economy Since the 1920s*, Manchester: Manchester University Press.

O'Halpin, E. (1992) 'Policy Making', in Coakley, J. and M. Gallagher (eds) *Politics in the Republic of Ireland*. Galway: PSAI Press.

O'Hagan, J. W. (ed.) (1995) *The Economy of Ireland: Policy and Performance of a Small European Economy*. Dublin: Gill and Macmillan.

O'Hara, P. and P. Commins (1998) 'Rural Development: Towards the New Century', in Healy, S. and B. Reynolds (eds) *Social Policy in Ireland: Principles, Practice and Problems*. Dublin: Oak Tree Press.

O'Hearn, D. (1997) 'The Celtic Tiger: The Role of the Multinationals', in E. Crowley and J. McLoughlin (eds) *Under the Belly of the Tiger: Class, Race, Identity and Culture in the Global Ireland*. Dublin: Irish Reporter Publications.

——(1998) *Inside the Celtic Tiger: The Irish Economy and the Asian Model*. London: Pluto Press.

Olson, M. (1968) *The Logic of Collective Action: Public Goods and the Theory of Groups*. New York: Schocken Books.

O'Mally, E. (1989) *Industry and Economic Development: The Challenge for the Latecomer*. Dublin: Gill and Macmillan.

——(1992) *The Pilot Programme for Integrated Rural Development 1988–90*. Dublin: The Economic and Social Research Institute.

O'Neill, G. (1997) 'A Study of the Involvement of Local Community Organisations in the LEADER Rural Development Programme in South-west Mayo, 1991–1994'. Unpublished MRD thesis, Department of Economics, University College Galway.

O'Reilly, P. (1994) 'Whose Plan Is It Anyway? Struggles Over the Attribution of Meaning in the Planning Process'. Unpublished MA thesis, Department of Political Science and Sociology, University College Galway.

O'Riordan, M. (1996) 'Towards a European Social Pact: The Irish Experience'. Paper presented to European Trade Union Institute Conference, Brussels, 1996.

O'Shea, E., Donnison, D., Larragy, J. *et al.* (1991) *The Role and Future Development of Nursing Homes in Ireland*. Dublin: National Council for the Elderly.

——(1992) *Coming of Age in Europe*. Brussels: Directorate-General 5, European Commission.

——(1993) *The Impact of Social and Economic Policies on Older People in Ireland*. Dublin: National Council for the Elderly.

——and Hughes, J. (1994) *The Economics and Financing of Long-term Care of the Elderly in Ireland*. Dublin: National Council for the Elderly.

O'Shea, M. (1993) *The Contribution of Private Nursing Homes to Care of the Elderly in County Galway*. UCG: Thesis, Faculty of Public Health Medicine in Ireland.

Parker, H. (1989) *Instead of the Dole: An Enquiry into the Integration of the Tax and Benefit Systems*. London: Routledge.

Peace, A. (1993) 'Environmental Protest, Bureaucratic Closure; The Politics of Discourse in Rural Ireland', in K. Milton (ed.) *Environmentalism: The View From Anthropology*. London: Routledge.

——(1994) 'Chemicals, Conflicts and the Irish Environmental Protection Agency', *Cork Environmental Alliance News*, No. 9, pp. 17–22.Ploug, N. and Kvist, J. (1996) *Social Security in Europe: Development or Dismantlement?* The Hague: Kluwer Law International.

Phillipson, C. (1993) 'The Sociology of Retirement', in J. Bond *et al.* (eds) *Ageing in Society*. London: Sage, pp. 180–99.

——and Walker, A. (eds) (1986) *Ageing and Social Policy: A Critical Assesment*. London: Gower.

Pickvance, C. and E. Preteceille (1991) 'Introduction: The Significance of Local Power in Theory and Practice', in Pickvance, C. and E. Preteceille (eds) *State Restructuring and Local Power*. London: Pinter.

Piore M. and C. Sabel (1984) *The Second Industrial Divide: Possibilities for Prosperity*. New York: Basic Books.

Pollert, A. (1988) 'The Flexible Firm: Fixation or Fact?' *Work Employment and Society,* Vol 2., pp. 281–316.

Poverty 3, Central Unit (1992) 'Community Programme to Foster Economic and Social Integration of the Least Privileged Groups up to the year 2000', Conference on Combating Social Exclusion, Fostering Integration, Brussels, 2–3 April.

Pringle, D. G., Walsh, J. and M. Hennessy (eds) (1999) *Poor People, Poor Places: A Geography of Poverty and Deprivation in Ireland*, Dublin: Oak Tree Press.

Purcell, J. (1991) 'The Rediscovery of the Management Prerogative: The Management of Labour Relations in the 1980s', *Oxford Review of Economic Policy*. Vol. 7, pp. 33–43.

Ray, C. (1996) *The Dialectic of Local Development: The Case of the EU LEADER I Rural Development Programme*. Newcastle: Centre for Rural Economy, Department of Agricultural Economics and Food Marketing, University of Newcastle upon Tyne.

Report of the Expert Working Group on the Integration of the Tax and Social Welfare Systems (1996). *Integrating Tax and Social Welfare*. Dublin: Stationery Office.

Report of the Pensions Board (1998) *Securing Retirement Income: National Pensions Policy Initiative*. Dublin: The Pensions Board.

Rhodes, M. (1998) 'Globalisation, Labour Markets and Welfare States: A Future of Competitive Corporatism?', in Rhodes, M. and Y. Meny, *The Future of European Welfare: A New Social Contract?* London: Macmillan.

Riley, M. and Riley, J. (1986) 'Longevity and Social Structure: the Potential of the

Added Years', in Alan Pfifer and Lydia Bronte (eds) *Our Aging Society: Paradox and Promise*. New York: Norton, pp. 53–7.

Roche, W. K. (1997) 'Pay Determination, the State and the Politics of Industrial Relations', in T. V. Murphy and W. Roche (eds) *Irish Industrial Relations in Practice*, Dublin: Oak Tree Press.

Rolston, B. (1997) 'Overview of Community Development in Northern Ireland', *Inishowen Development Journal*, Summer: 15–19.

Room, G. (1995) 'Poverty in Europe: Competing Paradigms of Analysis', *Policy and Politics*, 23 (2): 103–13.

Rottman, D. and Reidy, M. (1988) *Redistribution Through State Social Expenditure in the Republic of Ireland: 1973–1980*. Dublin: National Economic and Social Council.

Rowthorn, R. E. (1992) 'Centralisation, Employment and Wage Dispersion', *Economic Journal*, Vol. 102.

Rubery, J. and F. Wilkinson (eds) (1994) *Employer Strategy and the Labour Market*. Oxford: Oxford University Press.

Sabel, C. (1995) *Ireland: Local Partnerships and Social Innovation*. Paris: OECD.

Sali-Martin, X. (1997) 'Transfers, Social Safety Nets, and Economic Growth', *IMF Staff Papers*, 44 (1), pp. 81–102.

Scannell, Y. (1989) *The Law and Practice Relating to Pollution Control in the Republic of Ireland*. Dublin: Graham and Trotman.

——(1990) 'Legislation and Toxic Waste Disposal in Ireland', in *Environmental Protection and the Impact of European Community Law*. Papers from the Joint Conference with the Incorporated Law Society of Ireland. Irish Centre for European Law, Trinity College, Dublin.

——(1993) 'Agriculture and Environmental Law', in Feehan, J. (ed.) *Environment and Development in Ireland*. Dublin: The Environmental Institute.

——(1995) *Environmental and Planning Law in Ireland*. Dublin: The Round Hall Press.

Schaefer, G. F. (1991) 'The Subsidiarity Principle and European Environmental Policy', in *Subsidiarity: The Challenge of Change: Proceedings of the Jacques Delors Colloquium*. Maastricht: European Institute of Public Administration.

Sen, A. (1992) *Inequality Re-examined*. Oxford: Clarendon Press.

——(1993) 'Capability and Well-Being', in M. Nussbaum and A. Sen (ed.) *The Quality of Life*. Oxford: Clarendon Press.

Shucksmith, M. and P. Chapman (1998) 'Rural Development and Social Exclusion', *Sociologia Ruralis*, 38 (2): 225–42.

Springer, B. (1992) *The Social Dimension of 1992: Europe Faces a New EC*. New York: Praeger.

Stone, D. (1988) *Policy Paradox and Political Reason*. Glenview, Ill.: Scott Forestman.

Streeck, W. (1988) 'Comment on Ronald Dore, Rigidities in the Labour Market',

Government and Opposition, pp. 413–23

——(1992) *Social Institutions and Economic Performance: Studies of Industrial Relations in Advanced Capitalist Economies*. London: Sage.

——and P. C. Schmitter (1991) 'From National Corporatism to Transnational Pluralism: Organised Interests in the Single European Market', in *Politics and Society*, Vol. 19, pp. 133–64.

Sweeney, P. (1998) *The Celtic Tiger: Ireland's Economic Miracle Explained*, Dublin: Oak Tree Press.

Tansey, P. (1998) *Ireland at Work: Economic Growth and the Labour Market 1987–1997*, Dublin: Oak Tree Press.

Task Force on Integration of Local Government and Local Development Systems (1998) Dublin: Department of the Environment and Local Government.

Taylor, G. (1995) 'Rigidity and Flexibility in Macro-Political Bargaining: A Reply to M. J. Gobeyn', *Governance: An International Journal of Policy and Administration*. Vol. 8, pp. 419–30.

——(1996) 'Labour Market Rigidities, Institutional Impediments and Managerial Constraints: Some Reflections on the Recent Experience of Macro-Political Bargaining in Ireland', *The Economic and Social Review*, Vol. 27 (3).

——(1998) 'Conserving the Emerald Tiger: The Politics of Environmental Regulation in Ireland', in *Environmental Politics*, Vol. 7, no. 4, pp. 53–74.

——(1998a) 'Me Thinks thou Do'st Protest Too Much: Oral Hearings, Public Registers and Environmental Democracy in Ireland' *Irish Planning and Environmental Law Journal*. Vol. 5, no. 4, pp. 143–55.

Taylor-Gooby, P. (1991) 'Welfare State Regimes and Welfare Citizenship', *Journal of European Social Policy*, Vol. 1, no. 2, pp. 93–105.

Tussing, A. D. (1985) *Irish Medical Care Resources: An Economic Analysis*. Dublin: The Economic and Social Research Institute.

Van Kesbergen, K. (1995) *Social Capitalism. A Study of Christian Democracy and the Welfare State*. London: Routledge.

Varley, T. (1991) 'Power to the People? Community Groups and Rural Revival in Ireland', in Reynolds, B. and S. Healy (eds) *Rural Development Policy: What Future for Rural Ireland?* Dublin: Conference of Major Religious Superiors.

Victor, C. (1991) *Health and Health Care in Later Life*. Buckingham: Open University Press.

——(1994) *Old Age in Modern Society*. London: Chapman & Hall.

Walker, A. (1993) 'Poverty and Inequality in Old Age', in J. Bond *et al.* (eds) *Ageing in Society*. London: Sage, pp. 280–303.

Walsh, B. M. (1996) 'Stabilisation and Adjustment in a Small Open Economy: Ireland, 1979–95', *Oxford Review of Economic Policy*, Vol. 12 (3).

Walsh, J. (1993) 'Internalisation v. Decentralisation: An analysis of Recent Developments in Pay Bargaining', *British Journal of Industrial Relations*. Vol. 31, no. 3, p. 416.

——and Craig, S. and D. McCafferty (1998) *Local Partnership for Social Inclusion?* Dublin: Oak Tree Press in association with Combat Poverty Agency.

Ward, S. (1994) 'A Basic Income System for Ireland', in B. Reynolds and S. Healy (eds) *Towards an Adequate Income for All.* Dublin: Justice Commission, Conference of Religious in Ireland.

Warde, A. (1994) 'Consumers, Consumption and Post-Fordism', in R. Burrows and B. Loader (eds) *Towards a Post-Fordist Welfare State.* London: Routledge.

Watt, P. (1997) 'The Community Platform', in Fahy, K. (ed.) *Strategies to Encourage Participation.* Galway: Community Workers Co-operative.

Weale, A. (1992) *The New Politics of Pollution.* Manchester: Manchester University Press.

——(1996) 'Environmental Regulation and Administrative Reform in Britain', in G. Majone (ed.) *Regulating Europe.* London: Routledge.

Webster, C. M. (1991) 'How Far Can You Go? The Role of the Statutory Sector in Developing Community Partnership'. Unpublished MA thesis, University College Galway.

Western Health Board (WHB) (1985) *Services for the Aged.* Galway: WHB.

Whelan, C. (1995) 'Class Transformation and Social Mobility in the Republic of Ireland, in P. Clancy *et al.* (eds) *Irish Society: Sociological Perspectives.* Dublin: IPA.

——and Whelan, B. (1988) *The Transition to Retirement.* Dublin: The Economic and Social Research Institute.

White Paper on Education (1995) *Shaping Our Education Future*, Stationery Office.

Young, M. and Schuller, T. (1991) *Life After Work: The Arrival of the Ageless Society.* London: HarperCollins.

Government Publications

Delivering Better Government, 1994

Charting our Education Future

Labour Relations Commission Annual Reports 1991–96

Programme for National Economic Recovery 1987–90

Programme for Economic and Social Progress

Programme for Competitiveness and Work 1992

Partnership 2000

Shaping a Healthier Future: A Strategy for Effective Healthcare in the 1990s

Strategic Management Initiative

Index

Adnett, N., 73
Adshead, M., 82, 141
agricultural lobby, 82, 94–7
Ahern, B., 28
Alber, J., 58, 62
Allen, R., 82, 83
Anderson, R., 118
Anttonen, A., 62
area-based partnerships, 6, 129, 131–3, 142
Arensberg, C. M., 100–1
Atkinson, A. B., 70, 71, 77

Baker, S., 81
Barr, N., 71
Barrington, T., 139
Barry, F., 19–20
Barry, U., 83
Berger, J., 105
Beveridge, W., 60
Bradley, A. C., 99
Blackwell, J., 75
Blanchard, O., 20
Blank, R., 71
Bonoli, G., 60, 61
Boylan, T. A., 2, 3, 9, 12, 23, 30
Boyle, G. E., 131
Bradley, A. C., 99
Bradley *et al.*, 11
Bradley, J., 21, 25
B[illegible], 10, 108, 119, 120, 139
Breen, R., 102
Brown, T., 101
Brown, W. A., 32
Bruton, J., 18
Buller, H., 138
Burrows, R., 29
business lobby, 82–5, 90

Curtin, C., 6, 27
Callan *et al.*, 77
Callan, T. B., 27, 67, 77
Calmfors, L., 32
Caporaso, J. A., 75
celtic tiger, 1–3, 26–7, 38
changing employment patterns, 42, 43
Chapman, P., 132
Clancy, P., 101
Clark, S., 29
Coakley, J., 131
Cohen, G. A., 78
Commins, P., 131, 137, 149
community care, 103, 117–24
  and residualism, 102, 118–19
  and health promotion, 122–3
community employment schemes, 47–8
Conrad, P., 100–1
Conroy, P., 134
Control of Farmyard Pollution Scheme, 96–7
Corporatism, 31
Cousins, M., 61
Coyle, C., 81
Craig, S., 135, 136, 142, 148, 149
Creighton, S., 67
Crickley, A., 128
critical ethnography, 111
critical gerontology, 104–6
Crotty, R., 10
Crowley, E., 26
Culliton, J., 80

decommodification, 58
Deenihan, J., 96
D[illegible], J., [illegible]
Devereux, M. B., 20
Devlin, M., 128
Donnison, D., 102
Dore, R., 33, 35
Duffy, D., 11, 25
Dukes, A., 18

economic nationalism, 12
economic policy
  and economic crisis, 17–19
  and economic performance, 13–16

economic policy (*cont.*)
  and EEC, 13–14, 23
  and European Monetary Union, 22–3
  and protectionism, 14
  and stabilisation, 20–2
  and structural funds, 24–5
Eckersley, R., 87
Edmondson, R., 4, 5, 99, 100, 104
education, 24
Eipper, C., 130
Eleson, D., 83
environmental management, 91
Environmental Protection Agency
  and BATNEEC, 86–8
  and environmental auditing 88–9
  and independence, 93
environmental protest, 80, 81, 85, 97–8
environmental regulation
  and local authorities, 81–2, 89–90
Erikson, E. H., 124
Erikson, J. M., 124
Esping-Andersen, G., 58, 60, 61, 69–70, 78

Fahey, T., 109, 122
Fahy, K,. 144
Faughnan, P., 149
Feehan, J., 81
Ferrera, M., 53, 60
Finch, J., 101
fiscal expansion, 20–2
Fischer, F., 105
Fischer, S., 20
Fitzgerald, G., 18–19
Fitzgerald, J., 11, 25
flexible specialisation, 29, 49
Forester, J., 105
Frazer, H., 134

Gallagher, M., 131
Galligan, Y., 144
Gannon, B., 76
Geary, P. T., 71
Giavazzi, F., 20
Glyn, A., 71
Gilbert, N., 29
Gilmore, E., 90, 93
Girvin, B., 10
Gobeyn, M. J., 28, 31
Goldthorpe, J. H., 28, 30–1, 63
Gough, I., 35, 59
Gray, A., 10
Green, T. H., 99
Greer, J., 131
Guillemard, A., 102, 110
Gunnigle, P., 42

Habermas, J., 129
Hanan, D., 102
Hardiman, N., 38
Hareven, T., 101
Harney, M., 85, 90, 91
Harries, K., 112, 126
Hasse, T., 27, 141, 149
Hayek, F., 34
Healy, S., 27, 77, 140, 144, 149
Hearty, N., 42
Heath, A., 101
Hennessy, M., 27
Hills, J., 69
Hirst, P., 29, 129
Howlin, B., 91, 93, 96, 144
Honohan, P., 21, 25
Hyman, R., 29

IPC licensing, 86–7
Industrial Development Agency, 82–5

Jackman, R., 70
Jackson, P., 83
Jacobson, D., 144
Janicke, M., 87
Jarre, D., 59
Jones, C., 25 62, 63
Jones, T., 82, 83

Kaim-Caudle, P., 119
Kenny, G., 22
Katrougalos, G. S., 61
Keane, M., 76
Kearney, B., 131, 134, 139, 143
Kearney, I., 11, 25
Kelleher, C., 119
Kemeny, J., 60
Kennedy, V., 76
Kennelly, B., 4, 52
Keohane, K., 82, 83
Keynes, J. M., 60
Kimball, S., 100–1
Kirby, P., 144
Kivnick, H. Q., 124
Kosonen, P., 60
Krugman, P., 11, 30
Kuper, B. O., 73
Kvist, J., 58, 69

Labour Court, 41
labour market regulation, 33–4, 42
Labour Relations Commission, 40, 46, 49
Larragy, J., 33, 102
Lash, S., 28, 31
Laslett, P., 124
Lawson, N., 20
Layard, R., 70
Leddin, A. J., 16, 18, 19, 20, 21, 25
Lee, J. J., 1, 9, 82
Leech, B. C., 82
Le Grand, J., 78
Leonard, H. J., 82, 83
Liebfried, S., 60–1, 63, 74, 83
Lindbeck, A., 70
Lipsky, M., 148
Long, N., 148
Long, A., 148
Lumb, R., 138
Lundstrom, F., 102, 119, 122

Maastricht Treaty, 22, 73
macro-political bargaining
  and economic growth, 37, 38
  and flexibility, 30–5, 48–9
  and globalisation, 28–9
  and local bargaining, 32, 40–2, 45
  and rigidity, 30–7
  and the unemployed, 47–8
  and wage bargaining, 21–2
  and welfare state, 34–6
Majone, G., 74
Marsh, D., 33, 84
Mangan, I., 72
Mankiw, G. N., 25
Marshall, T. H., 74, 78
Mayer, K. U., 106
McAleese, D., 20
Mc Cafferty, D., 135
McCarthy, C., 132
McCarthy, D., 144
McEvoy, M., 149
McGettigan, D., 22
McKeown, K., 102, 119, 122, 135, 141
McLaughlin, E., 71
McLoughlin, J., 26
McSharry, R., 19
Meade, J. E., 77
Meny, Y., 34
Mernagh, M., 137
Middlemas, K., 22
Midgley, J., 129
Miliband, D., 71
Milton, K., 81
Mishra, R., 59
Moane, G., 76
modern growth theory, 25
Mogensen, G. V., 70
Morley, M., 42
Muiri, C. O., 76
Muller, W., 106
Murphy, A., 27
Murphy, C., 6
Murphy, T., 101
Murphy, T. V., 26
Murray, M., 131
Murray, P., 76, 109, 122

national debt, 16
National Economic and Social Forum, 47, 76, 144
National Heritage Areas, 95
Neugarten, B., 105
Neugarten, D., 105
Nickell, S., 70
Nolan, B., 27, 65–6, 67–8, 132
Nolan, P., 86
nursing homes, 112–17
Nussbaum, N., 78
nutrient management plan, 94

O'Cearbhaill, D., 144
O'Connell, P. J., 63, 66
O'Connor, J. S., 60
O'Donnell, R., 33, 38, 144
O'Donoghue, C., 77
O'Donovan, O., 129, 142, 144
O'Grada, C., 10, 17
O'Halpin, E., 131
O'Hagan, J. W., 17, 20, 23
O'Hara, P., 149
O'Hearn, D., 26, 27
older people
  and argumentational analysis, 105
  and public policy, 99–104, 124–6
Olson, M., 130
O'Malley, E., 10, 131
O'Neill, C., 77
O'Neill, G., 147
oral hearings, 91–2
O'Reilly, P., 136
O'Riordan, M., 38, 45, 46–8,
O'Shea, E., 4, 52, 76, 102, 109, 112, 115, 117, 124

Pagano, M., 20
Parker, H., 77
Partnership 2000, 49, 144
Pearson, R., 83
pensions, 107–12
Pfaller, A., 35
Phillipson, C., 103, 105, 107, 108
Pickvance, C., 146
Pierson, P., 74
Ploug, N., 58, 69
Pollert, A., 29
political regulation, 35–6
Preteceille, E., 146
Pringle, D. G., 27
Programme for Competitiveness and Work, 45–8
Programme for Economic and Social Progress, 39–44, 47
Programme for National Recovery, 39
Purcell, J., 32

Regan, S., 94–5
Reidy, M., 65
Reynolds, B., 27, 77, 140, 144, 149
Rhodes, M., 34
Rhodes, R. A. W., 84
Roche, W. K., 26
Rolston, B., 144
Romer, D., 25
Room, G., 132
Rottman, D., 65, 102
Rottman, D. B., 63, 66
Rourke, S., 141
Rowthorn, R. E., 34
Rubery, J., 34, 49
Rural Environmental Protection Scheme, 94–5
rural development,
  and communitarian approaches, 128–9
  and community empowerment, 145–9
  and community participation, 137–45
  and elitist approaches, 130
  and implementation, 133–7
  and LEADER, 131, 133–6, 139–43, 148–9
  and Poverty 3, 132–3

Sabel, C., 6, 136, 144, 150
Sali-Martin, X., 71
Scannell, Y., 81, 82
Schuller, T., 124
Sen, A., 77–8
Shorthall, F., 11, 25
Shucksmith, M., 132
Sipila, J., 62
spatial development theory, 11
Springer, B., 73
Stone, D., 104
Streek, W., 28, 29, 30–1, 34, 35
strike activity, 43–4, 46–7
Sweeney, P., 26

Tansey, P., 23
Taylor, G., 3, 4, 6, 26, 29, 30, 32, 35, 80–3, 88, 91–2
Taylor-Gooby, P., 60
Thomas, D., 144
Tovey, H., 27
Tussing, A. D., 65

Urry, J., 28, 31

Van Kesbergen, K., 59
Varley, T., 6, 129, 140, 142, 144
Victor, C., 103
Voluntary Health Insurance, 66

Walker, A., 103, 105, 107, 108
Walsh, B. M., 16, 18, 19, 20, 21, 25
Walsh, J., 27, 32, 135
Walsh, J. A., 131
Walsh *et al.*, 143
Ward, E., 144
Ward, S., 77
Watt, P., 144
Weale, A., 87
Webster, C. M., 136
Weil, D. N., 25
welfare state
  and employment, 69–71
  European Union, 71–2
  and healthcare, 65–7
  Irish, 61, 63–9
  models of, 57–63
  and poverty, 67–9
  and social protection expenditure, 53–6
Whelan, B., 27, 64–7, 110, 125
Whelan, C., 27, 63–5, 67, 102, 110, 125, 132
Whelan, K., 21
Whelan, T., 67
Wilford, R., 144
Wilkinson, F., 34, 49
Williams, J., 67, 132
Woods, M., 119
Wright, J., 21
Wright, S., 138

Yearley, S., 81
Young, M., 124

Zeitlin, J., 29